I0729702

GRAFFBOOK 2

This book seeks to act as a document to encourage illustration and creativity.
It is created without the collaboration of the owners of the walls themselves.
As publishers we're obliged to say it's not meant to encourage graffiti where it is
illegal. So we have.

A catalogue record for this book is available from the British Library
ISBN 9781908211354
First Edition 2025
First published in Great Britain in 2025 under the imprint of Carpet Bombing Culture
Email books@carpetbombingculture.co.uk

Printed on natural recyclable products (ie paper).

www.carpetbombingculture.com

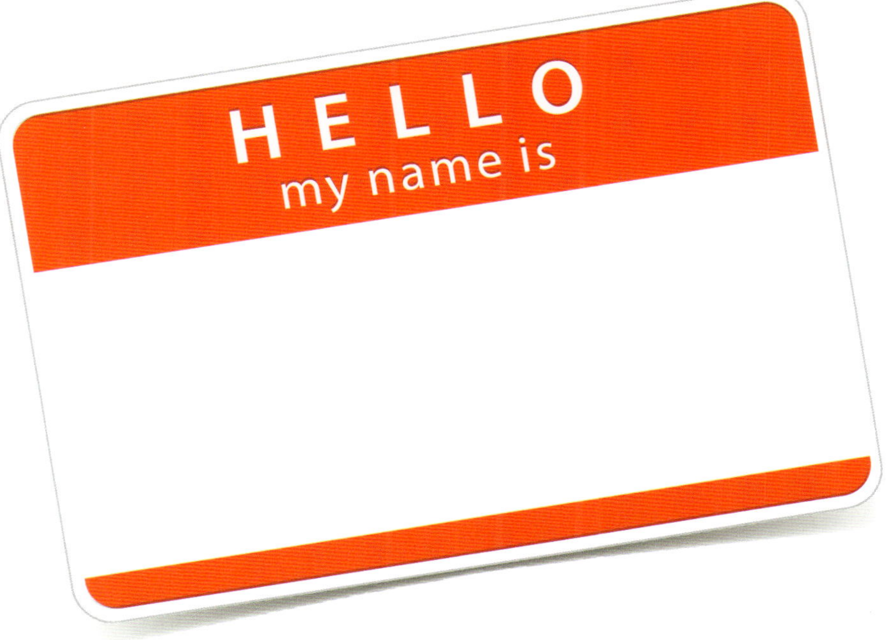

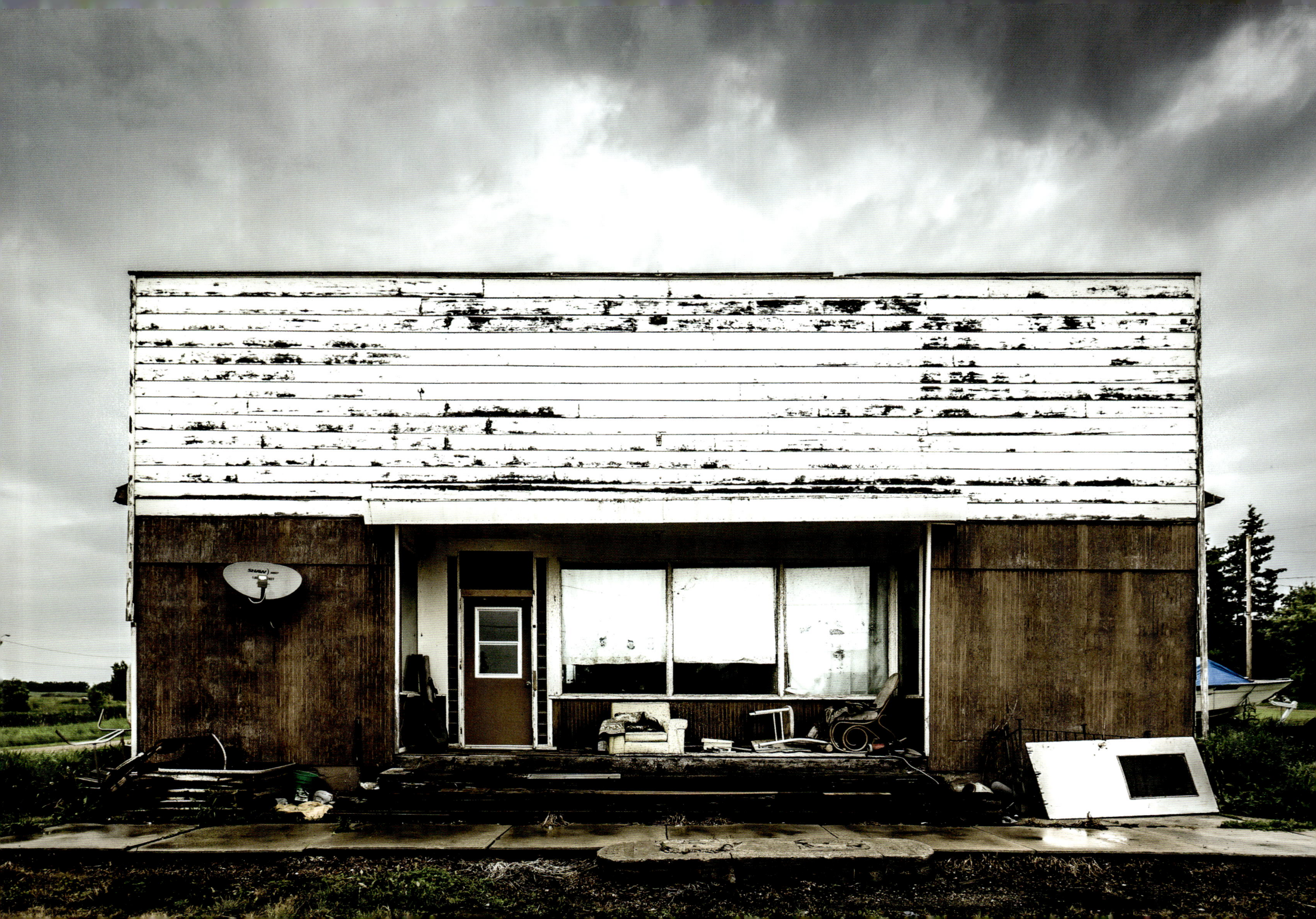

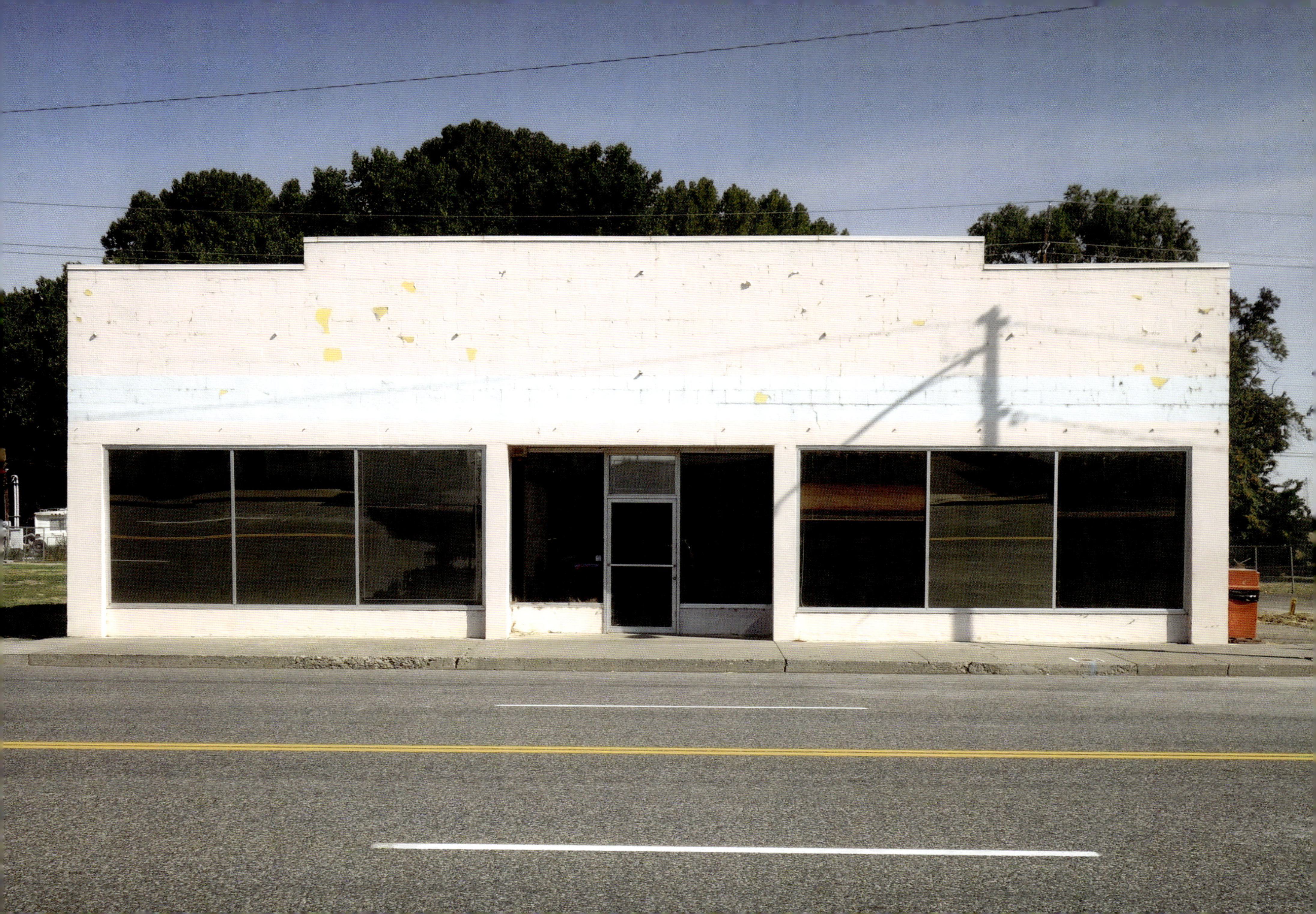

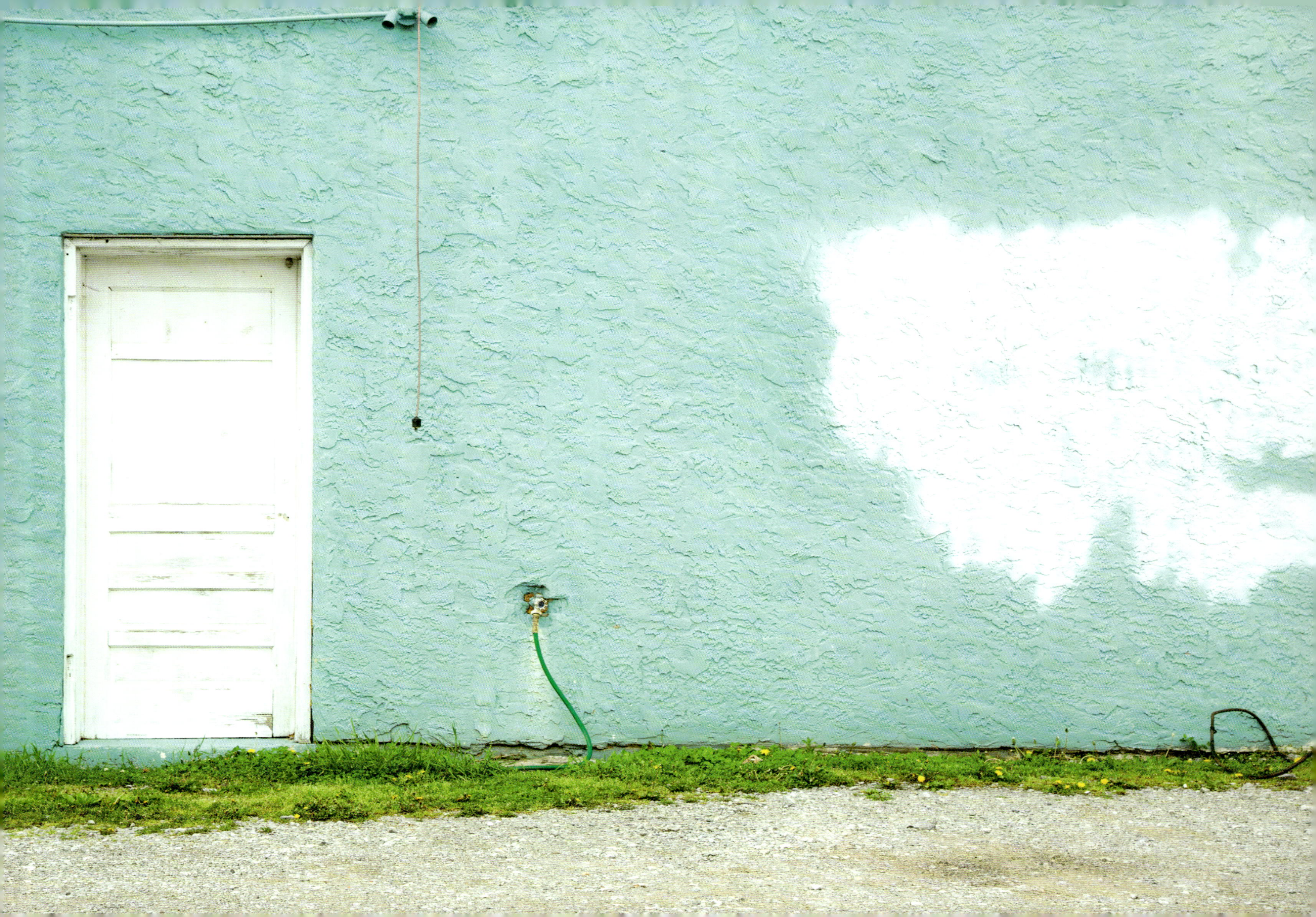

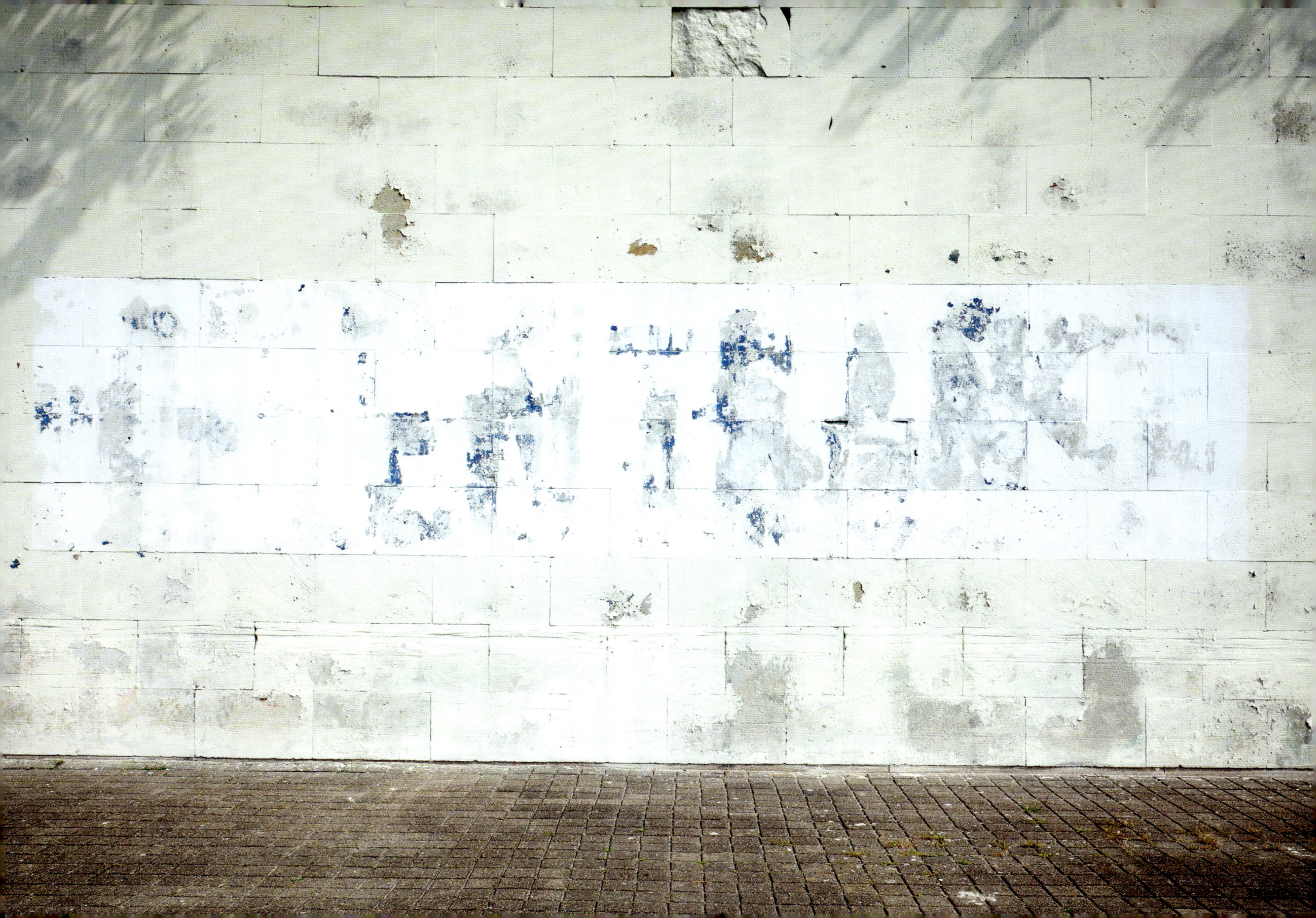

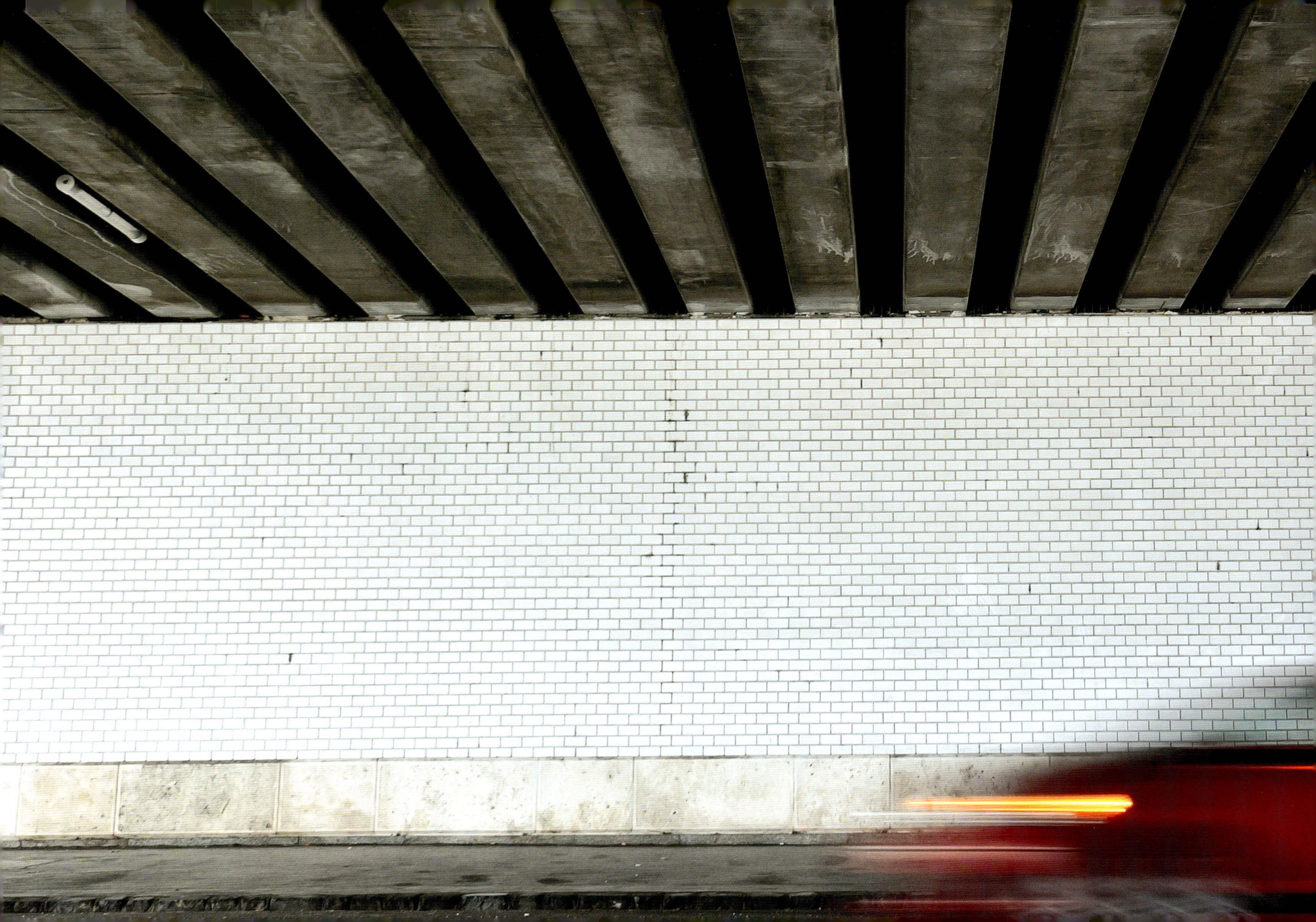

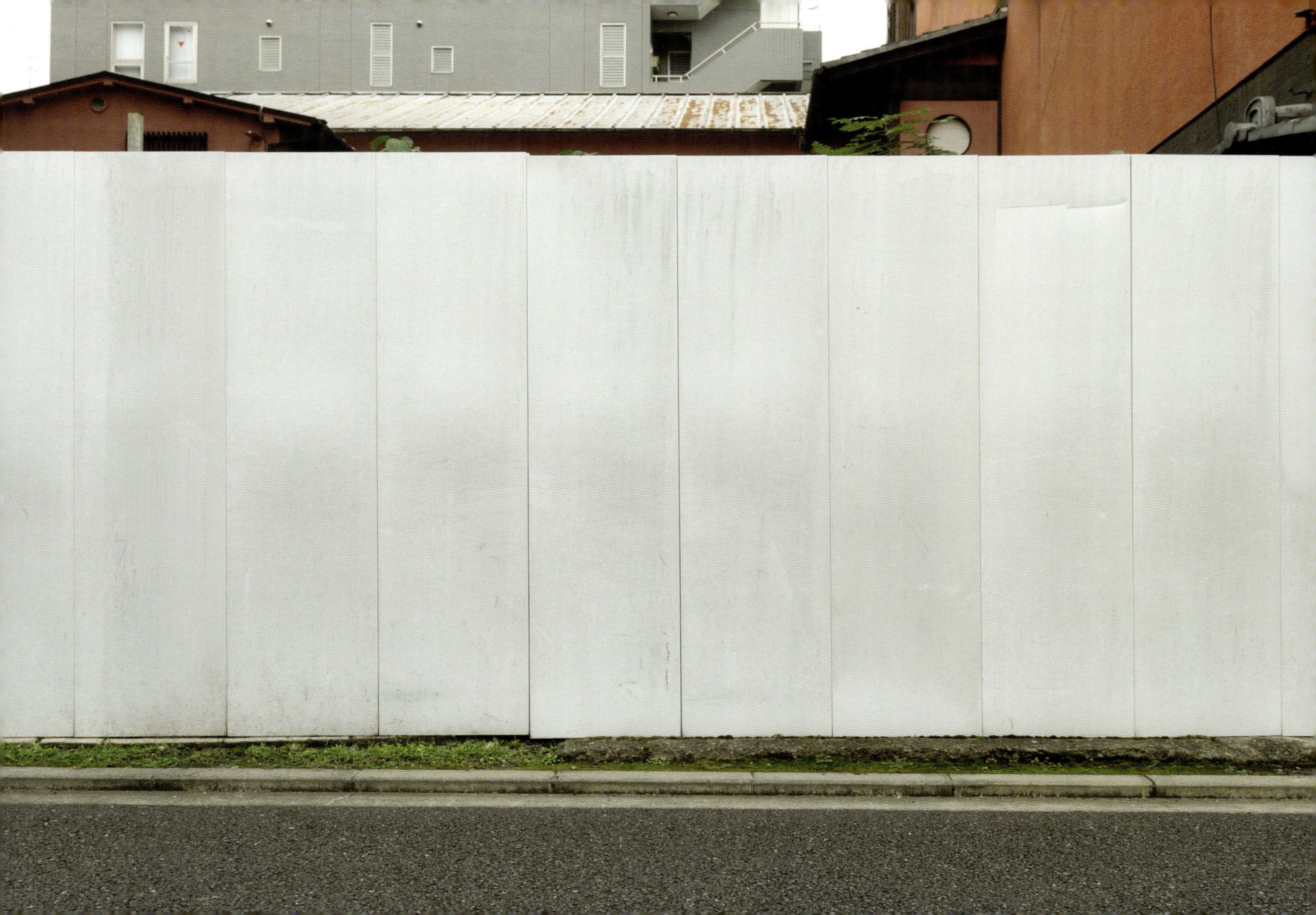

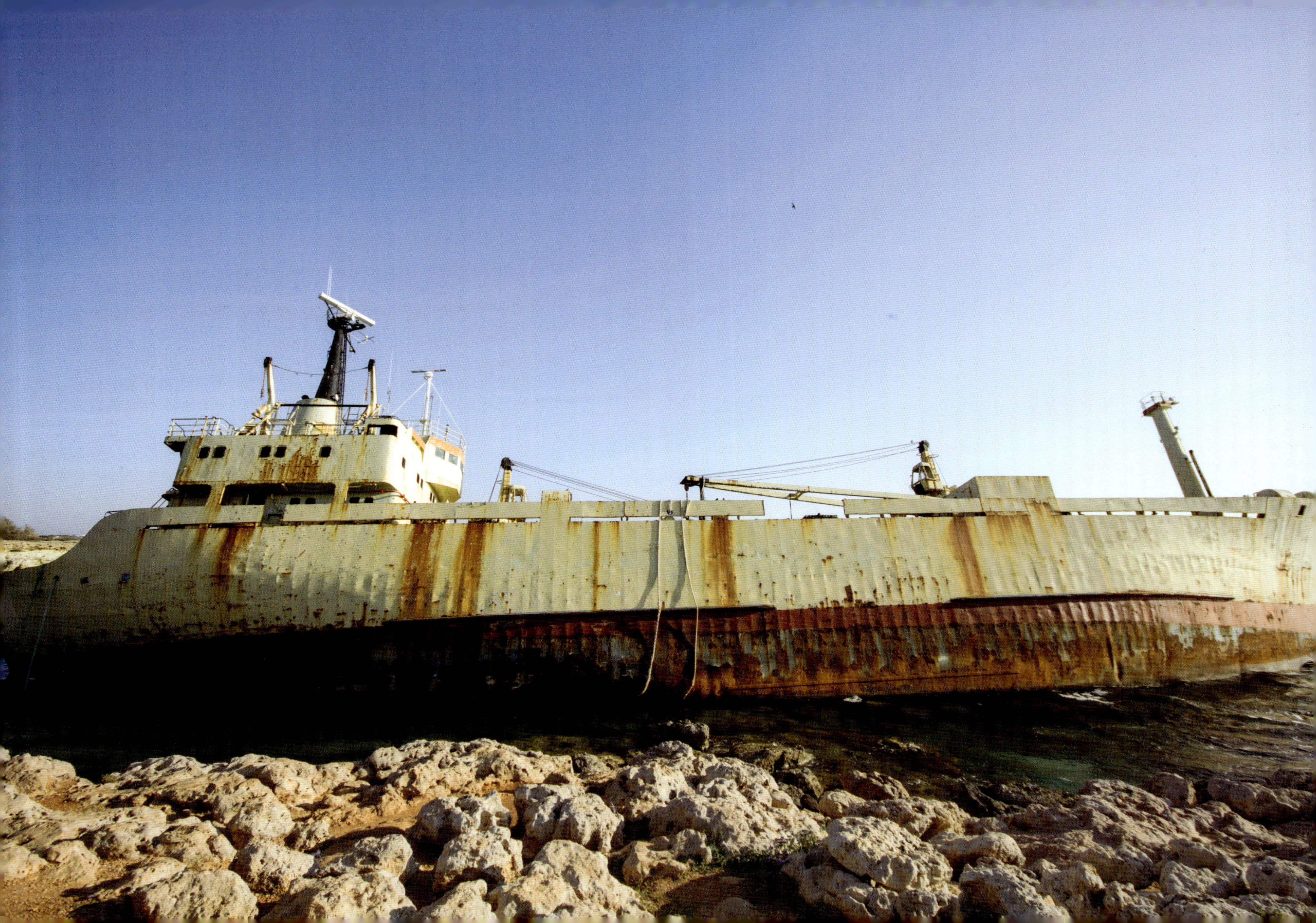

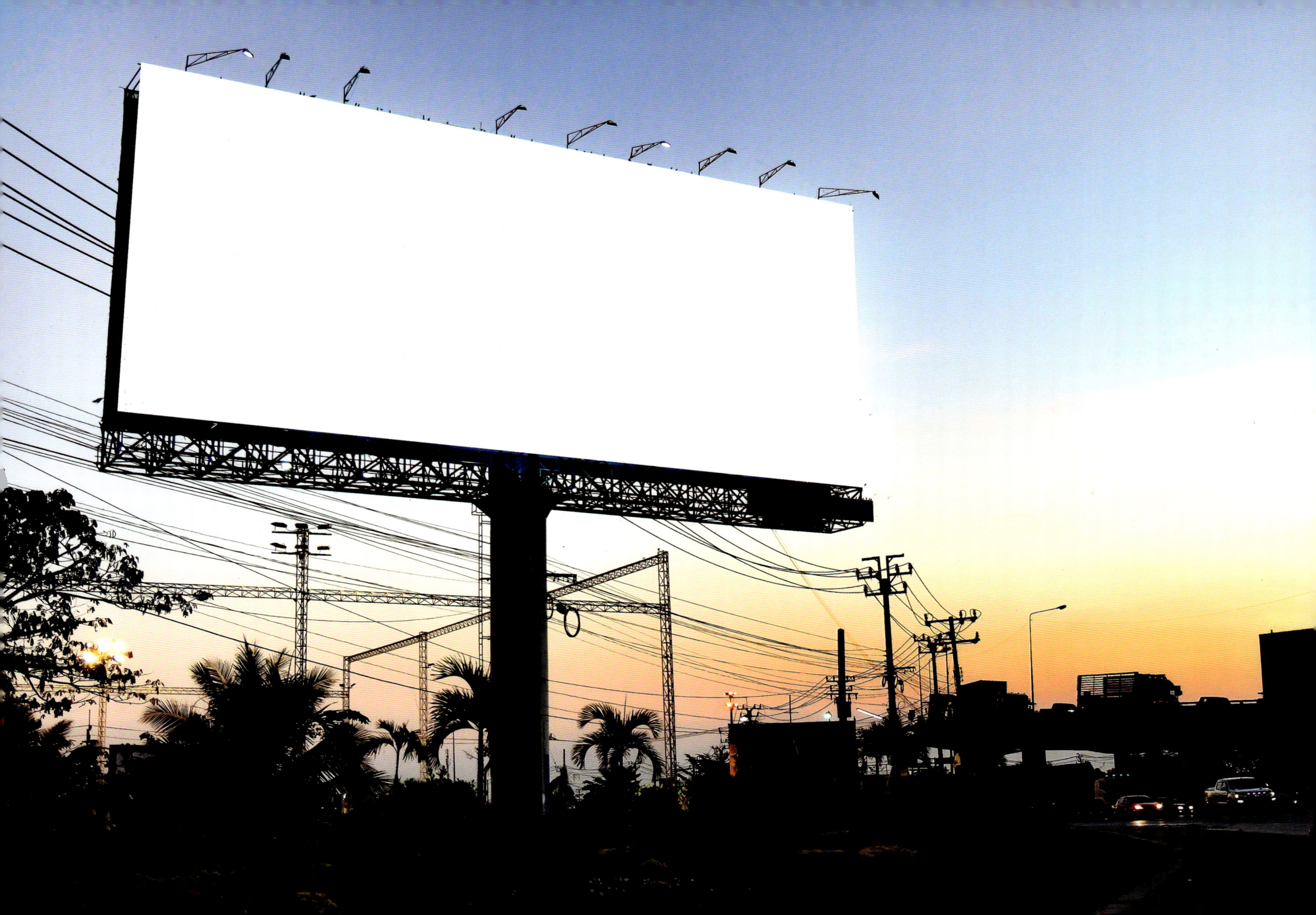

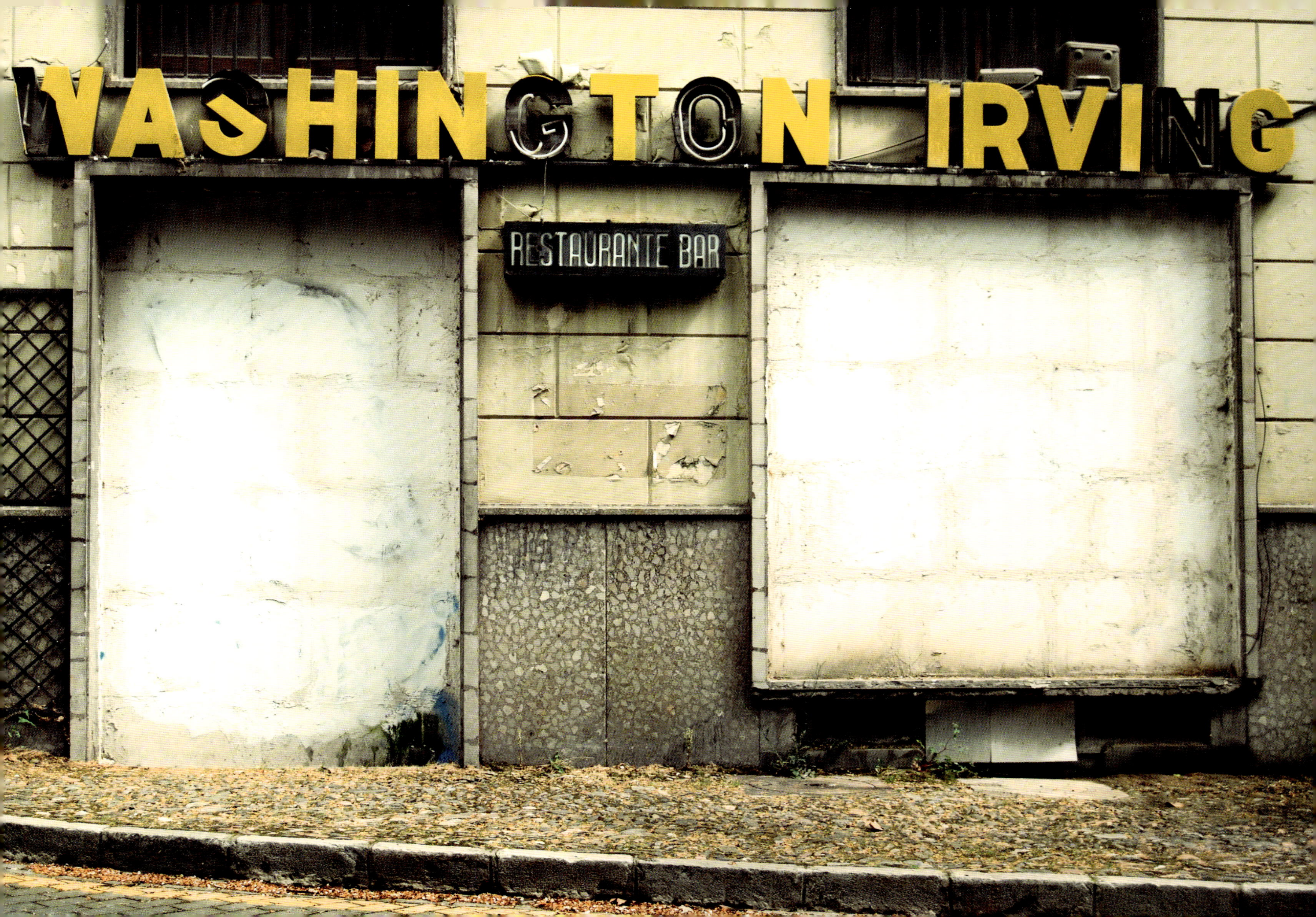
WASHINGTON IRVING
RESTAURANTE BAR

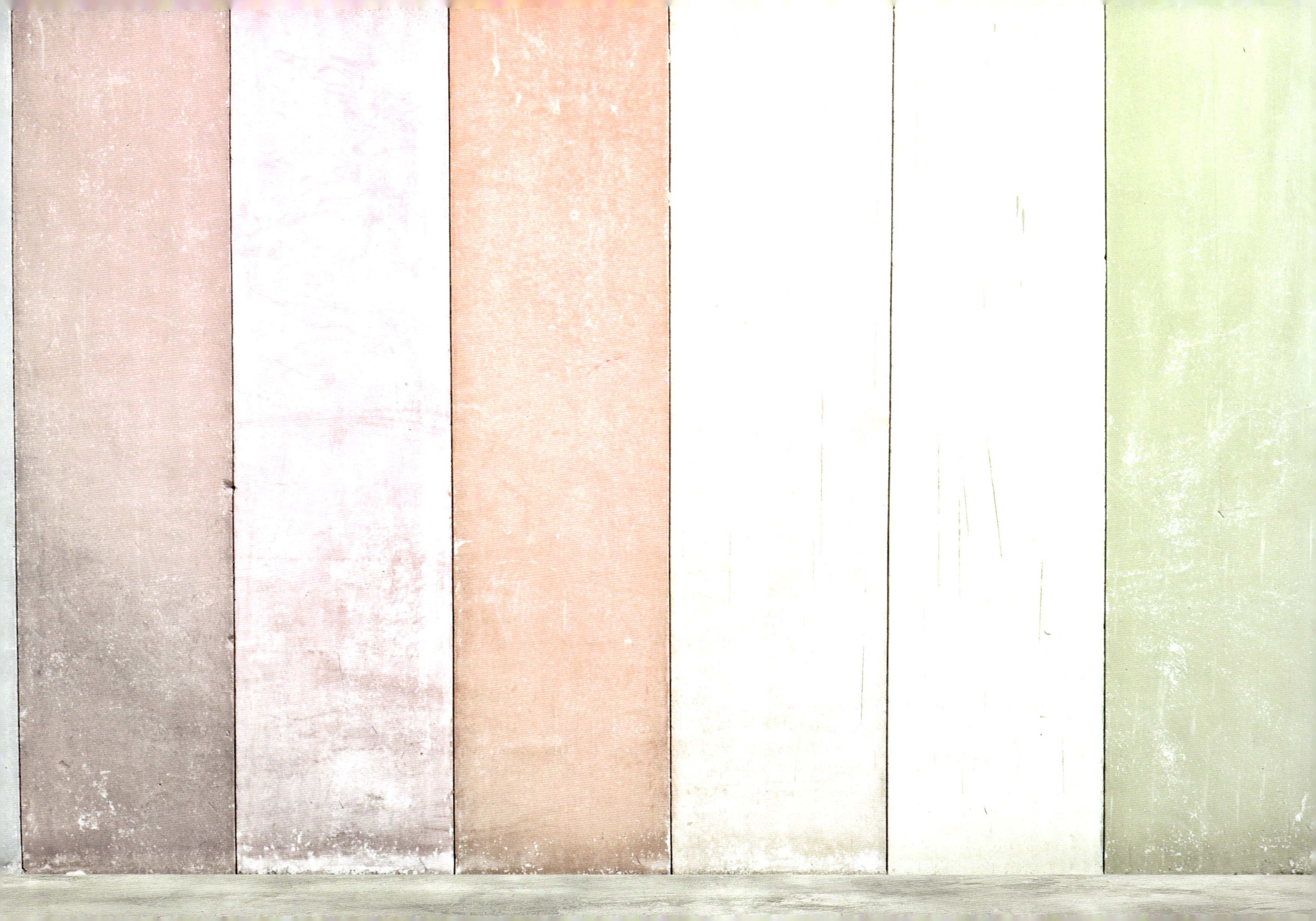

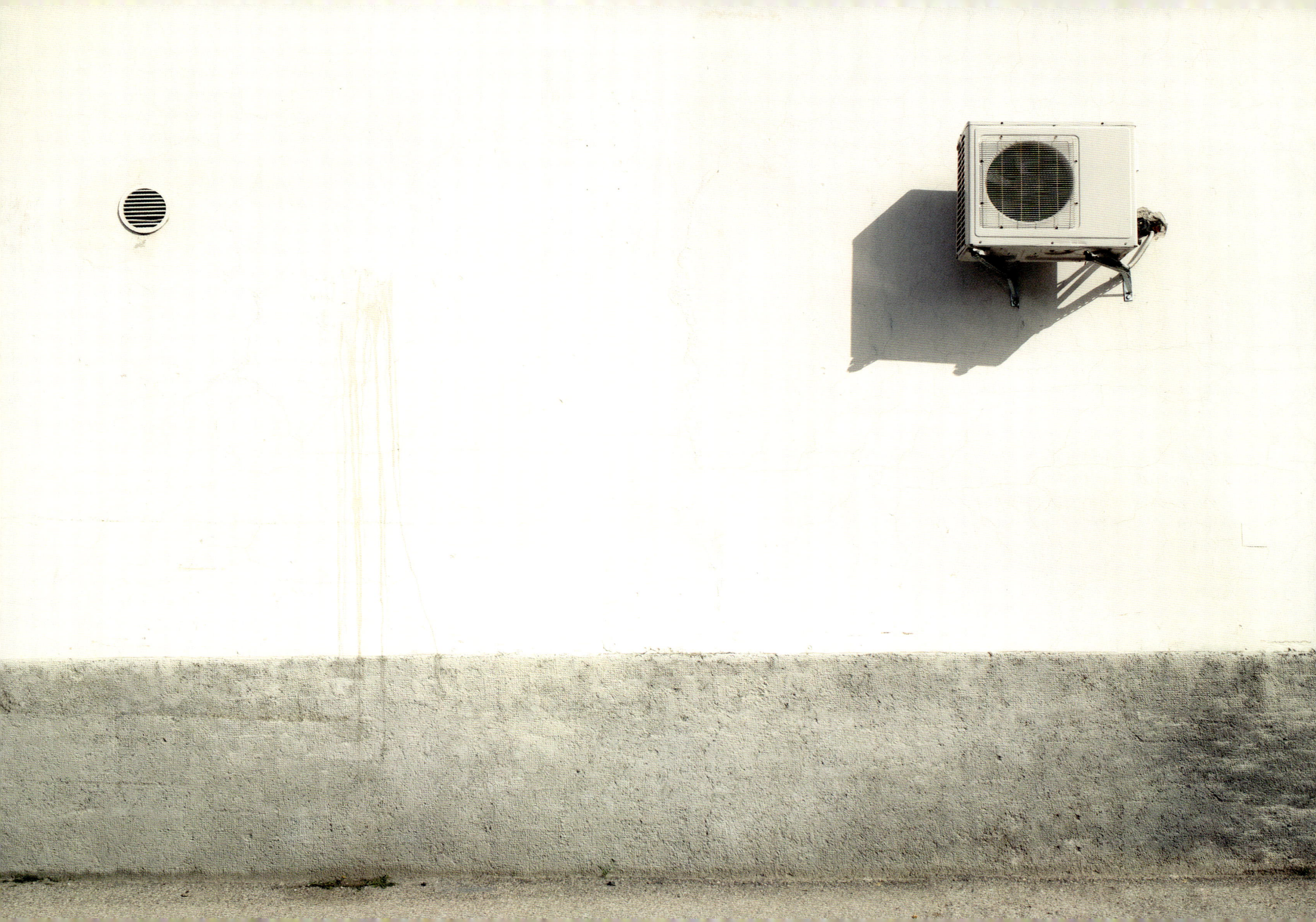

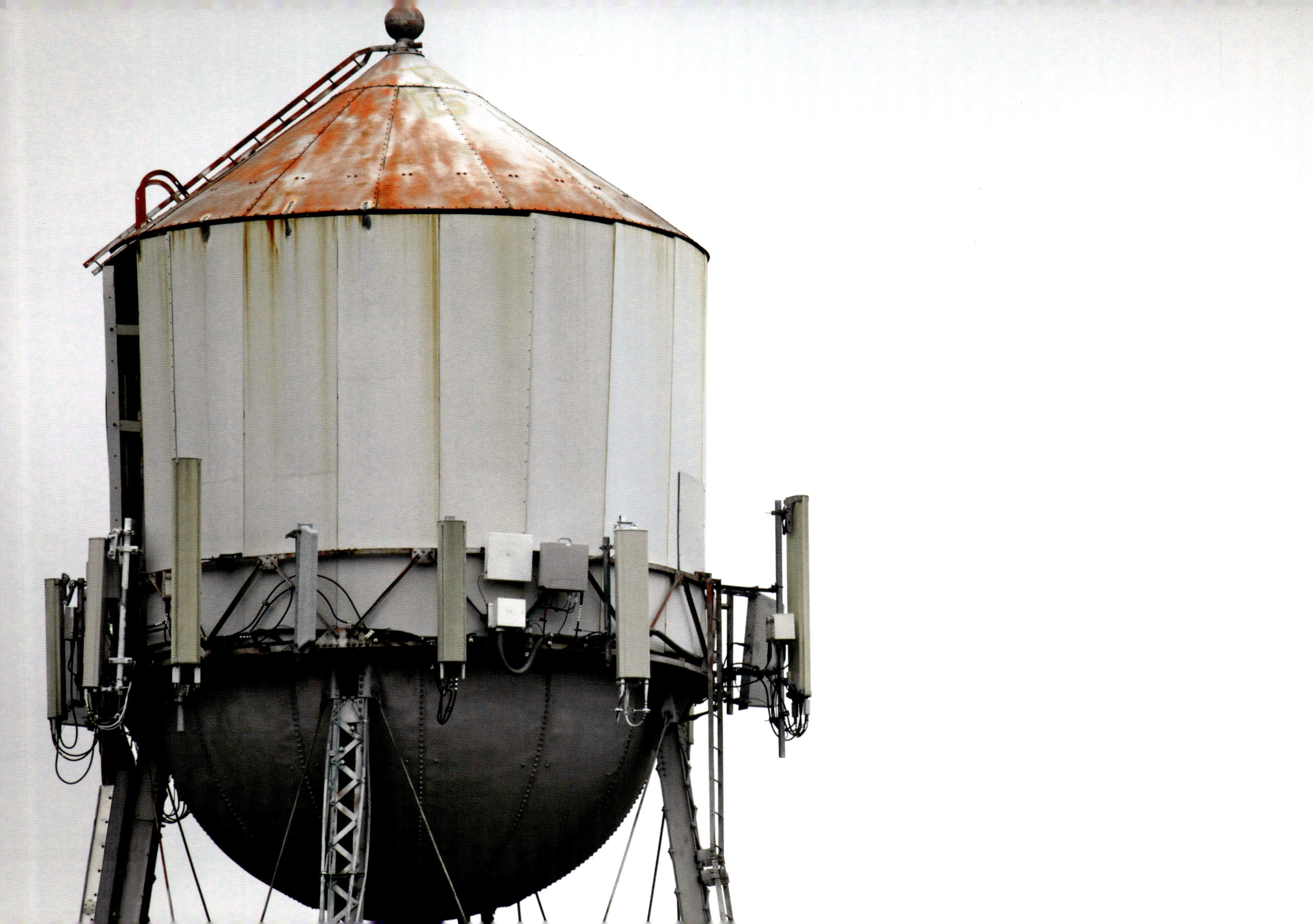

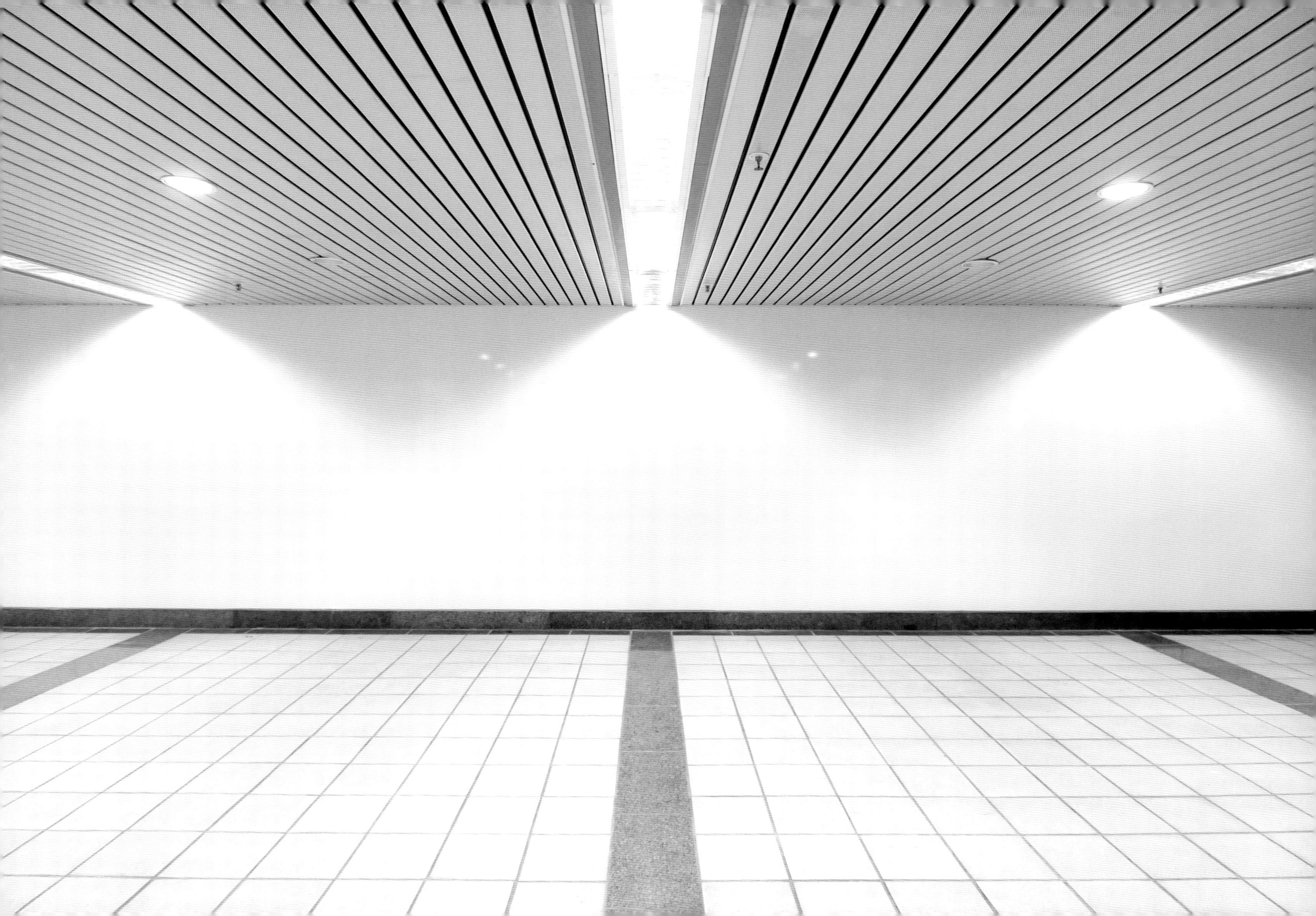

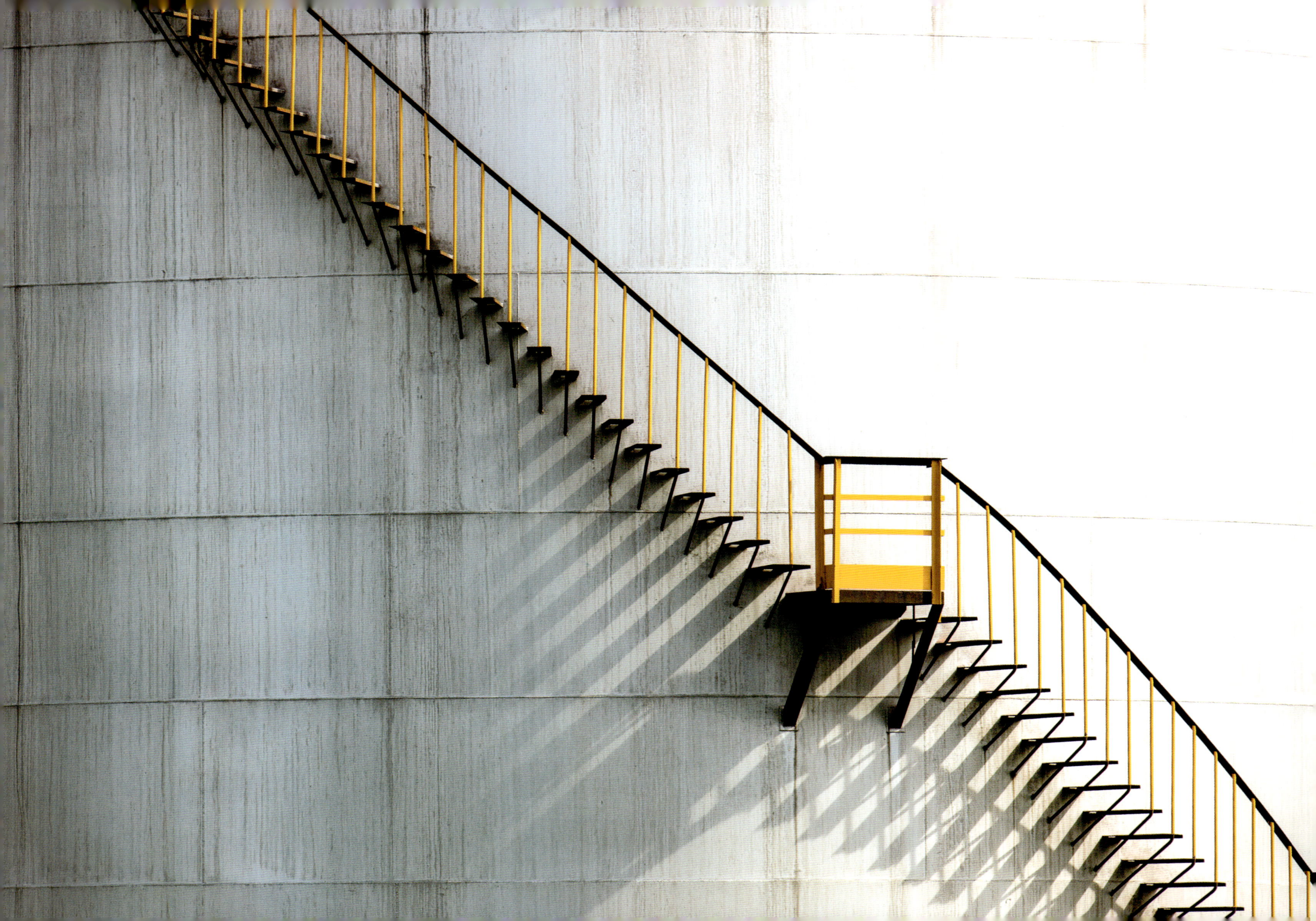

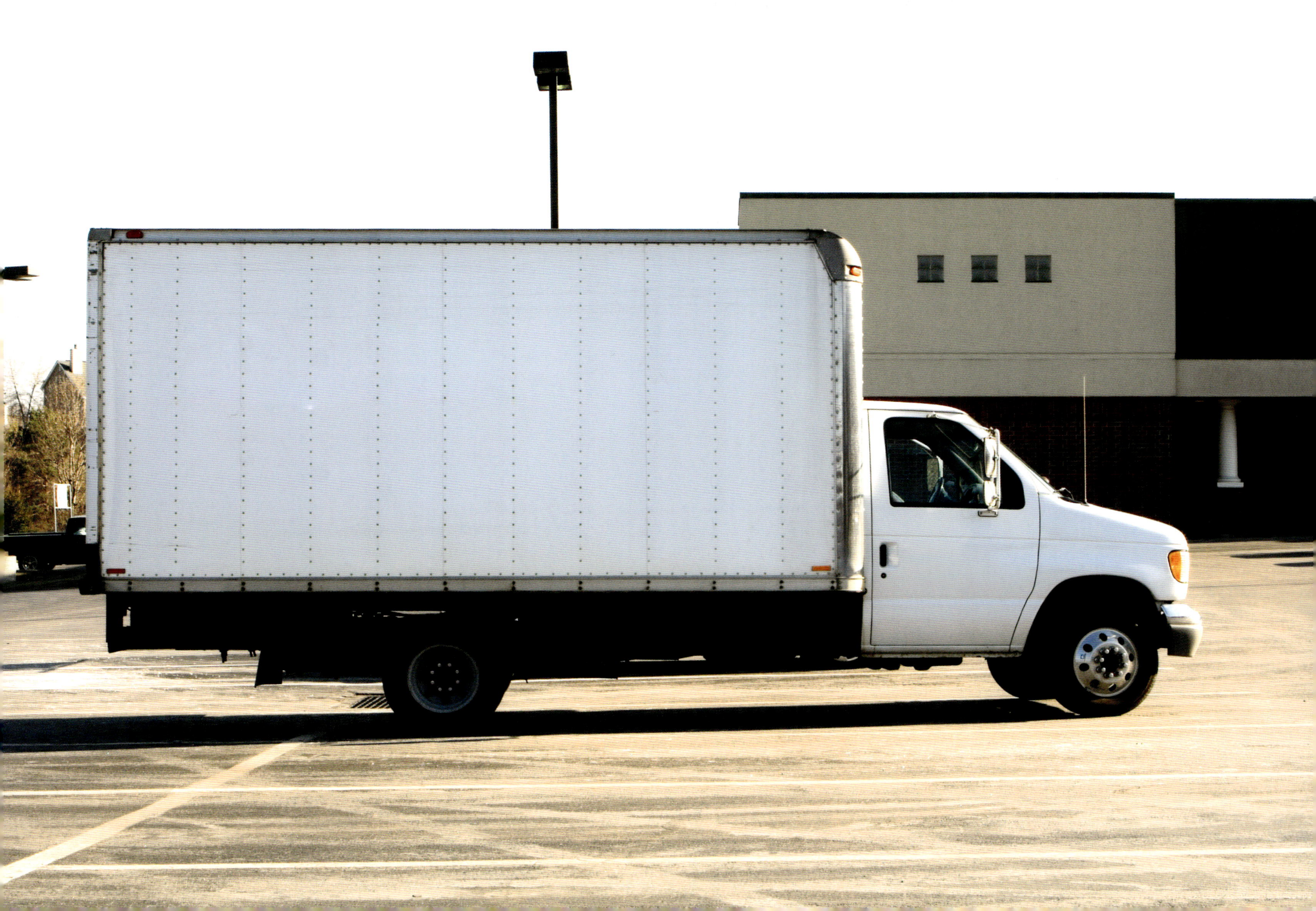

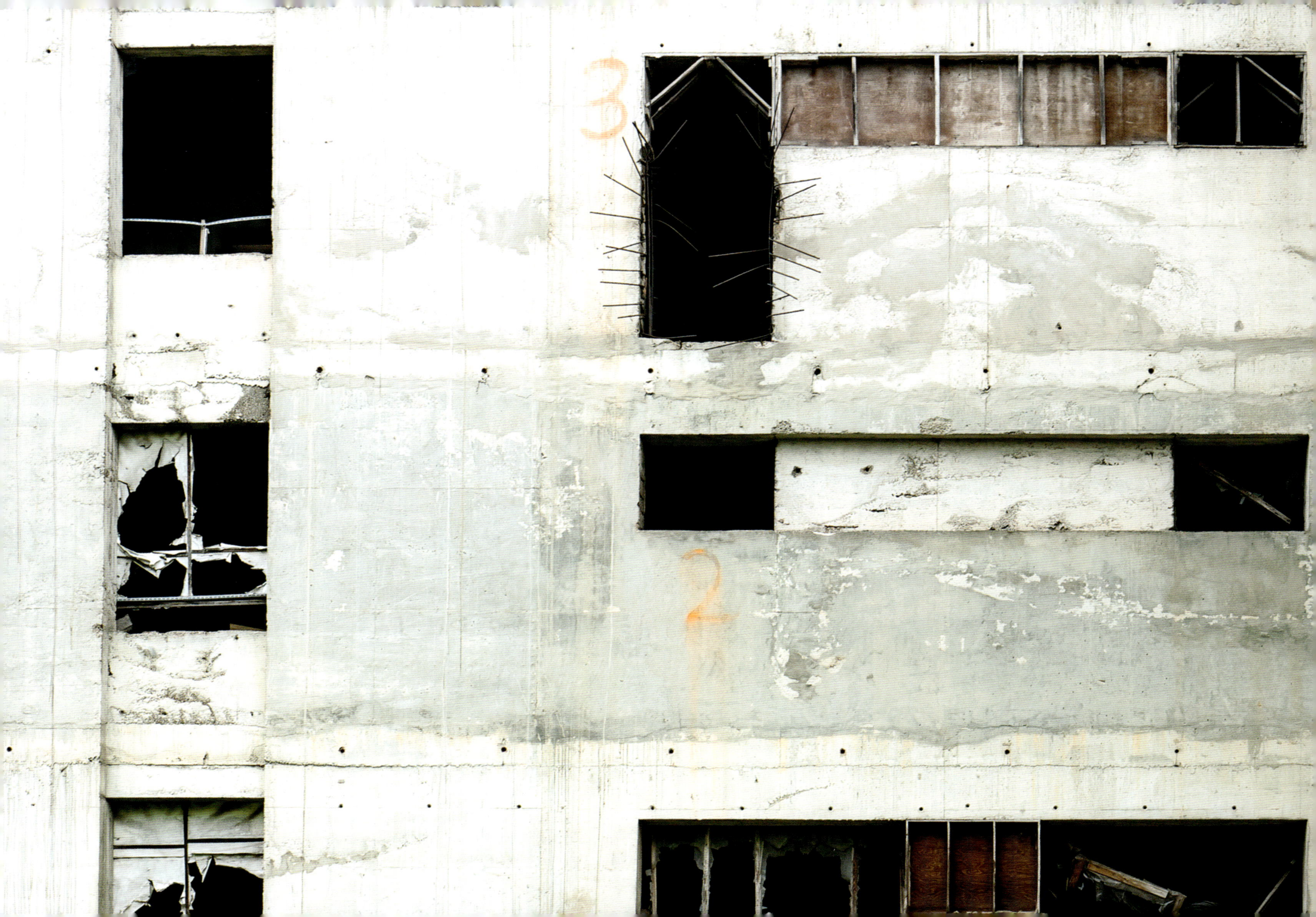

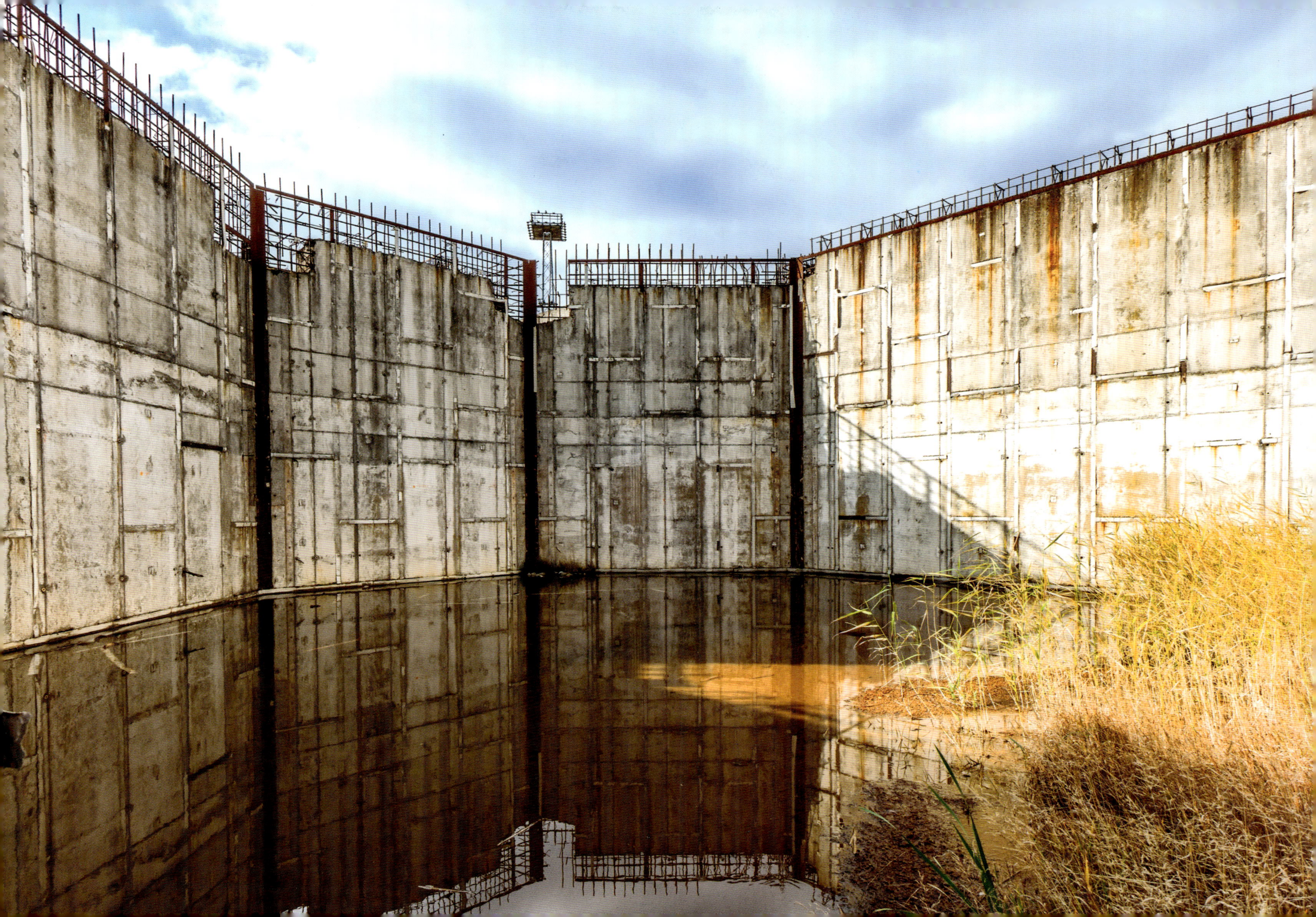

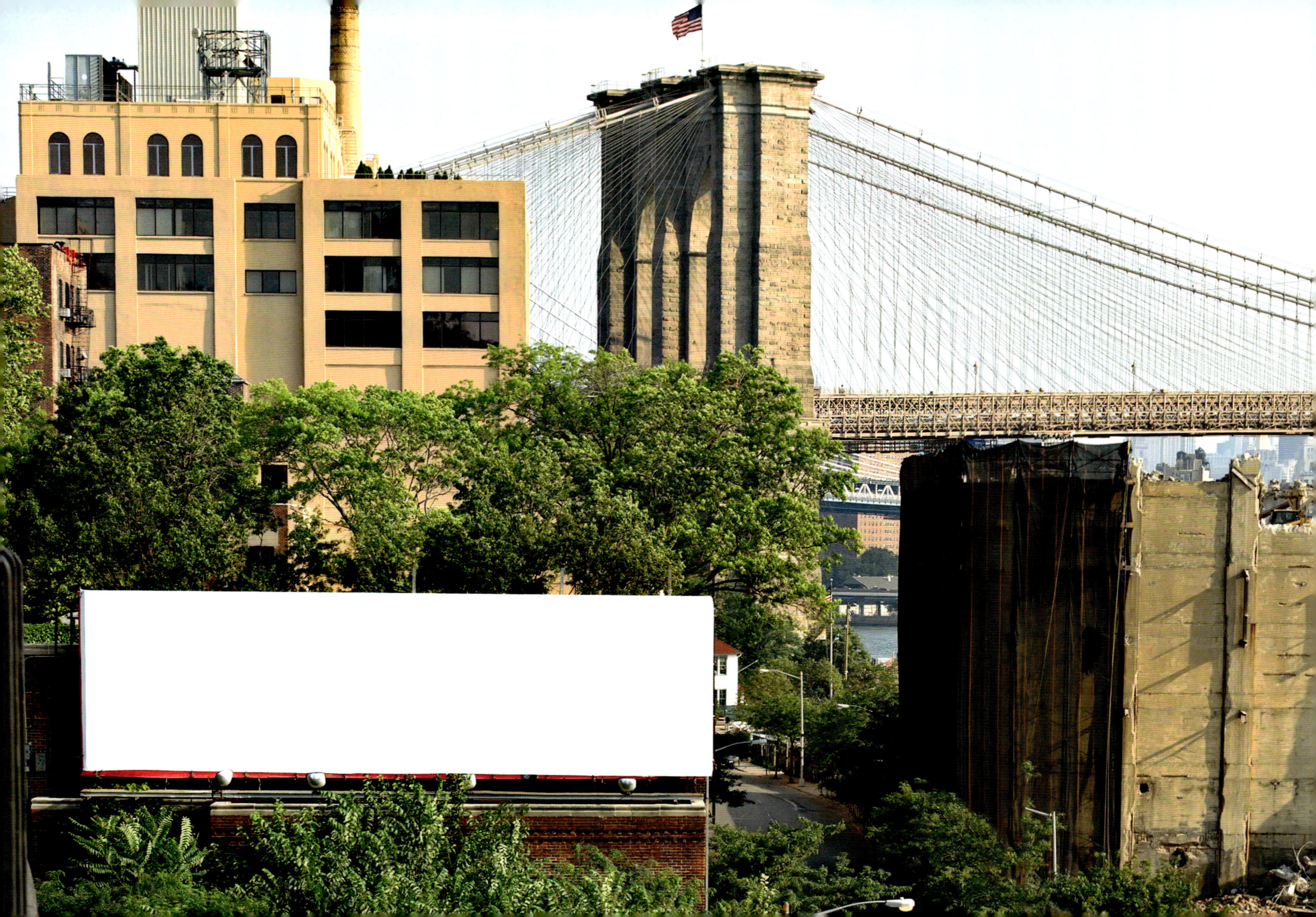

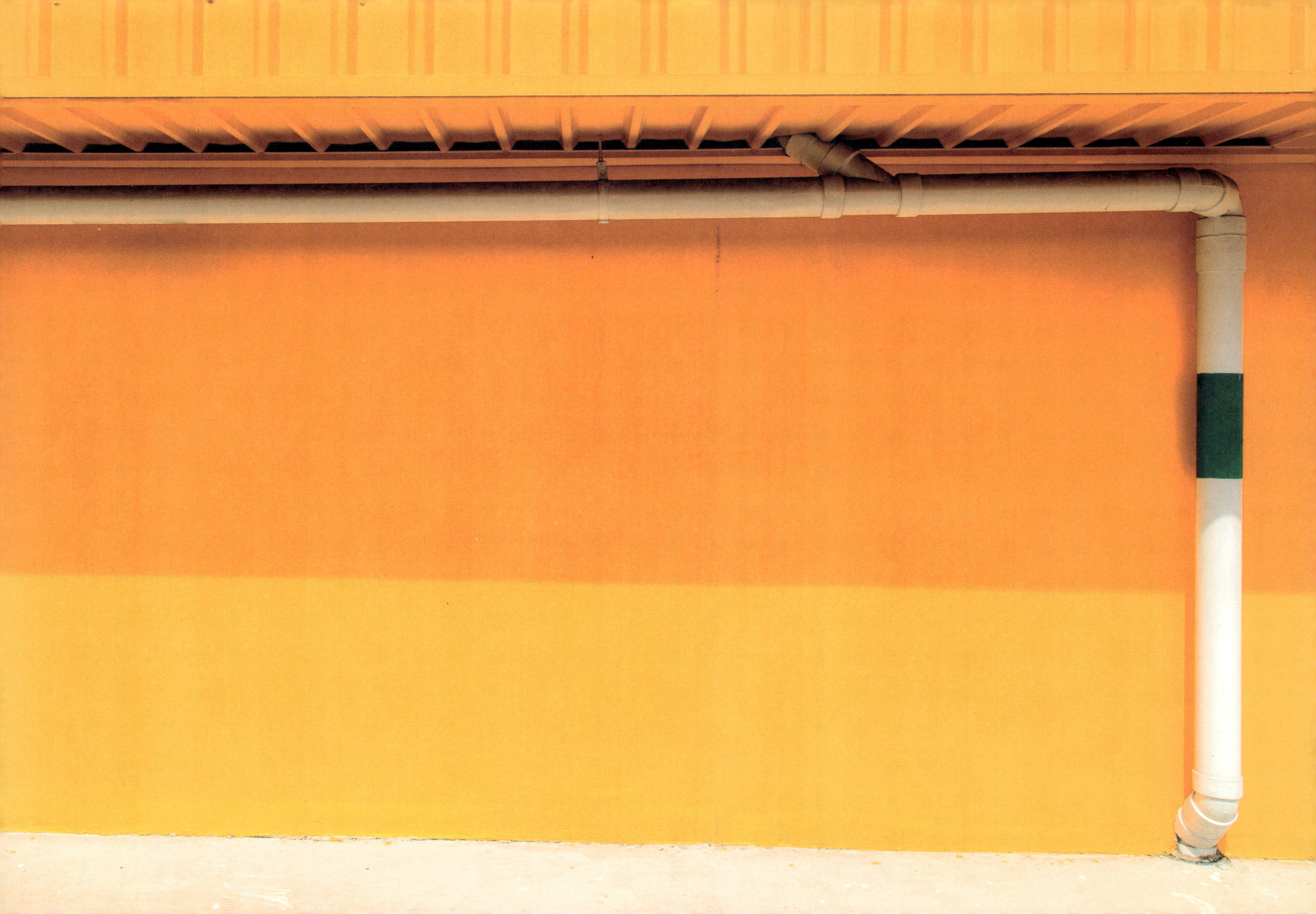

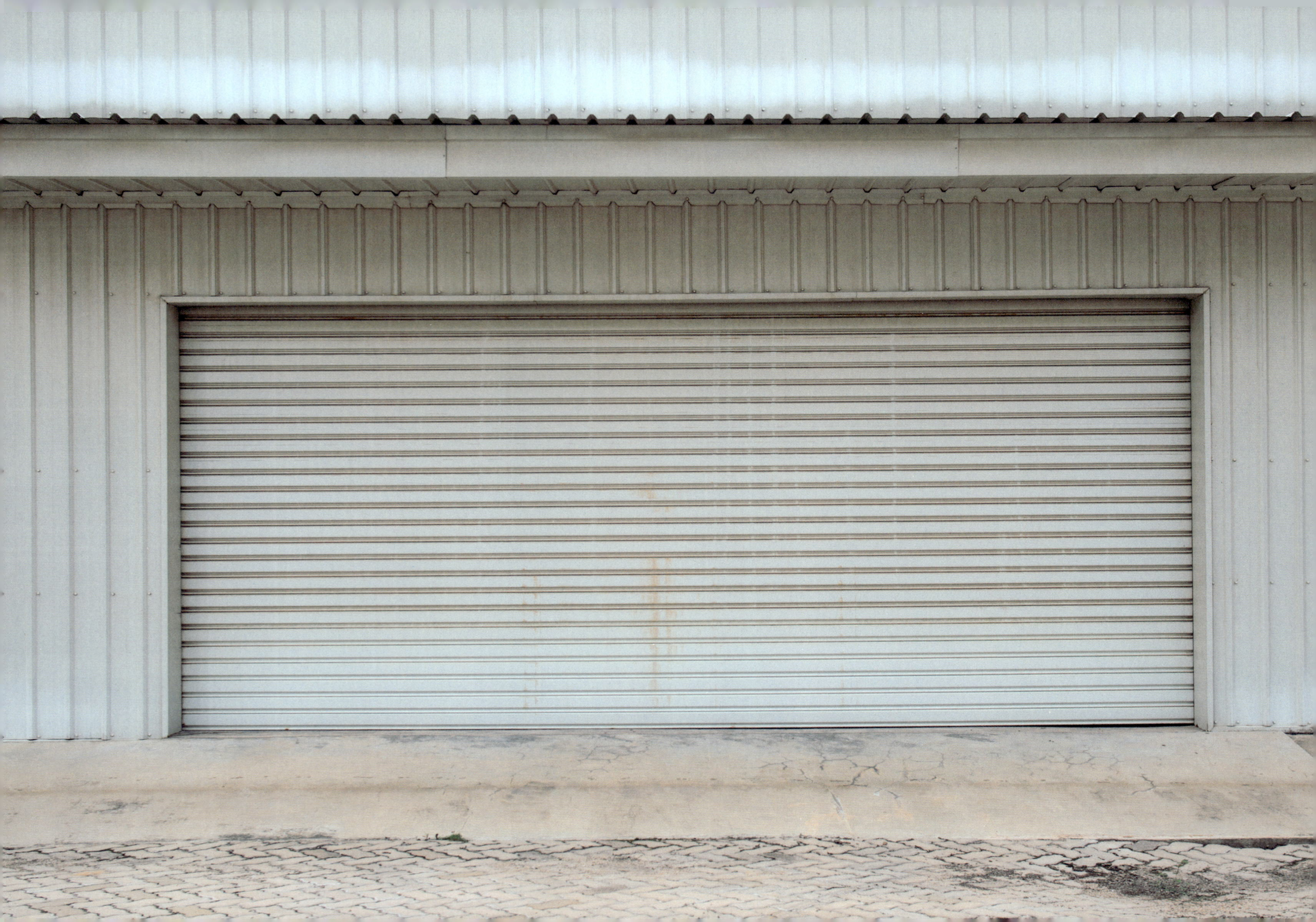

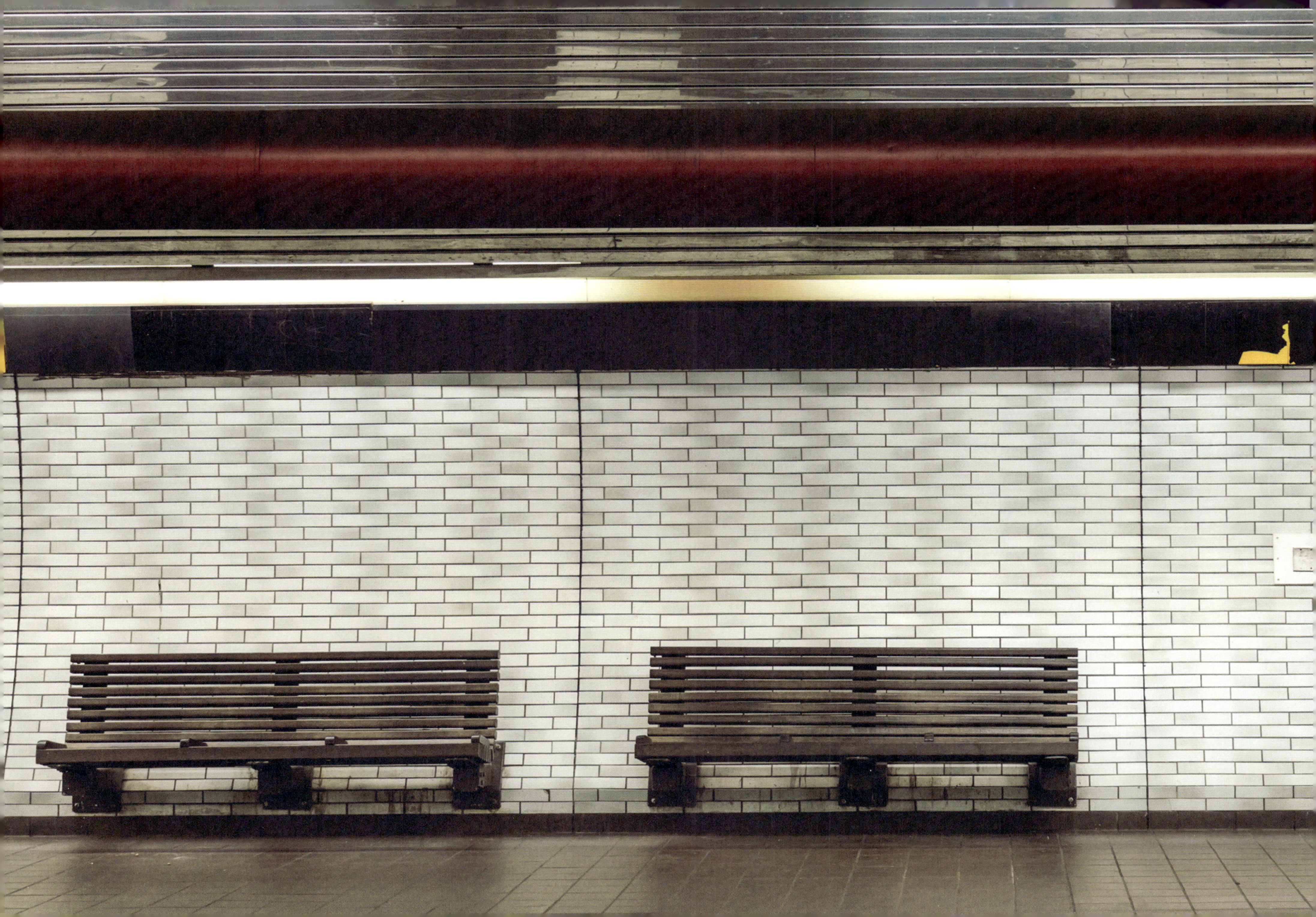

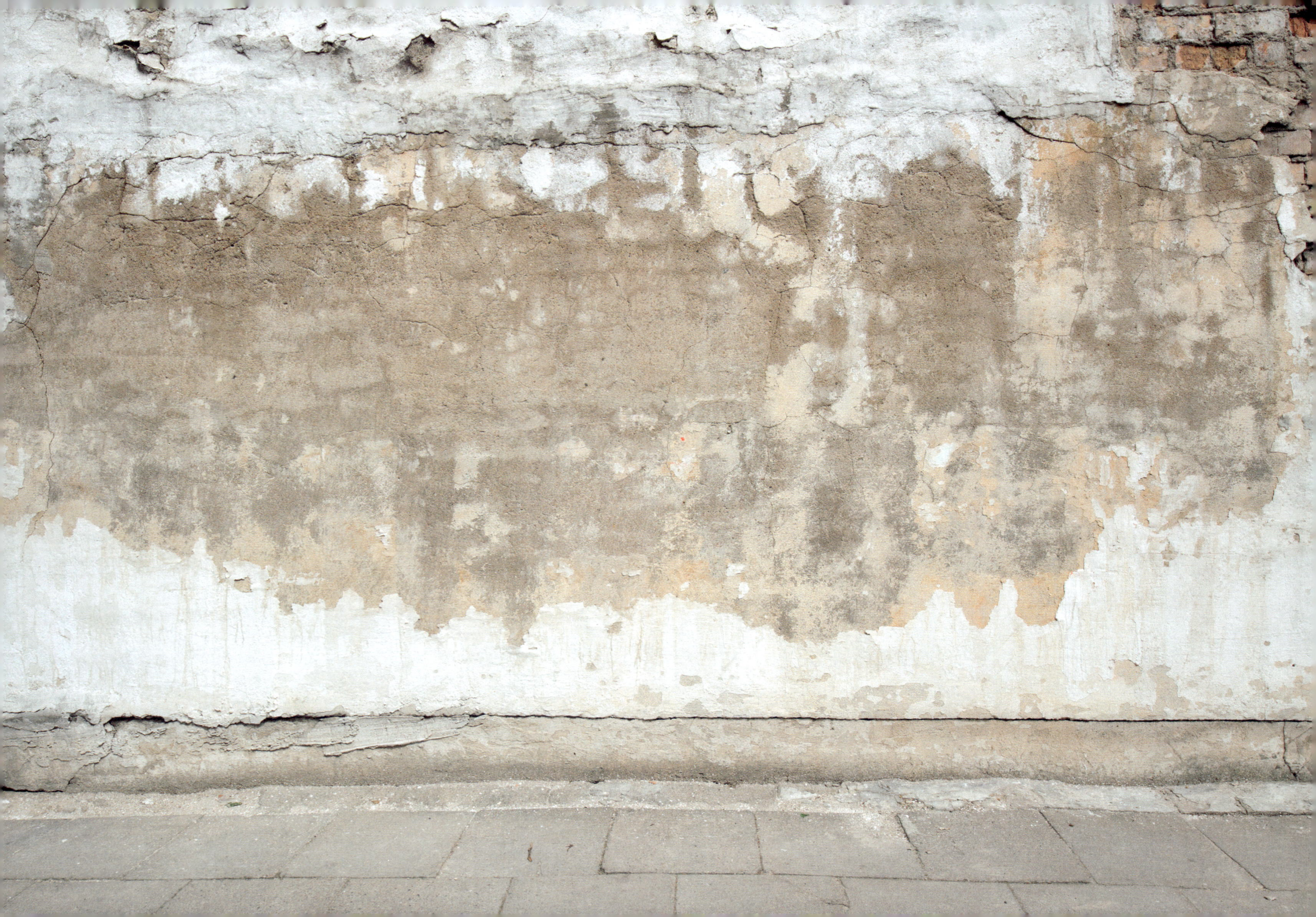

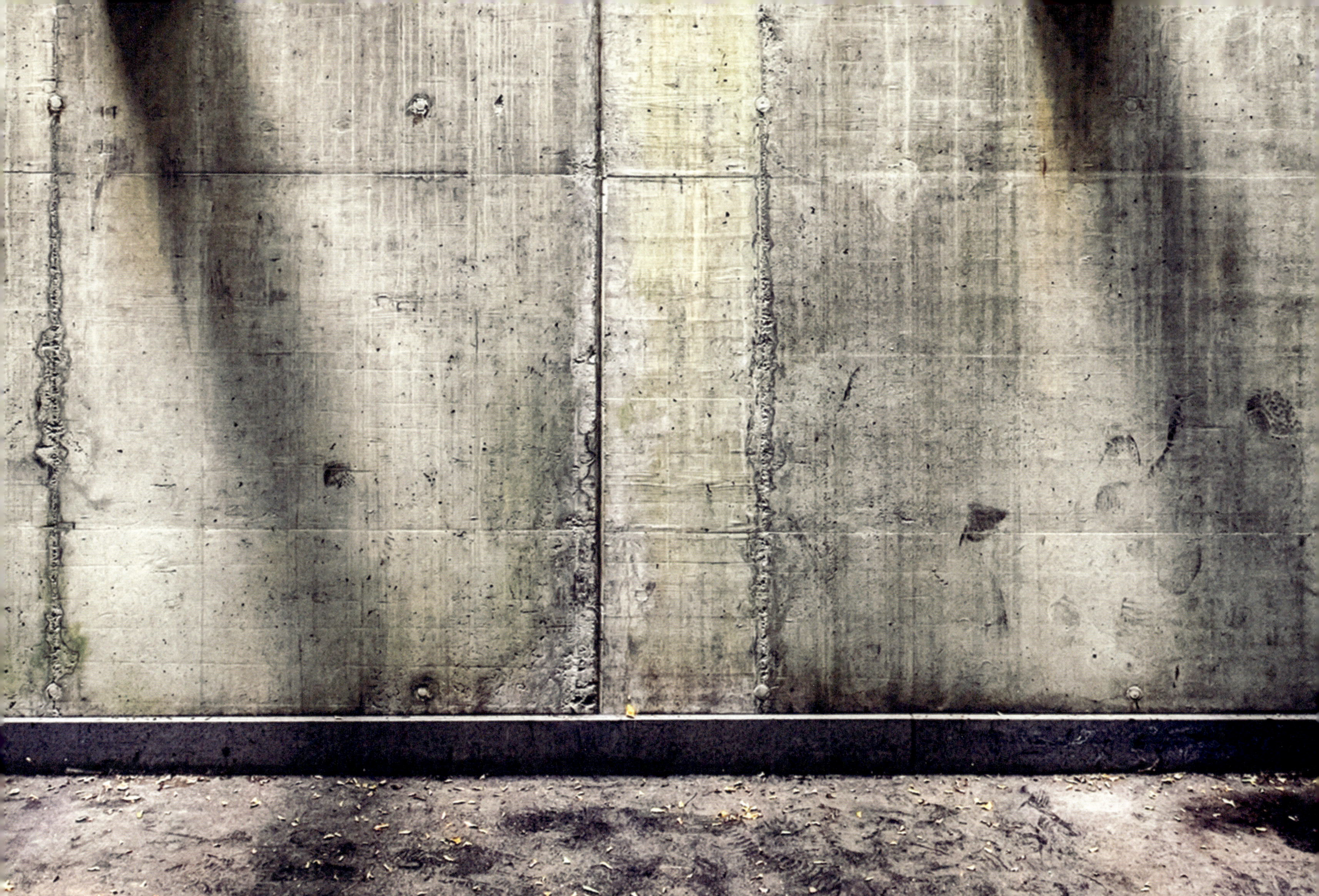

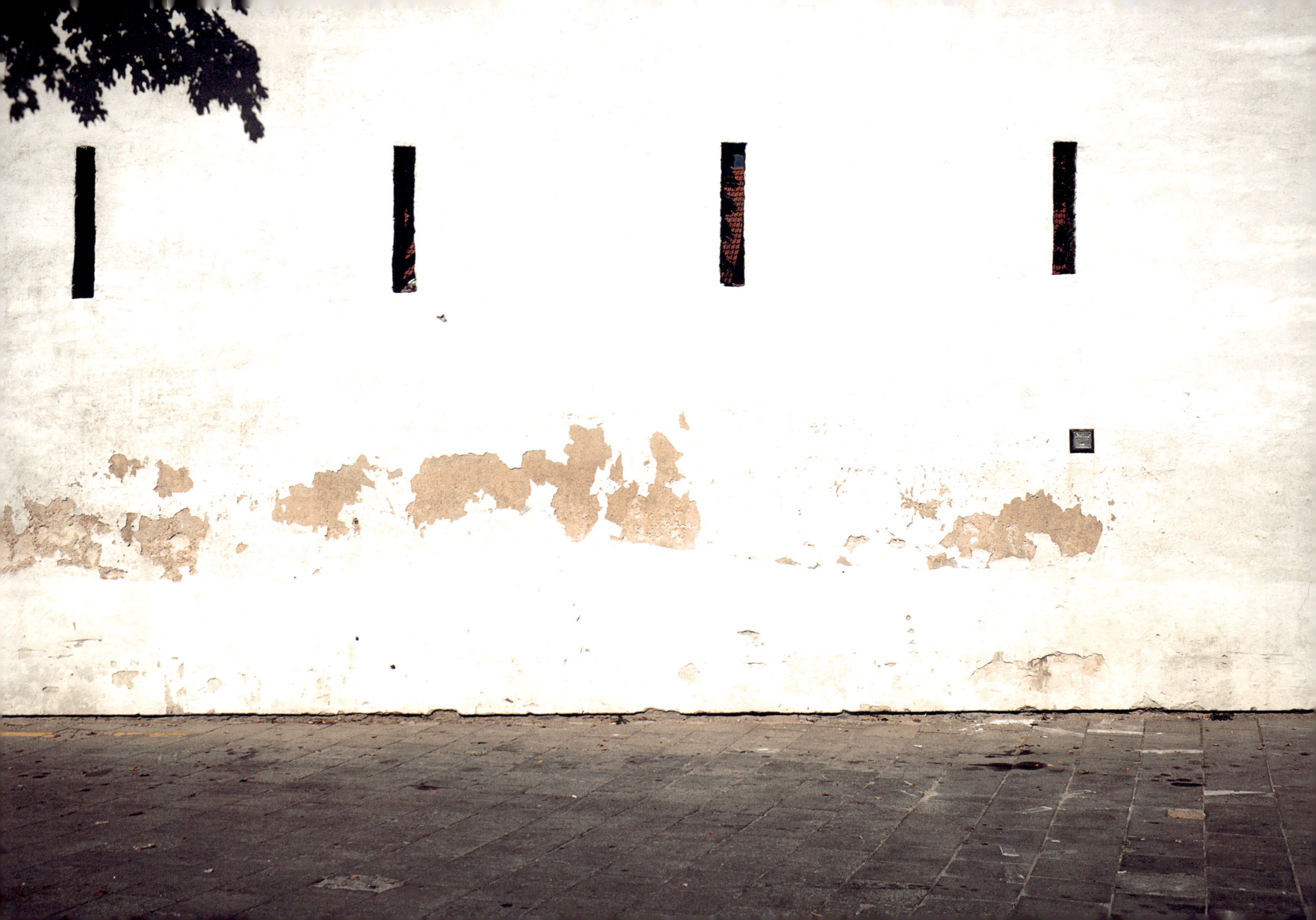

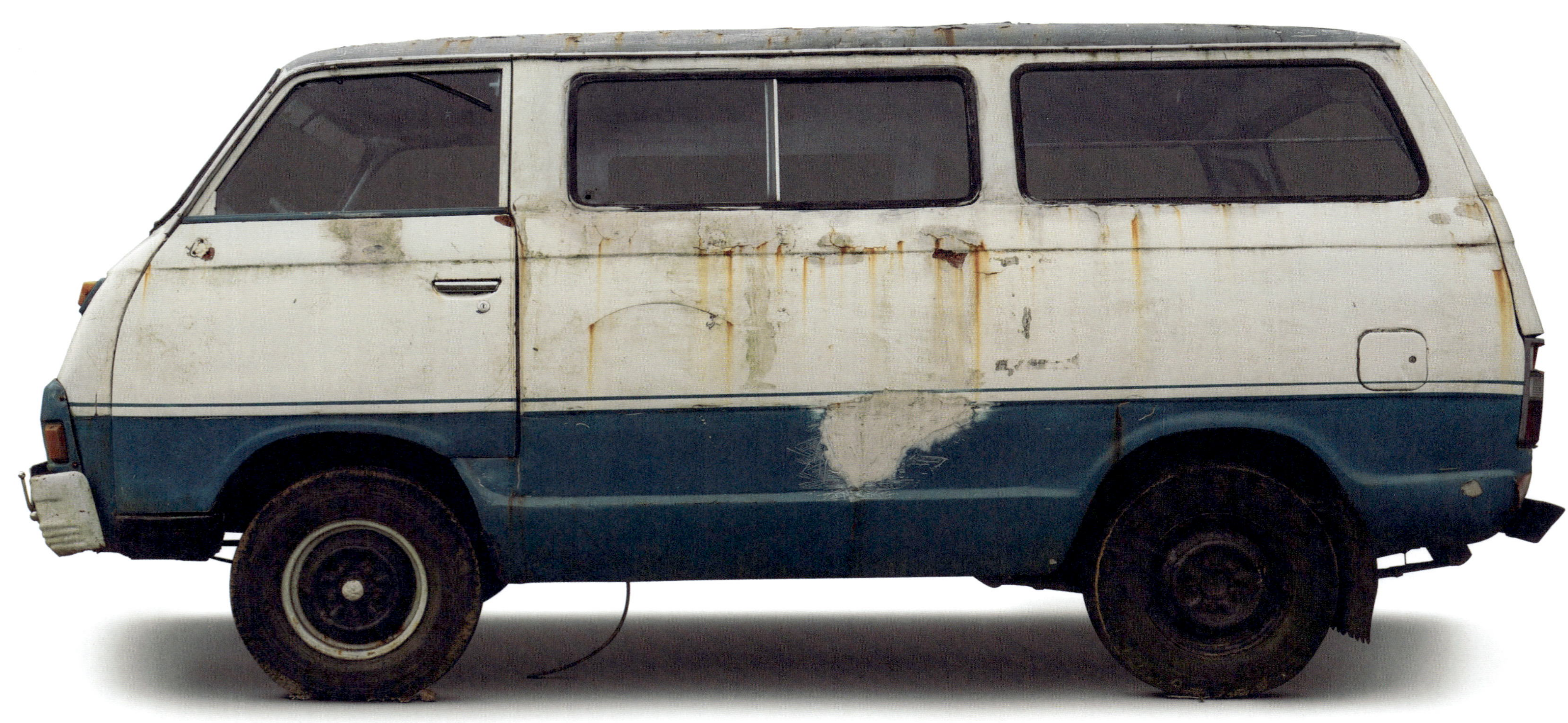

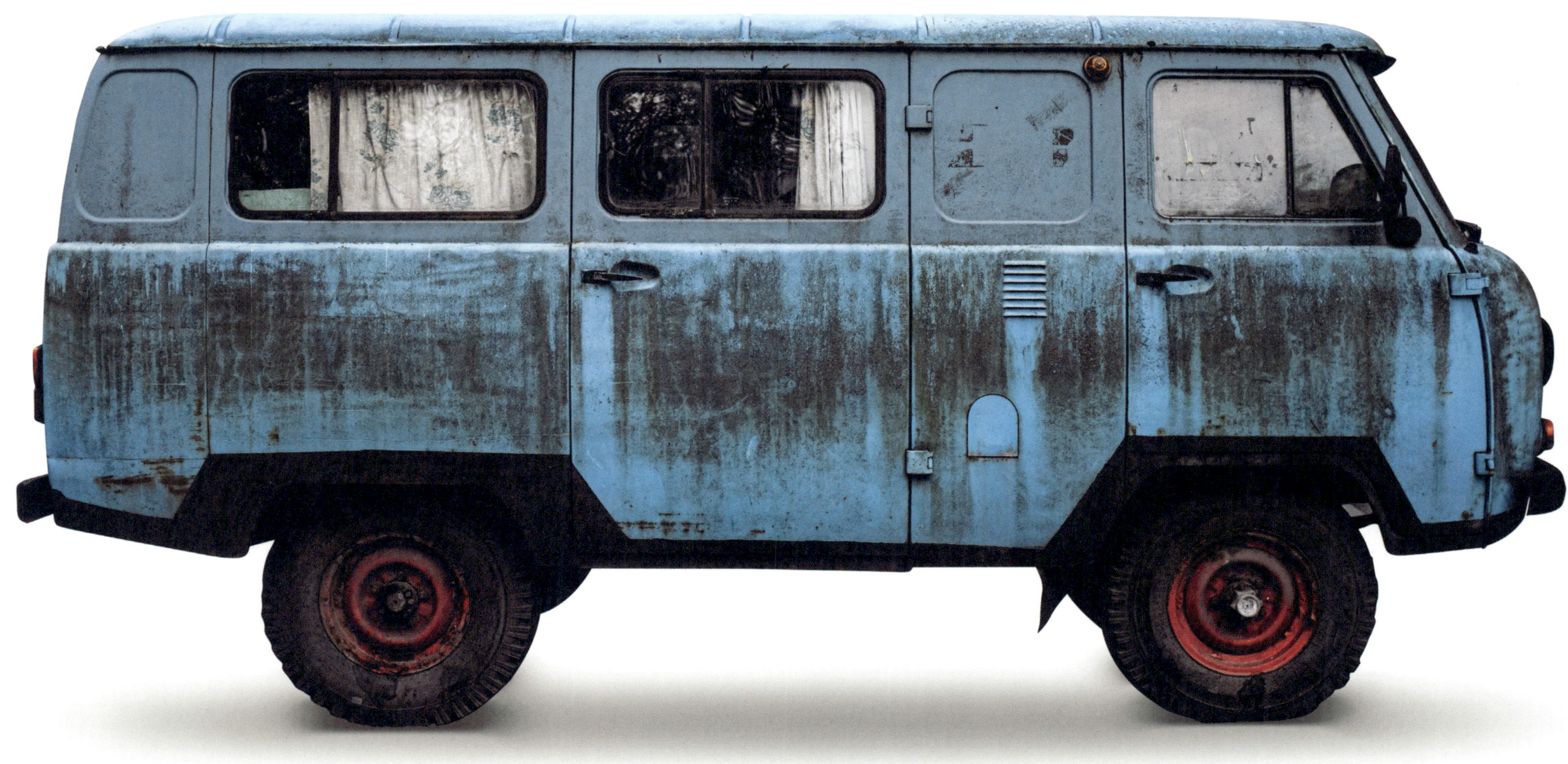

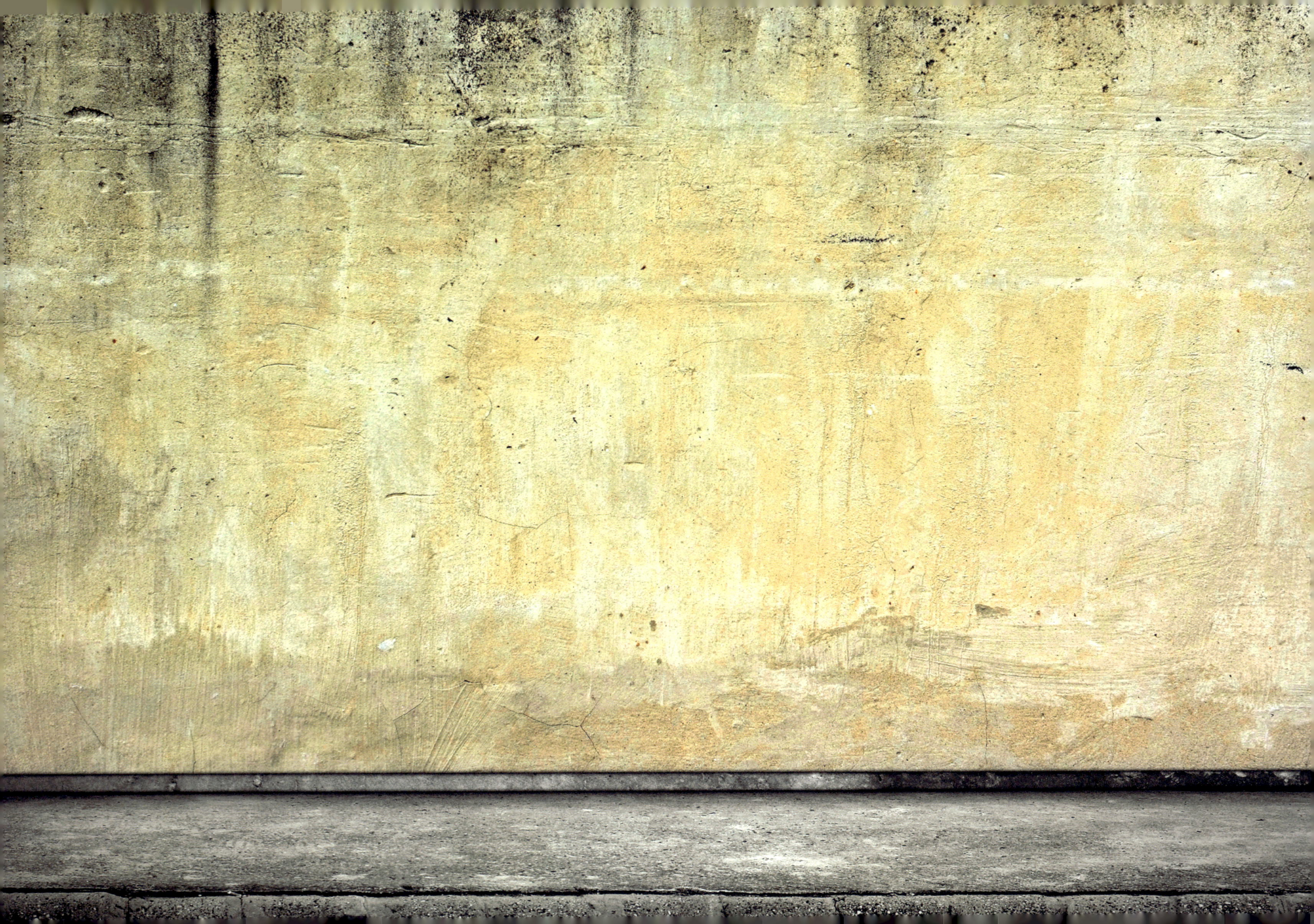

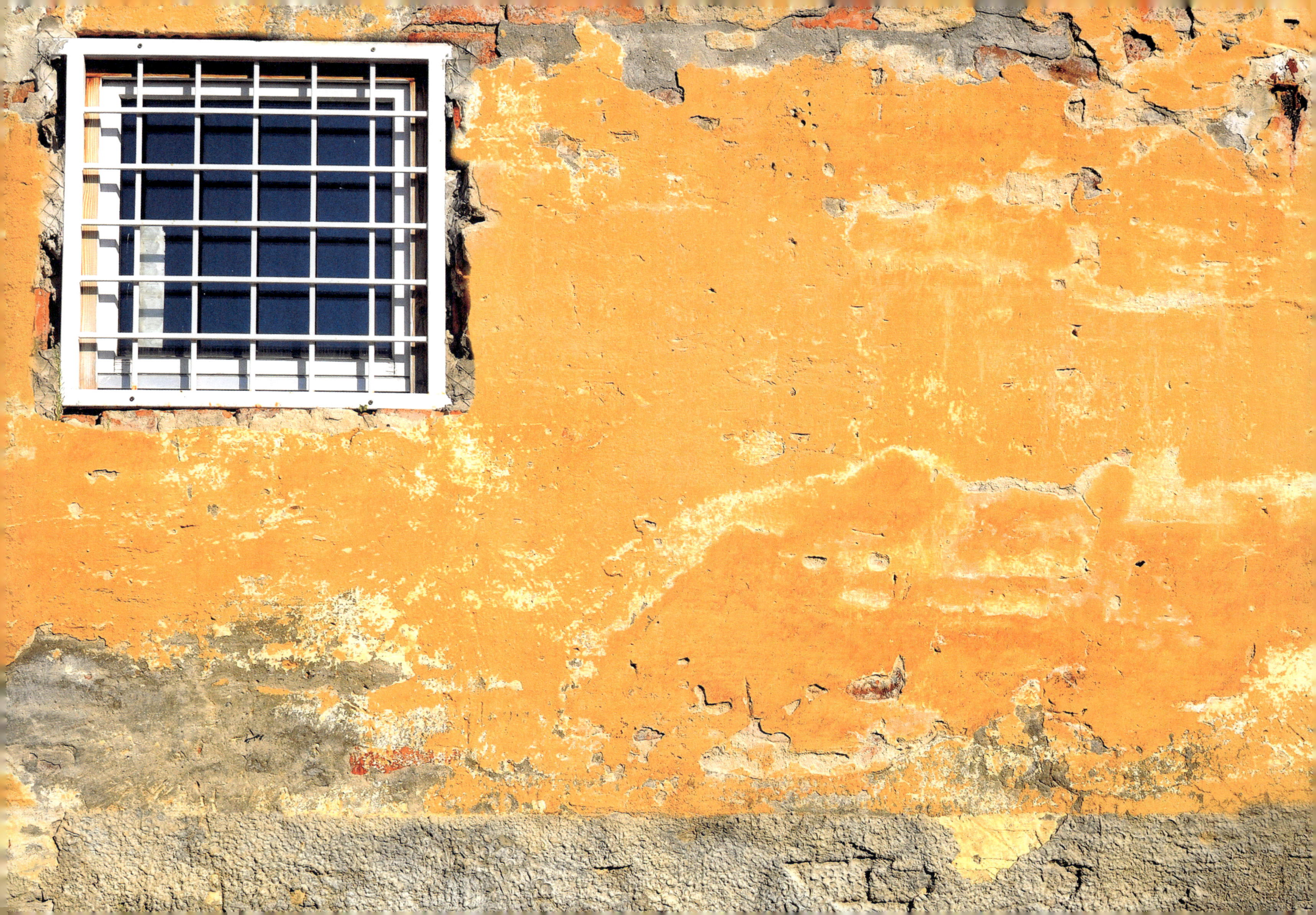

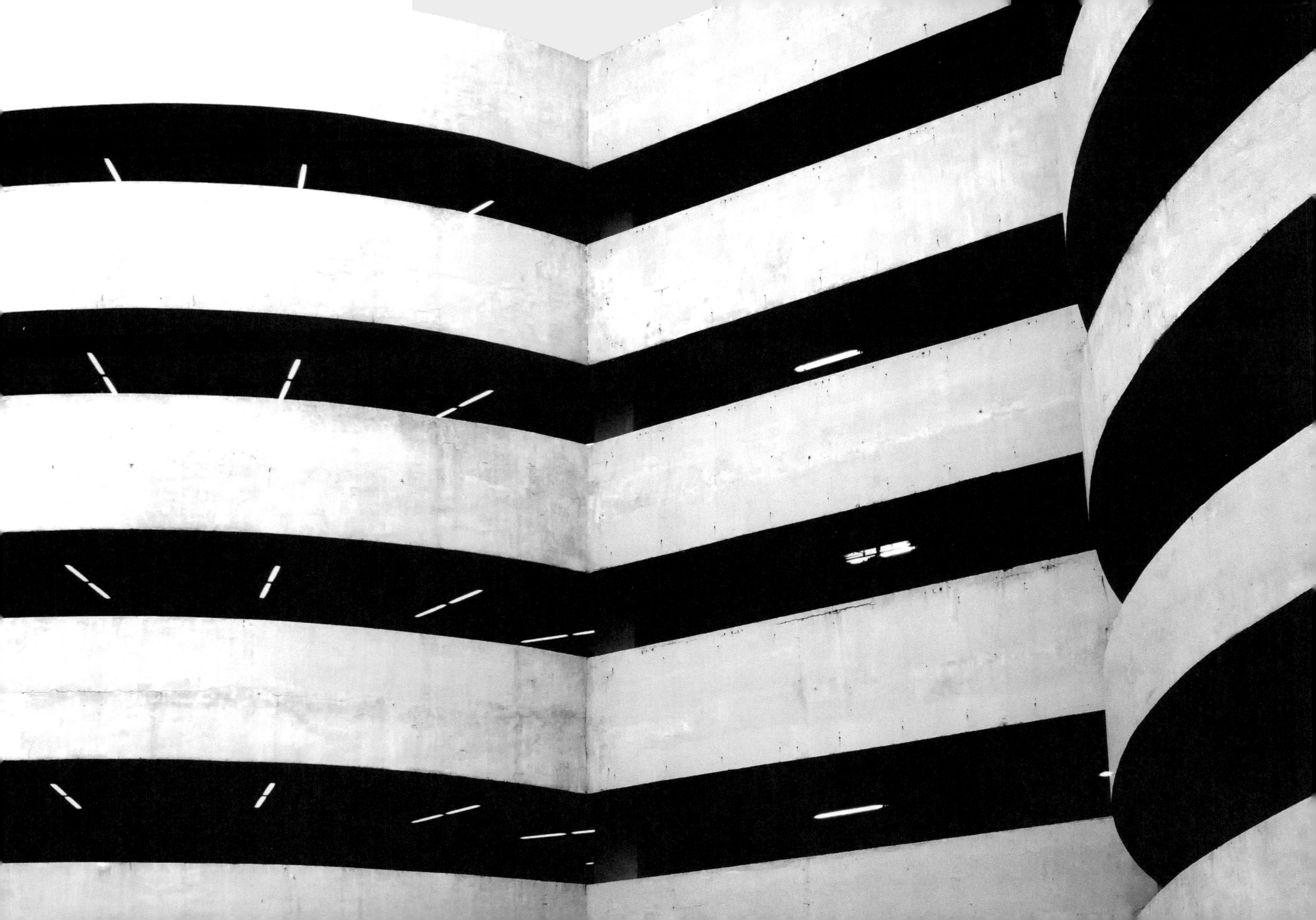

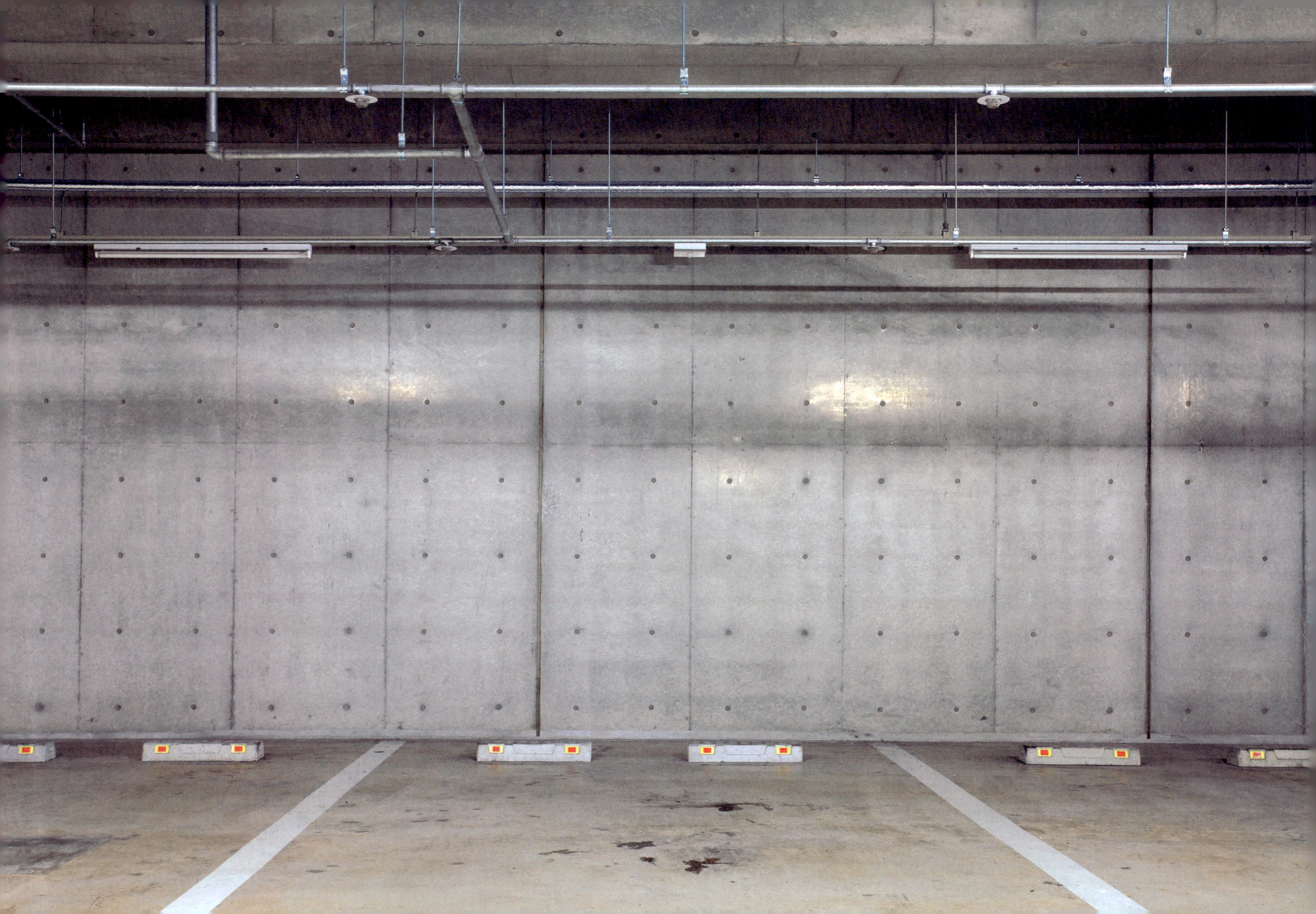

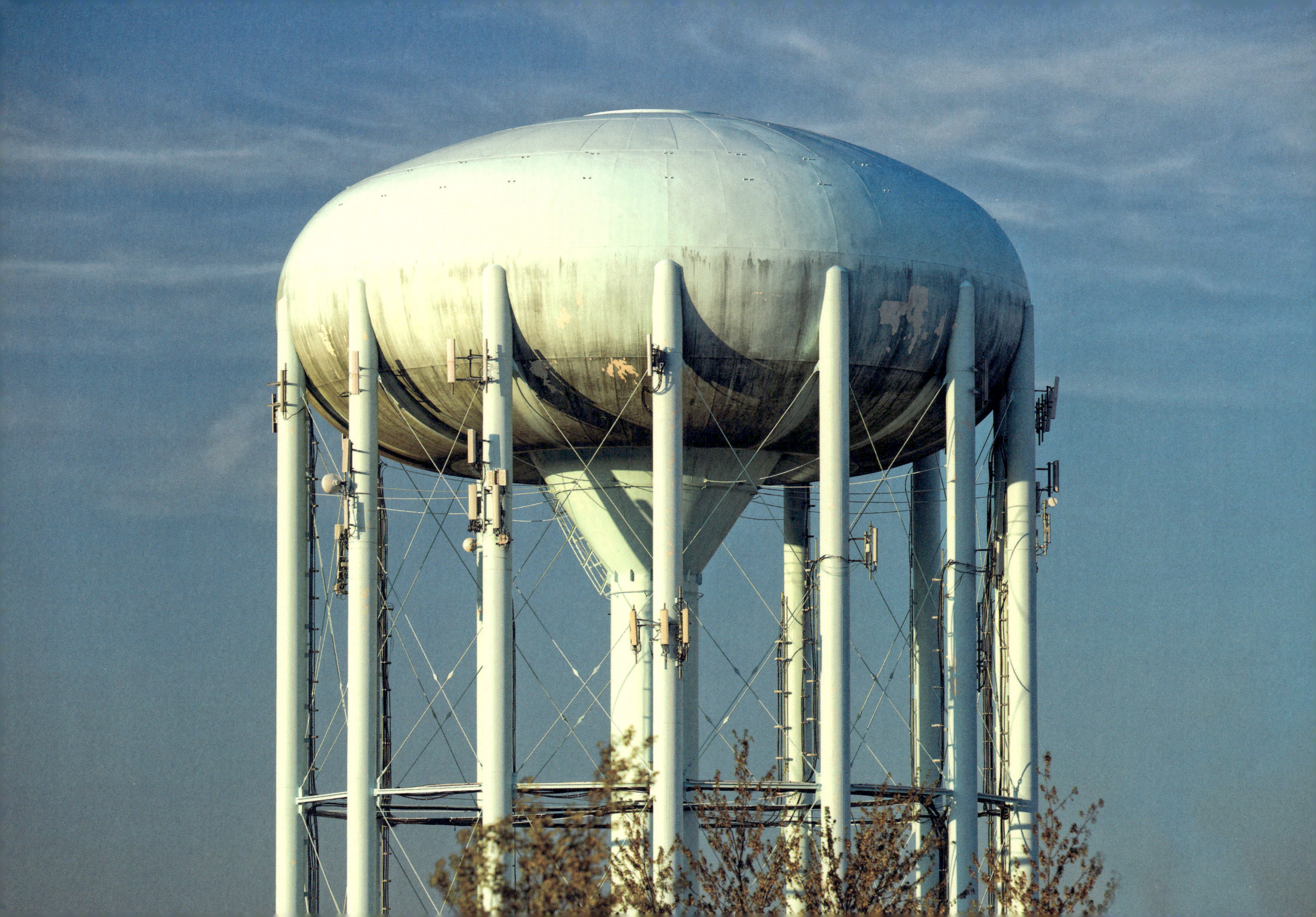

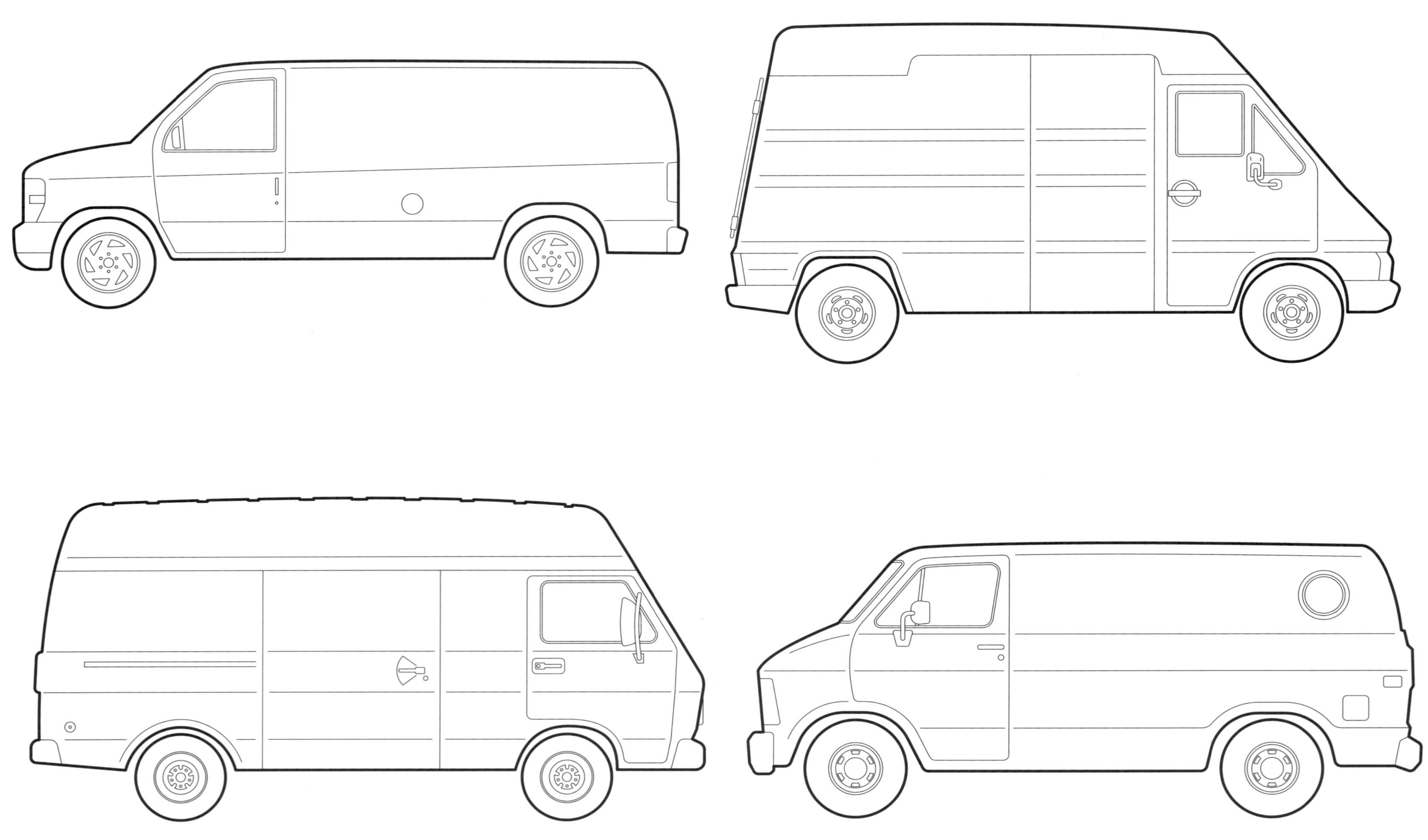

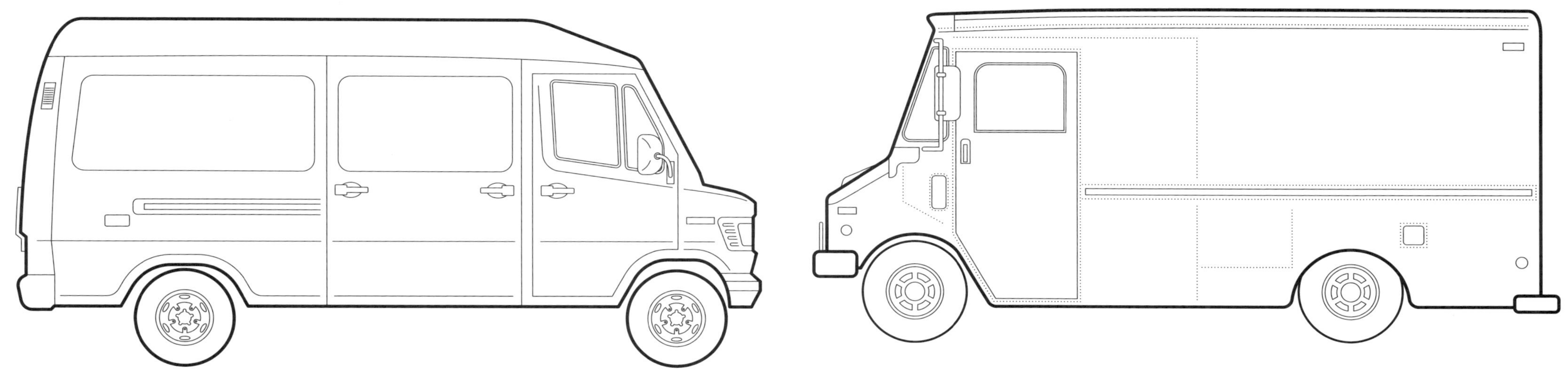

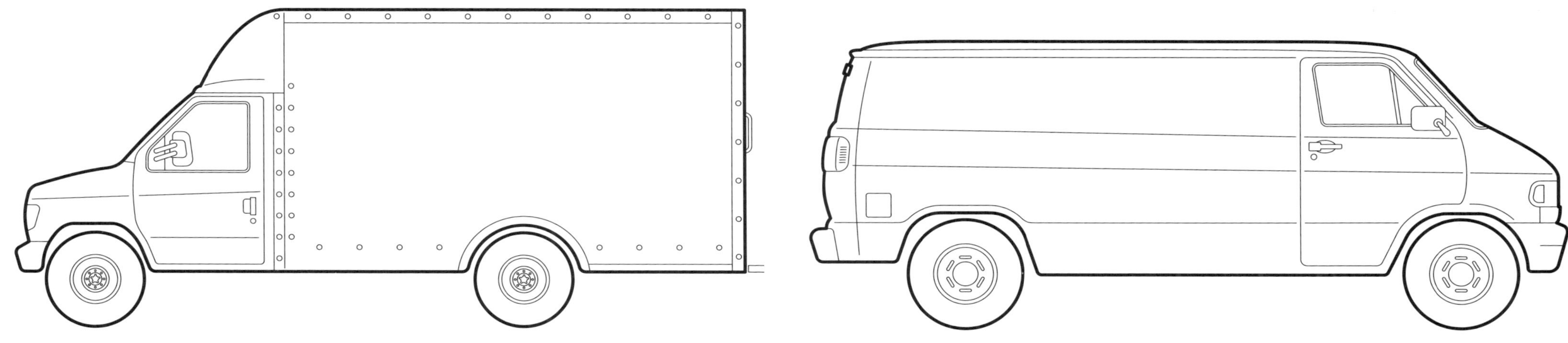

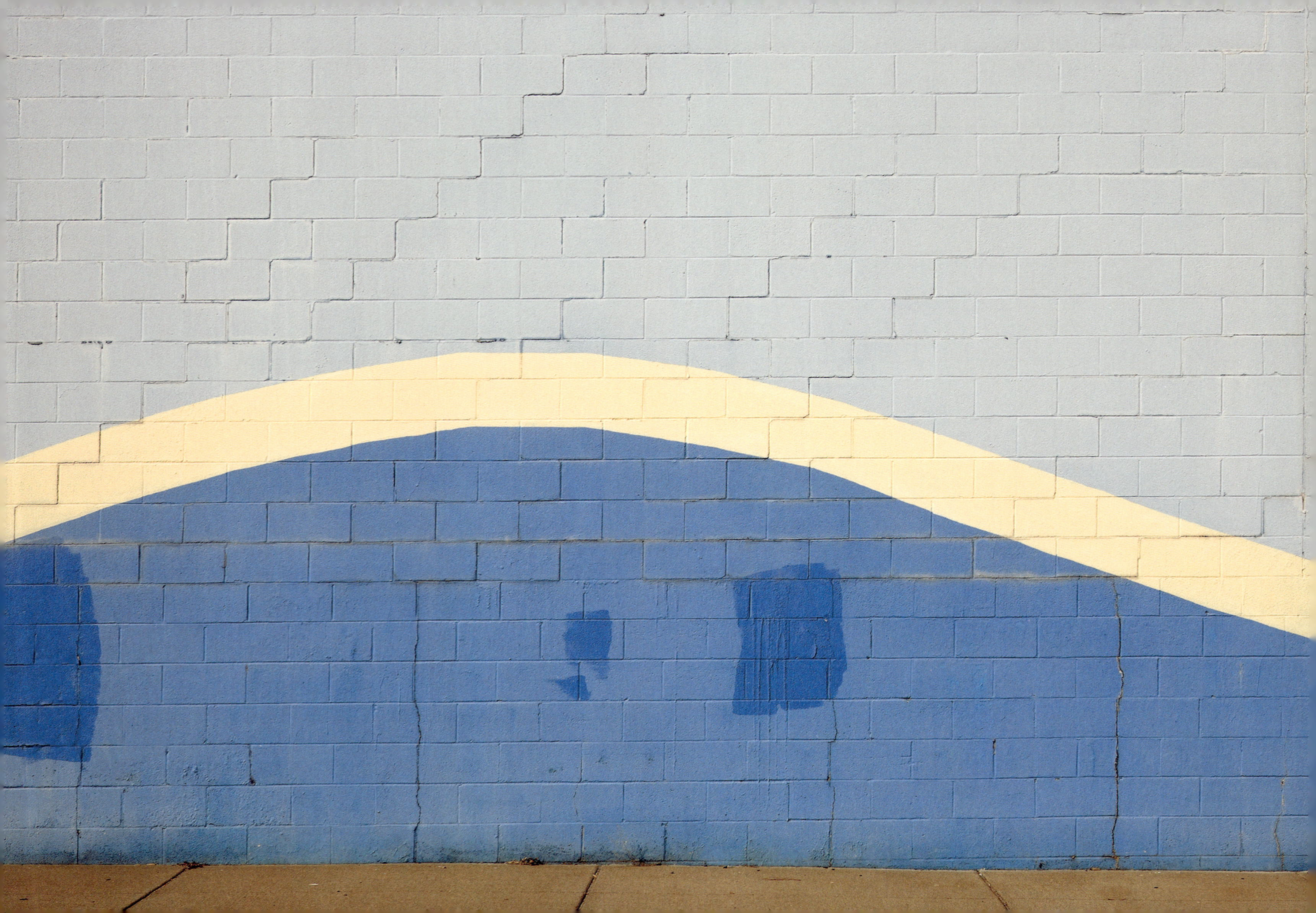

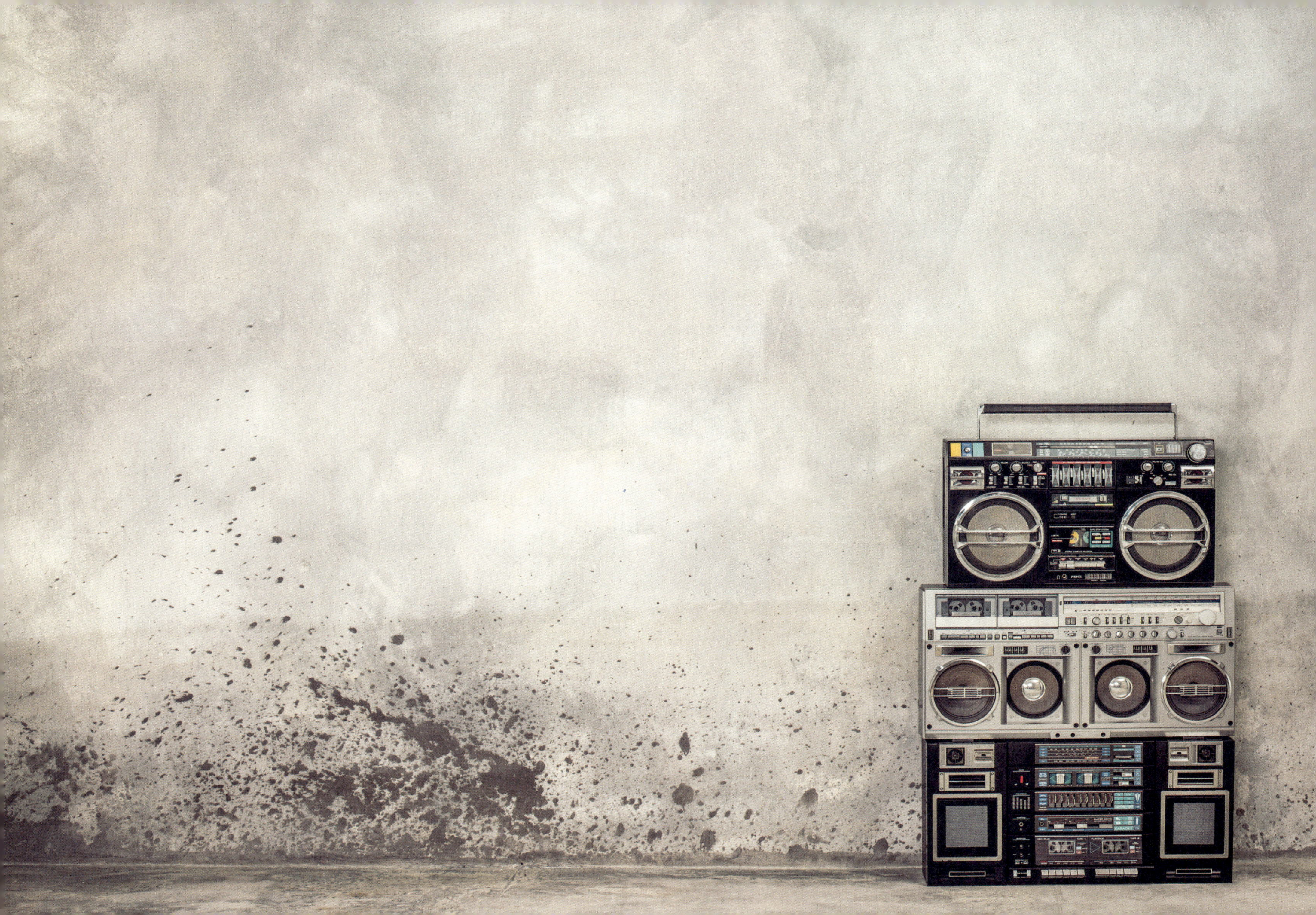

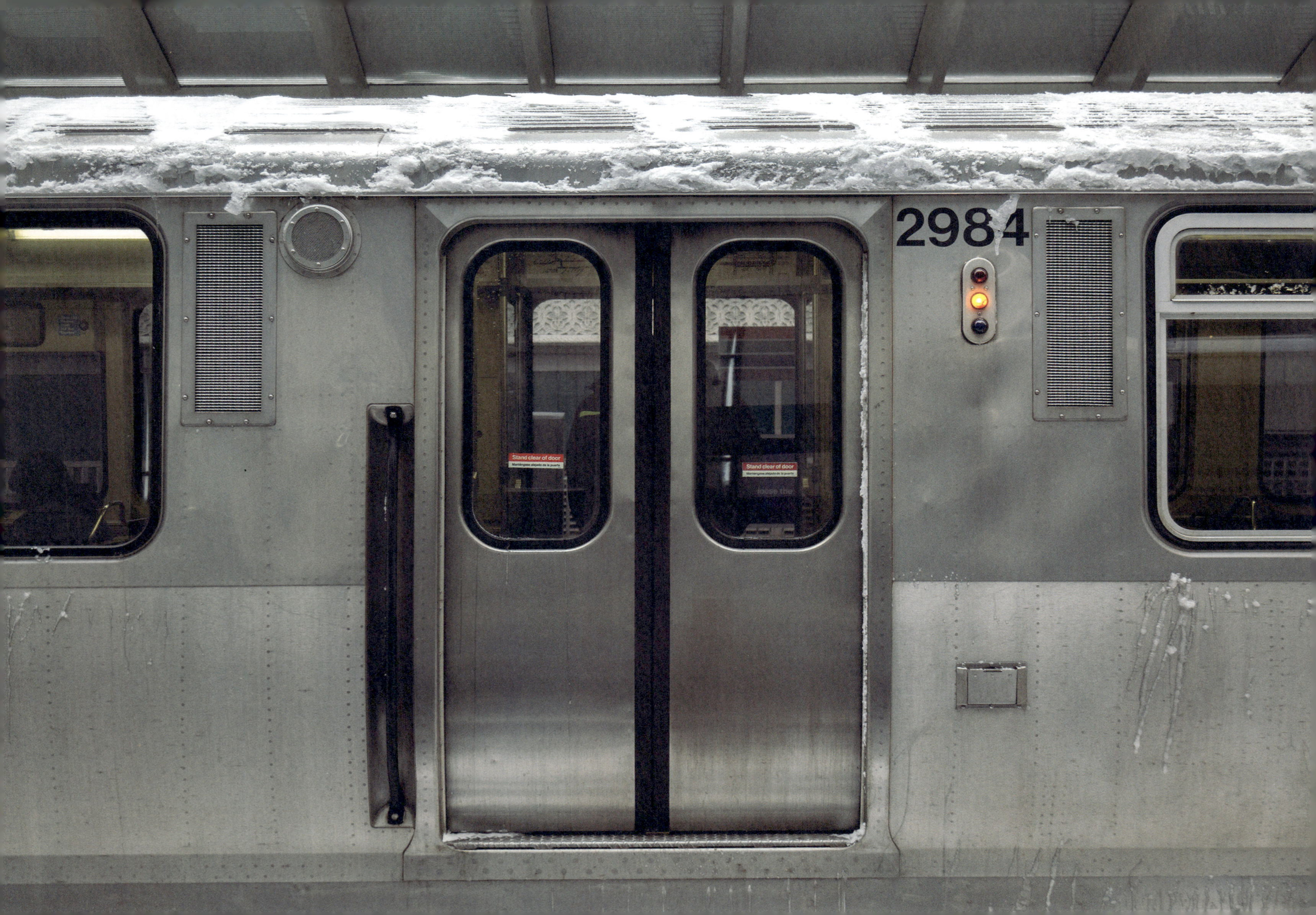
2984
Stand clear of door
Manténgase alejado de la puerta
Stand clear of door
Manténgase alejado de la puerta

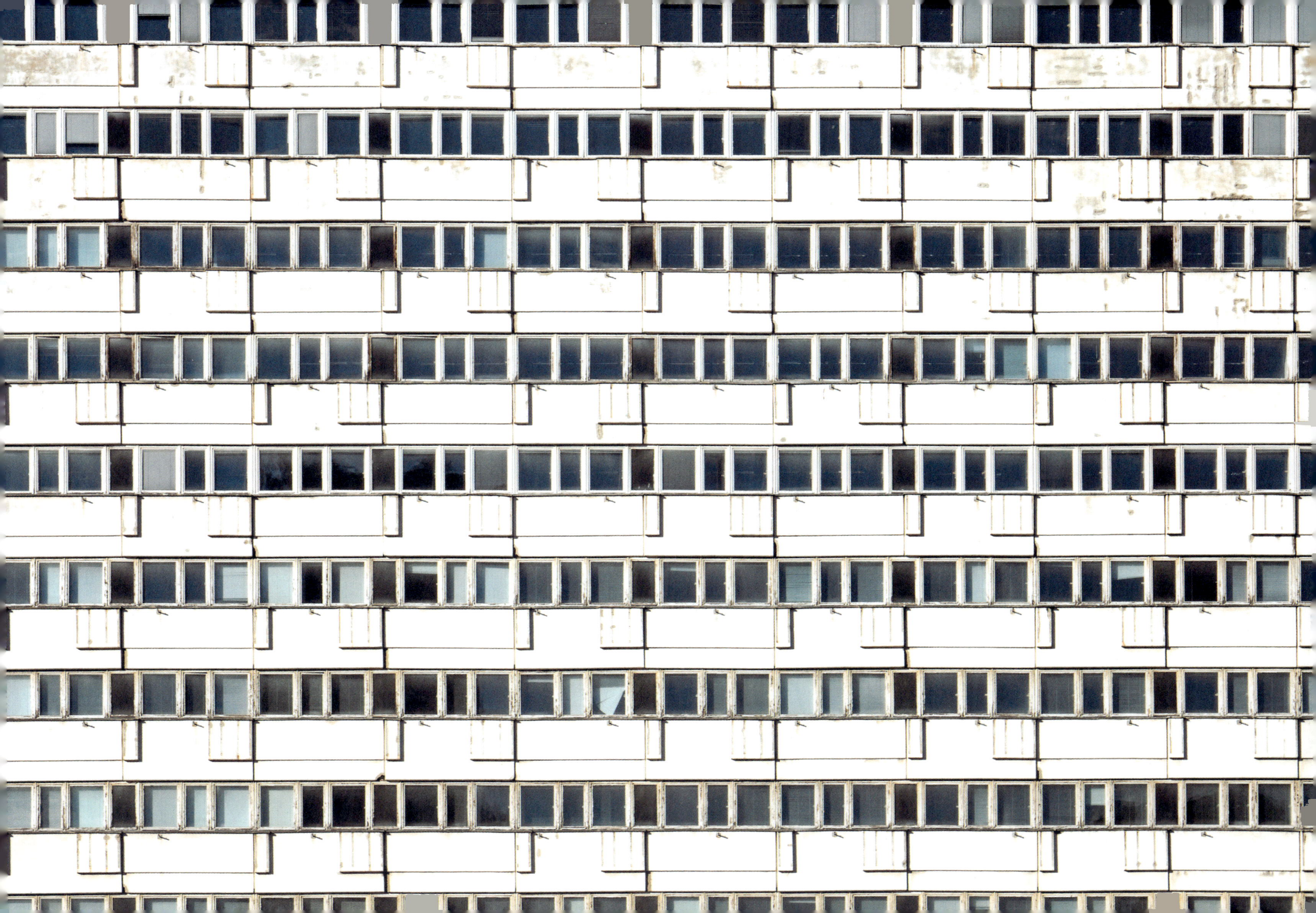

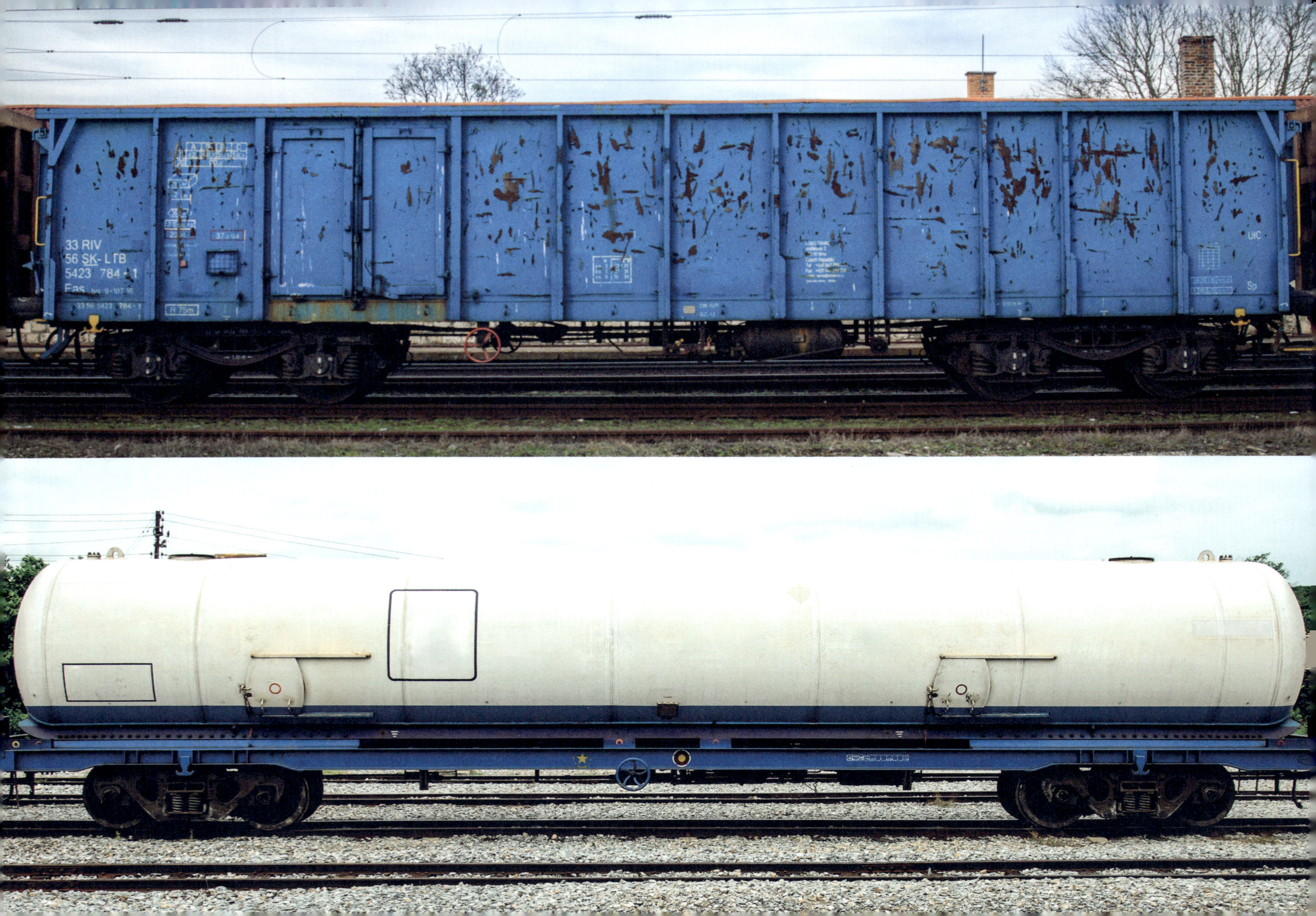

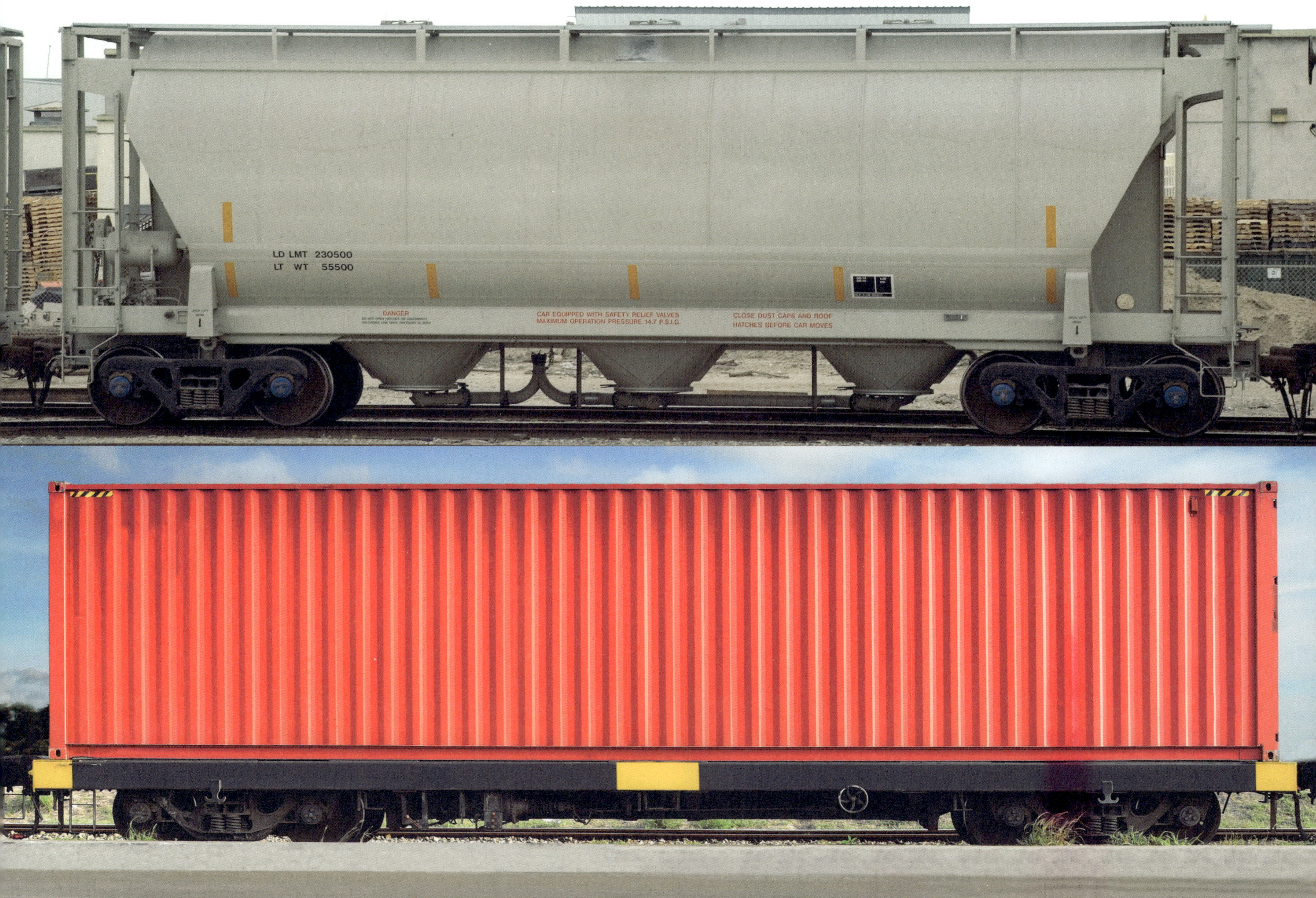

LD LMT 230500
LT WT 55500
DANGER
CAR EQUIPPED WITH SAFETY RELIEF VALVES
MAXIMUM OPERATION PRESSURE 14.7 P.S.I.G.
CLOSE DUST CAPS AND ROOF
HATCHES BEFORE CAR MOVES

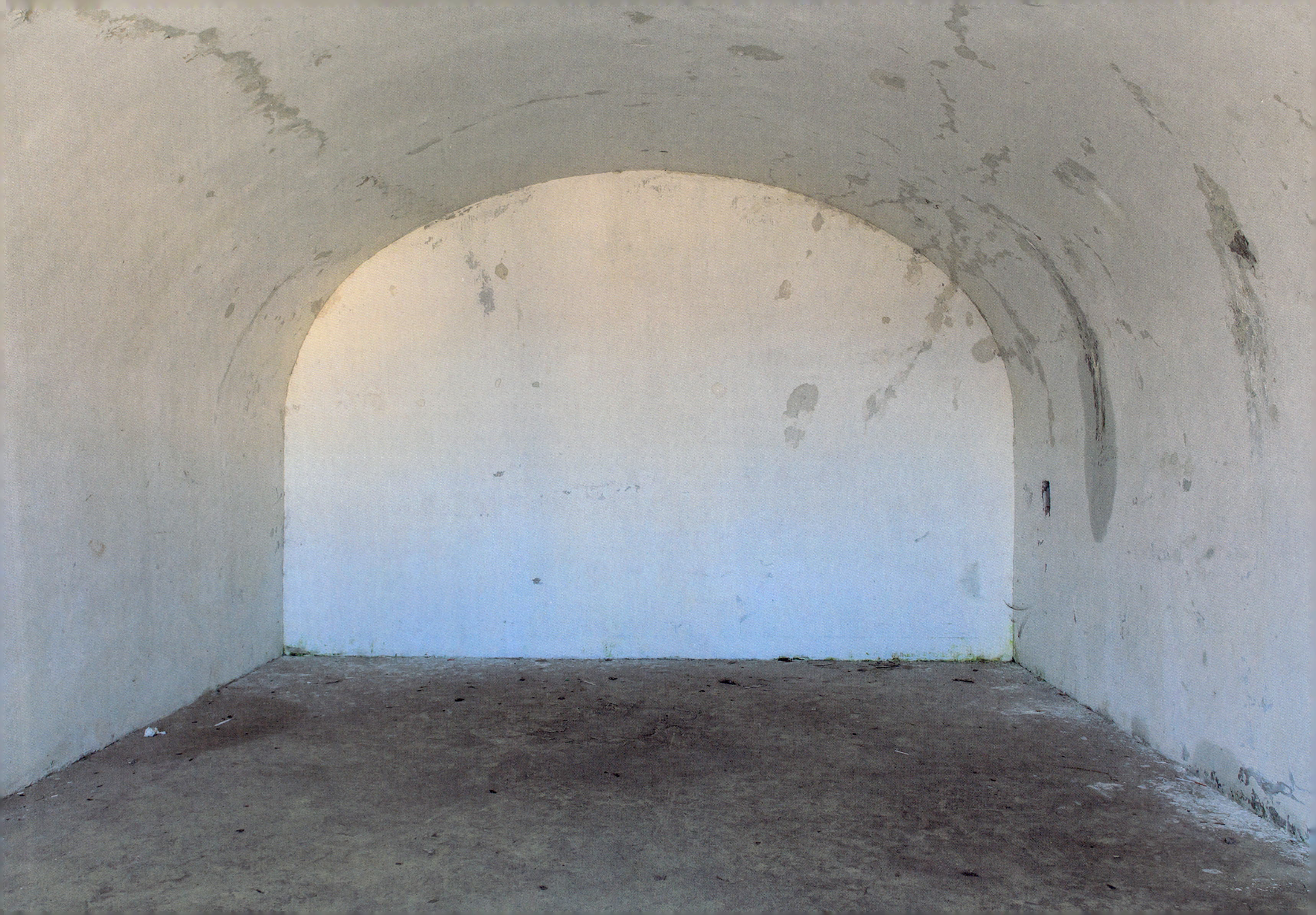

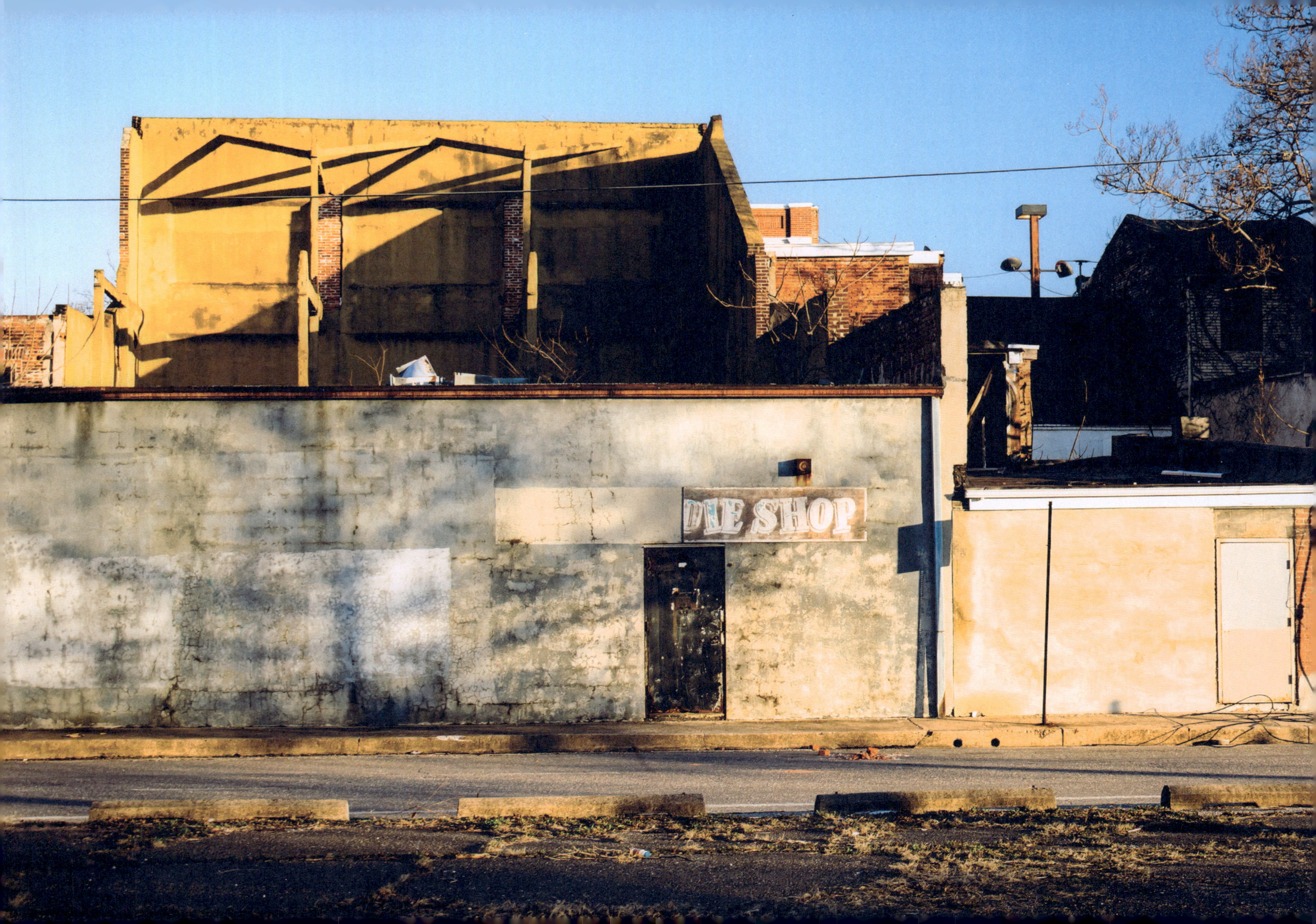
PIE SHOP

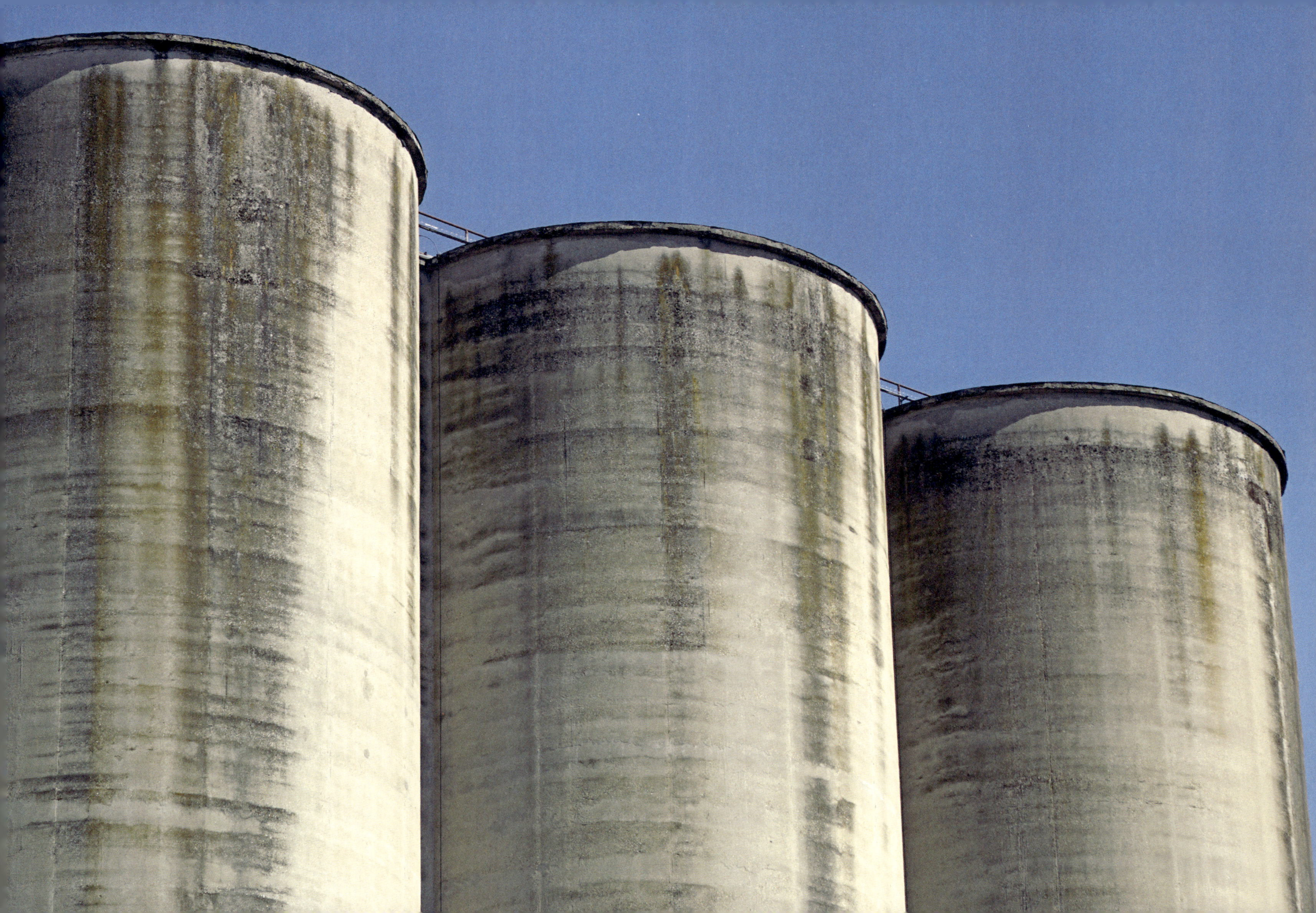

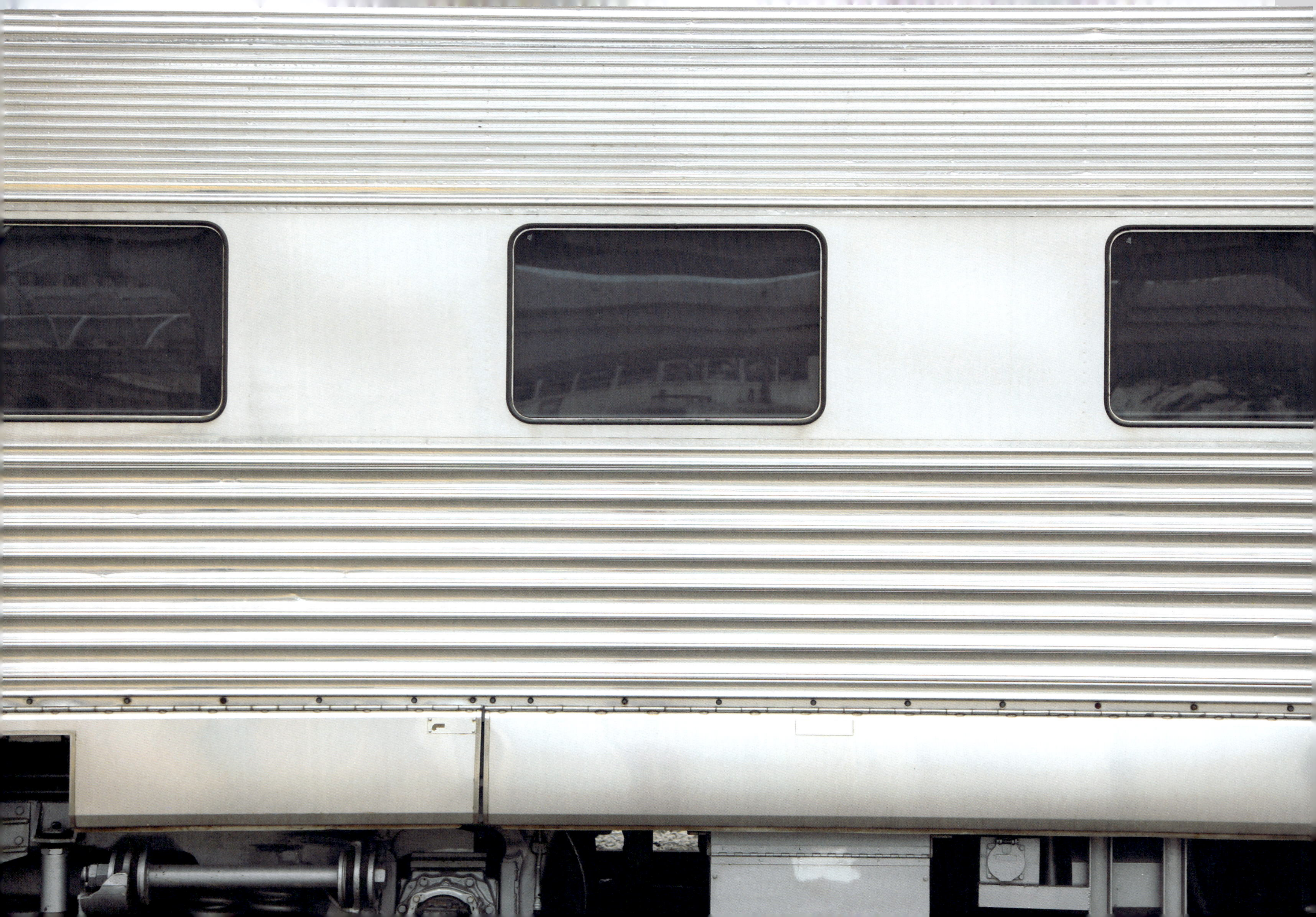

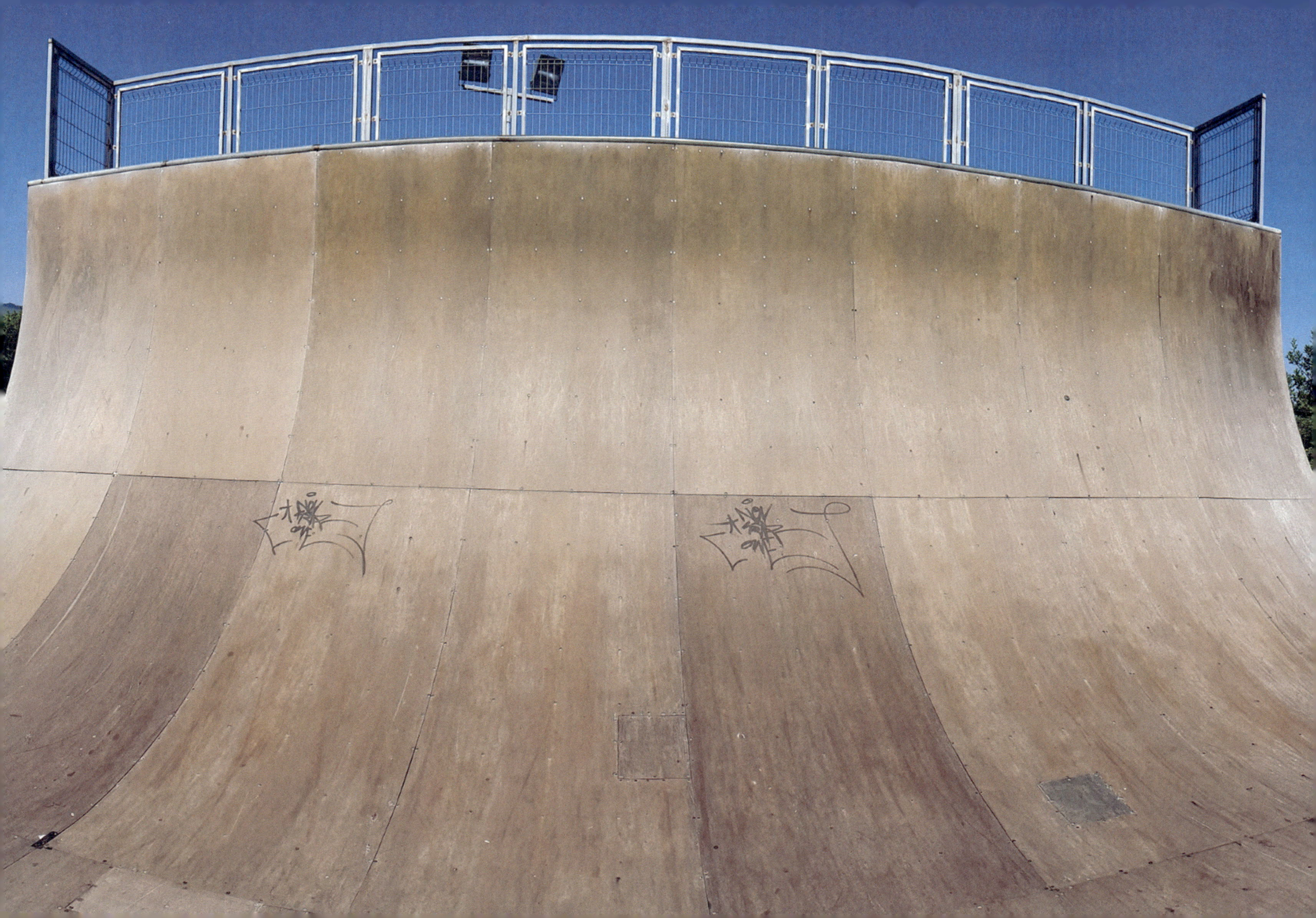

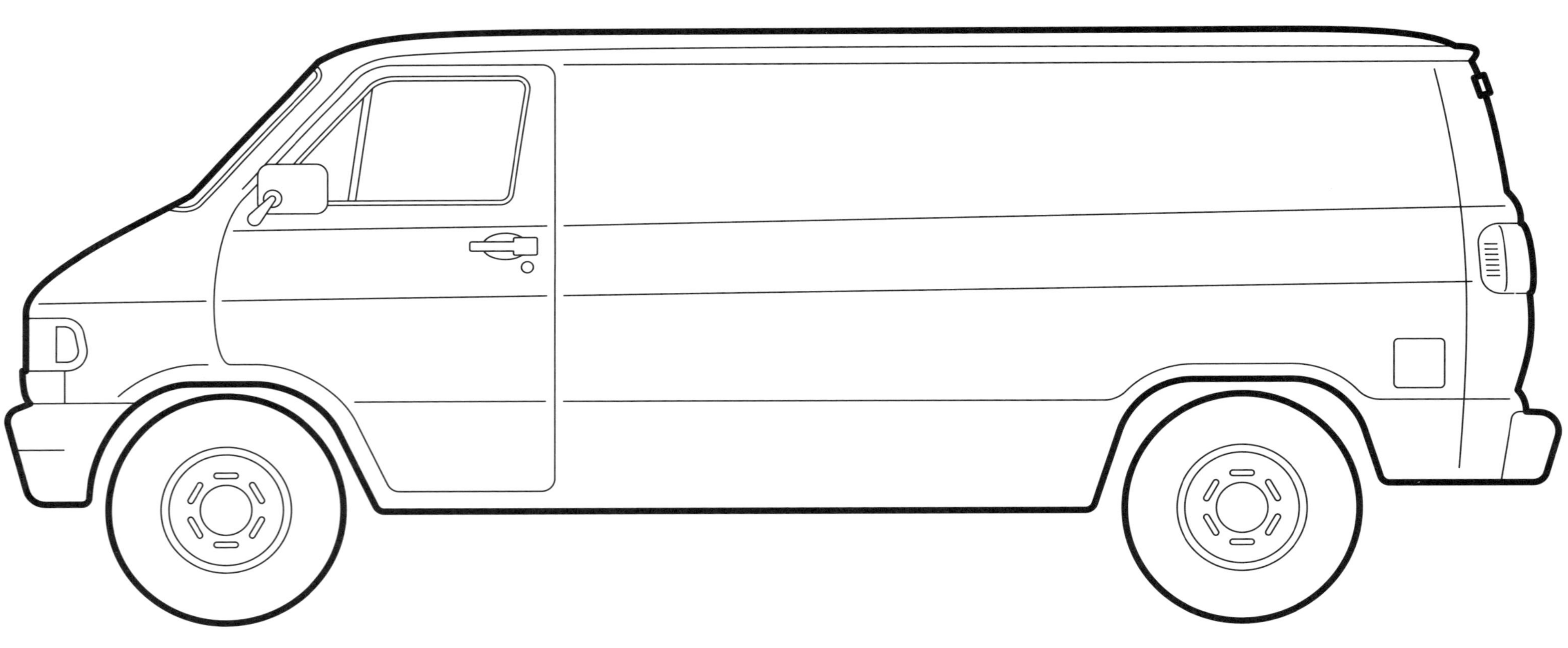

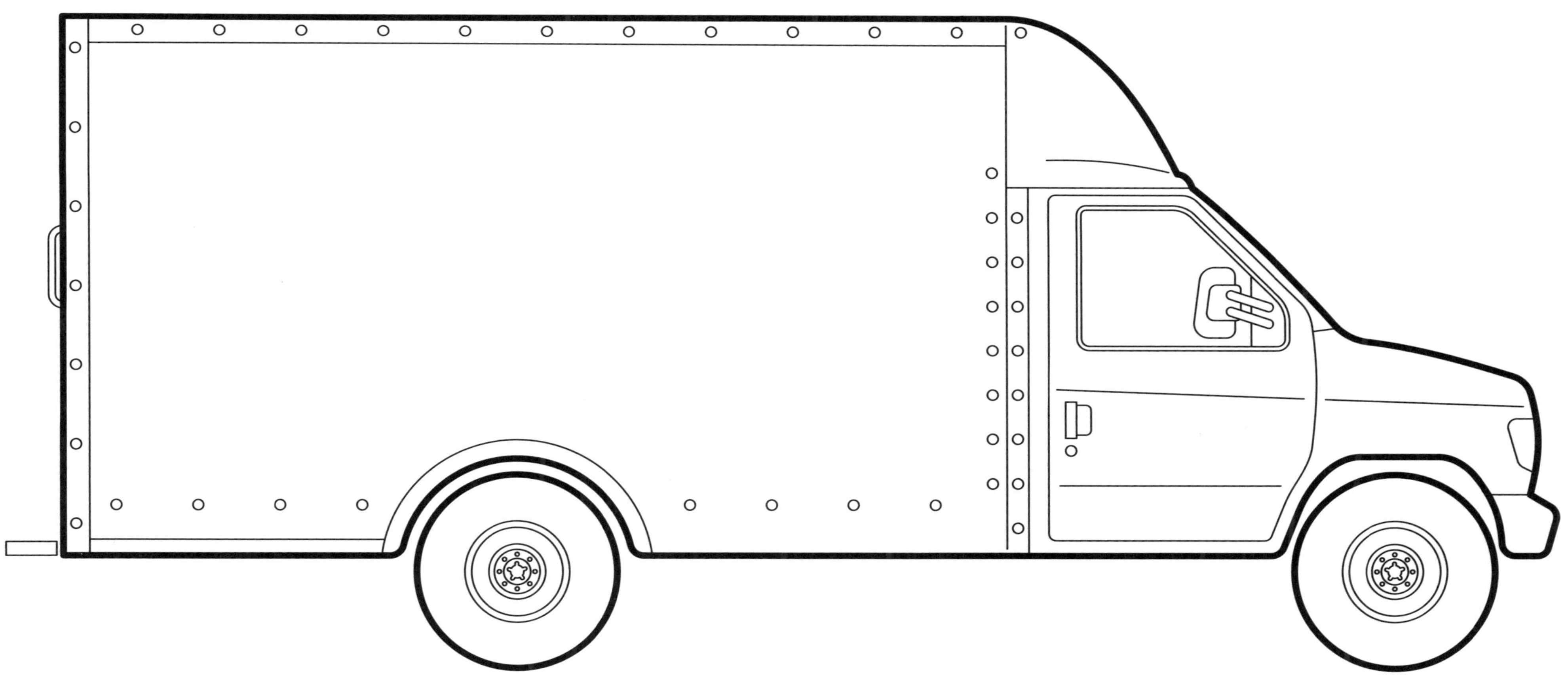

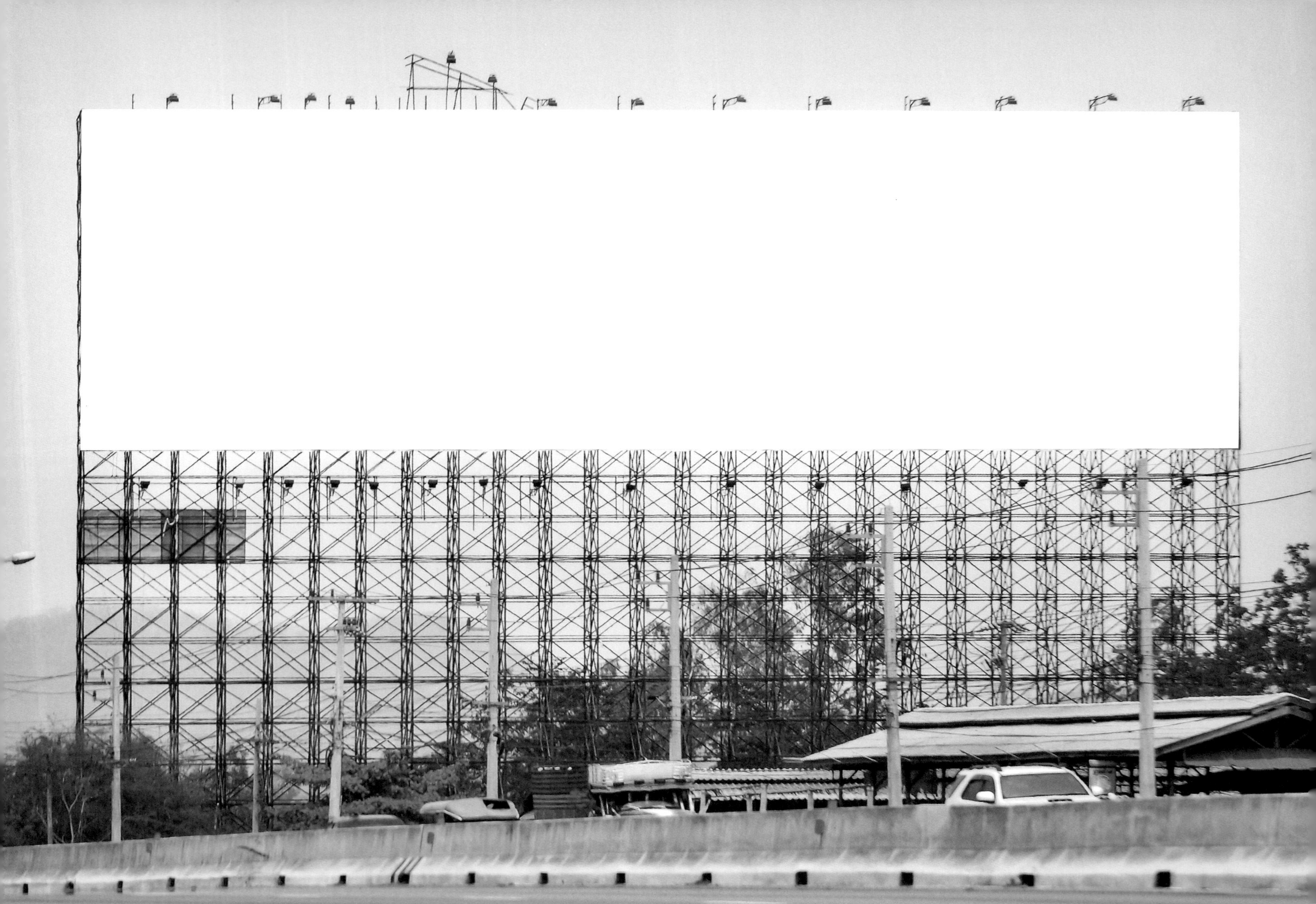

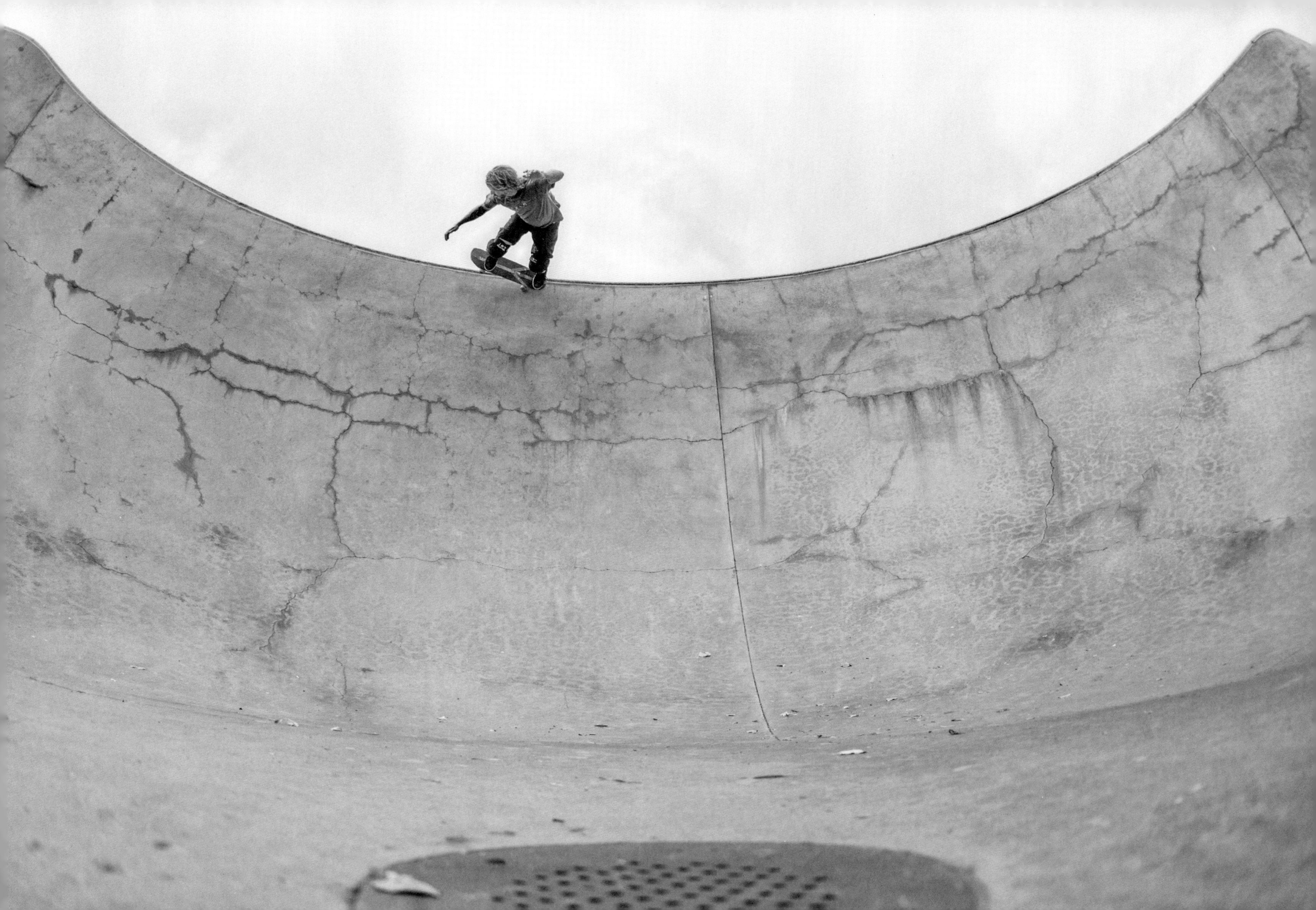

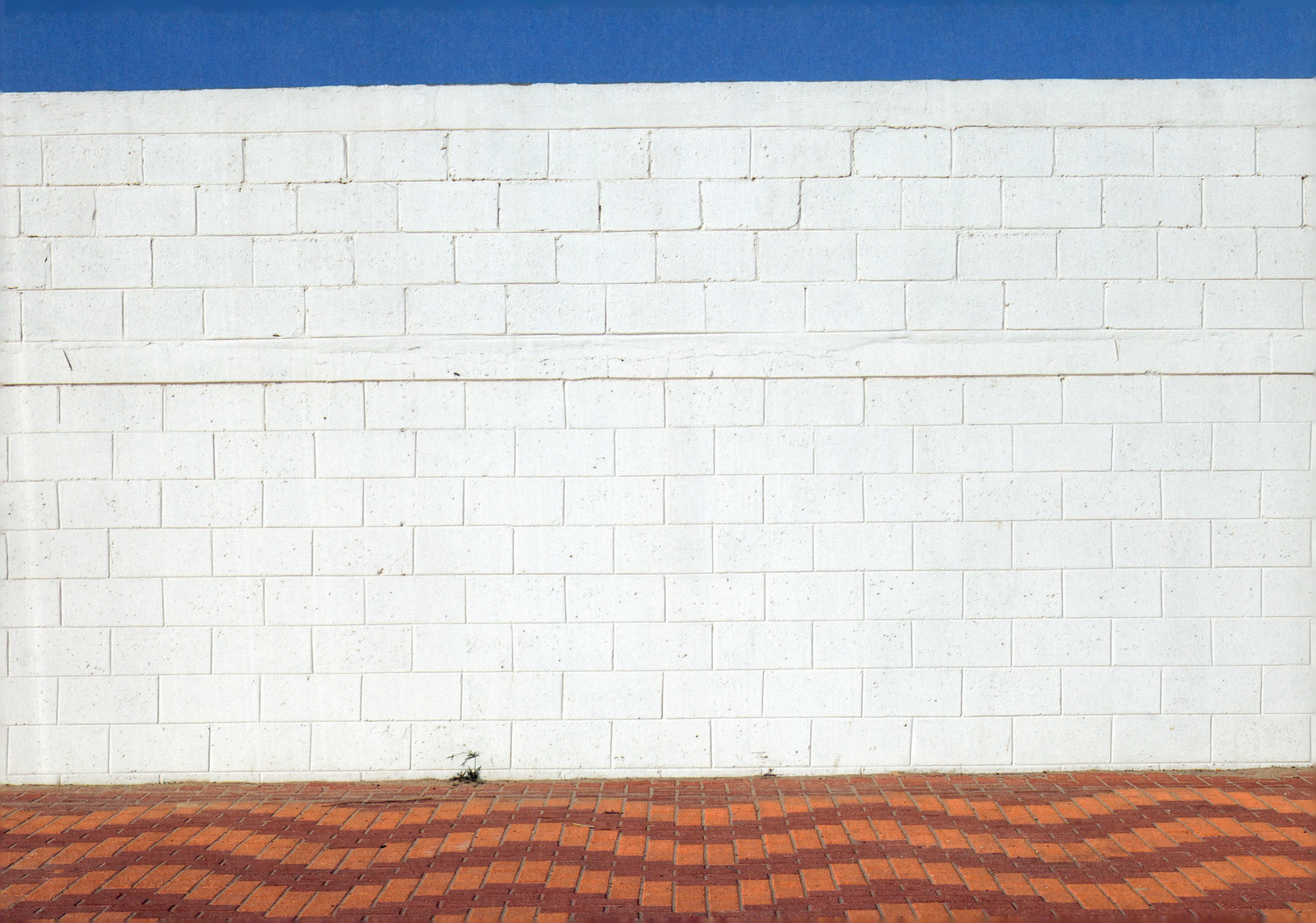

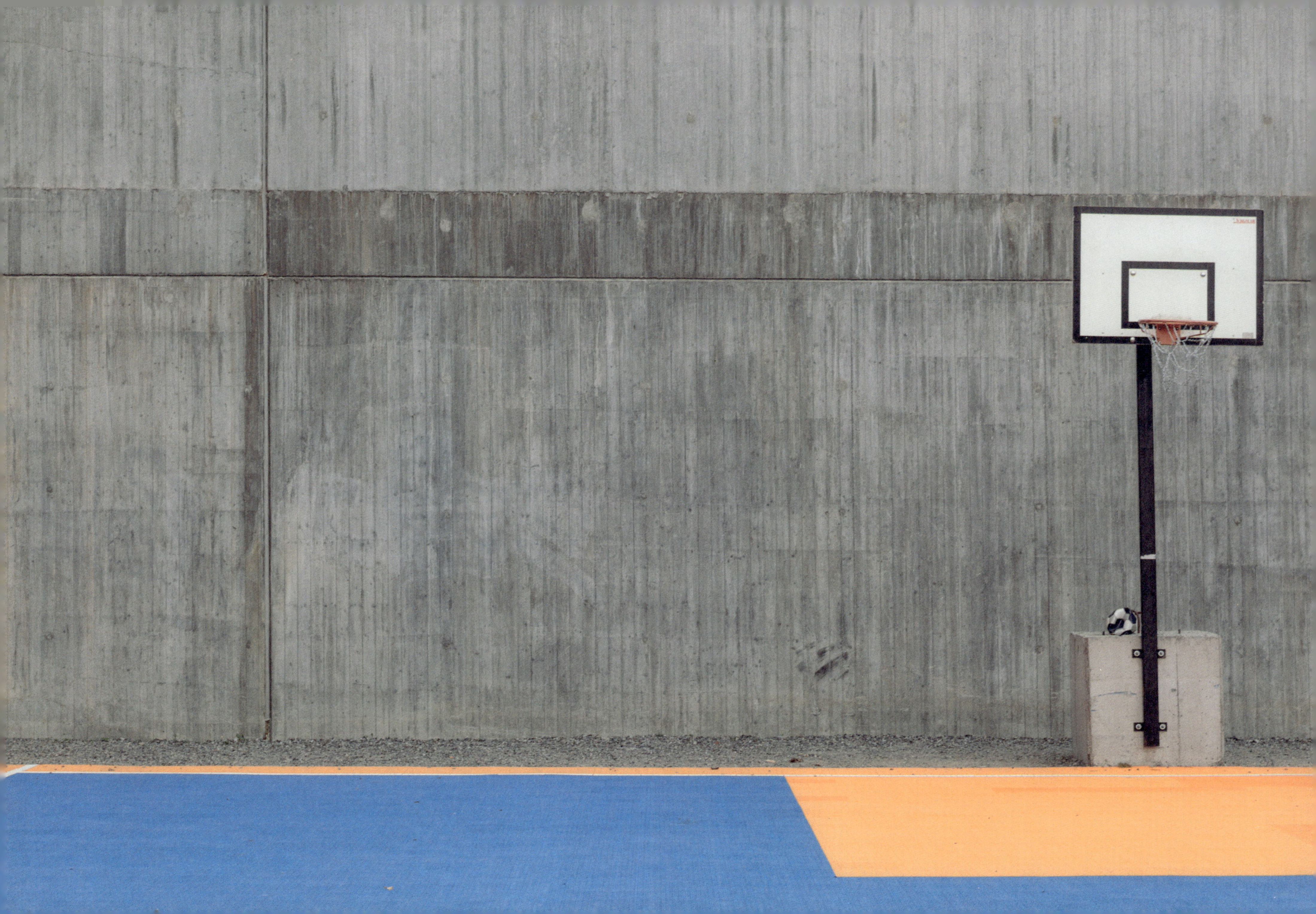

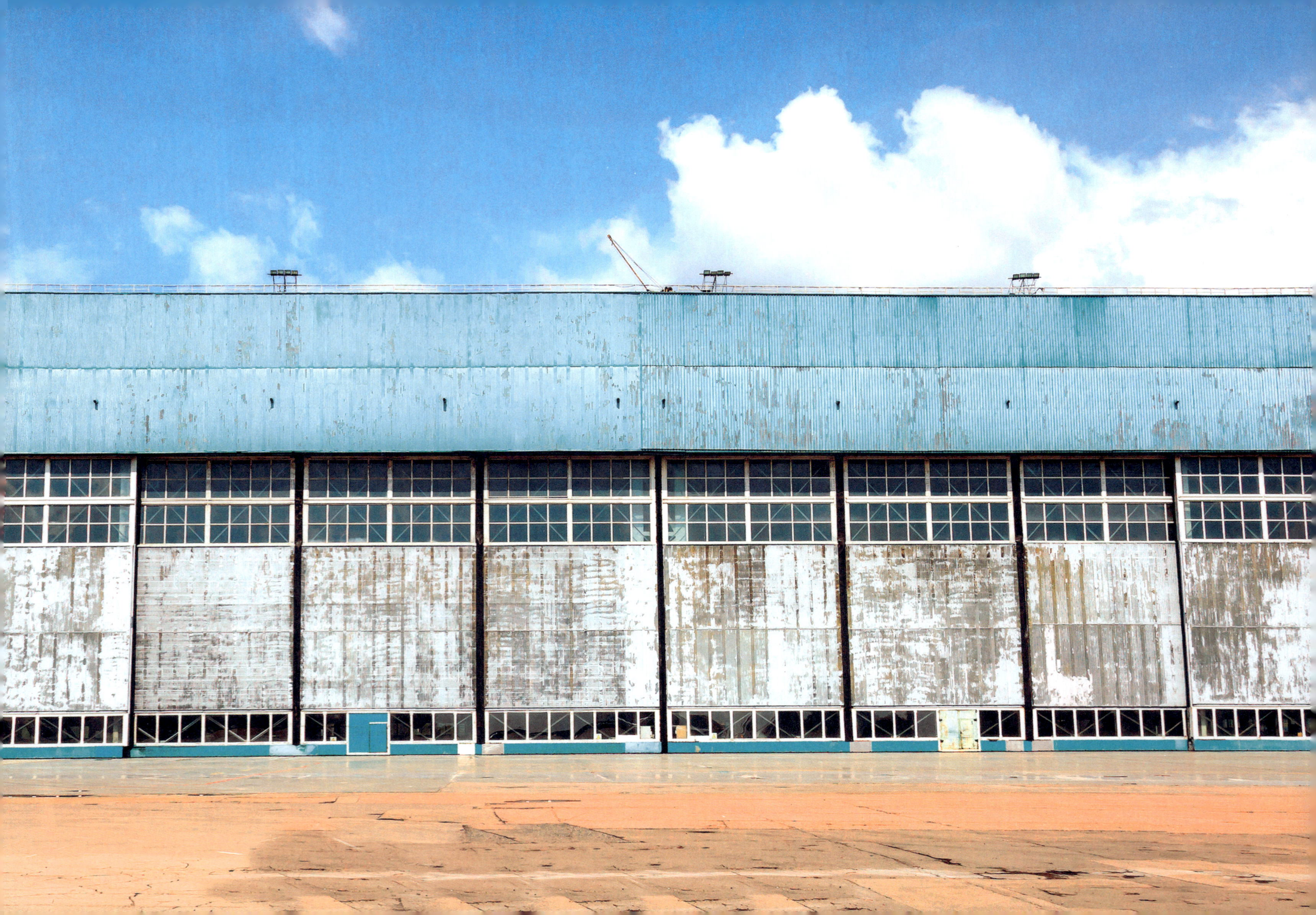

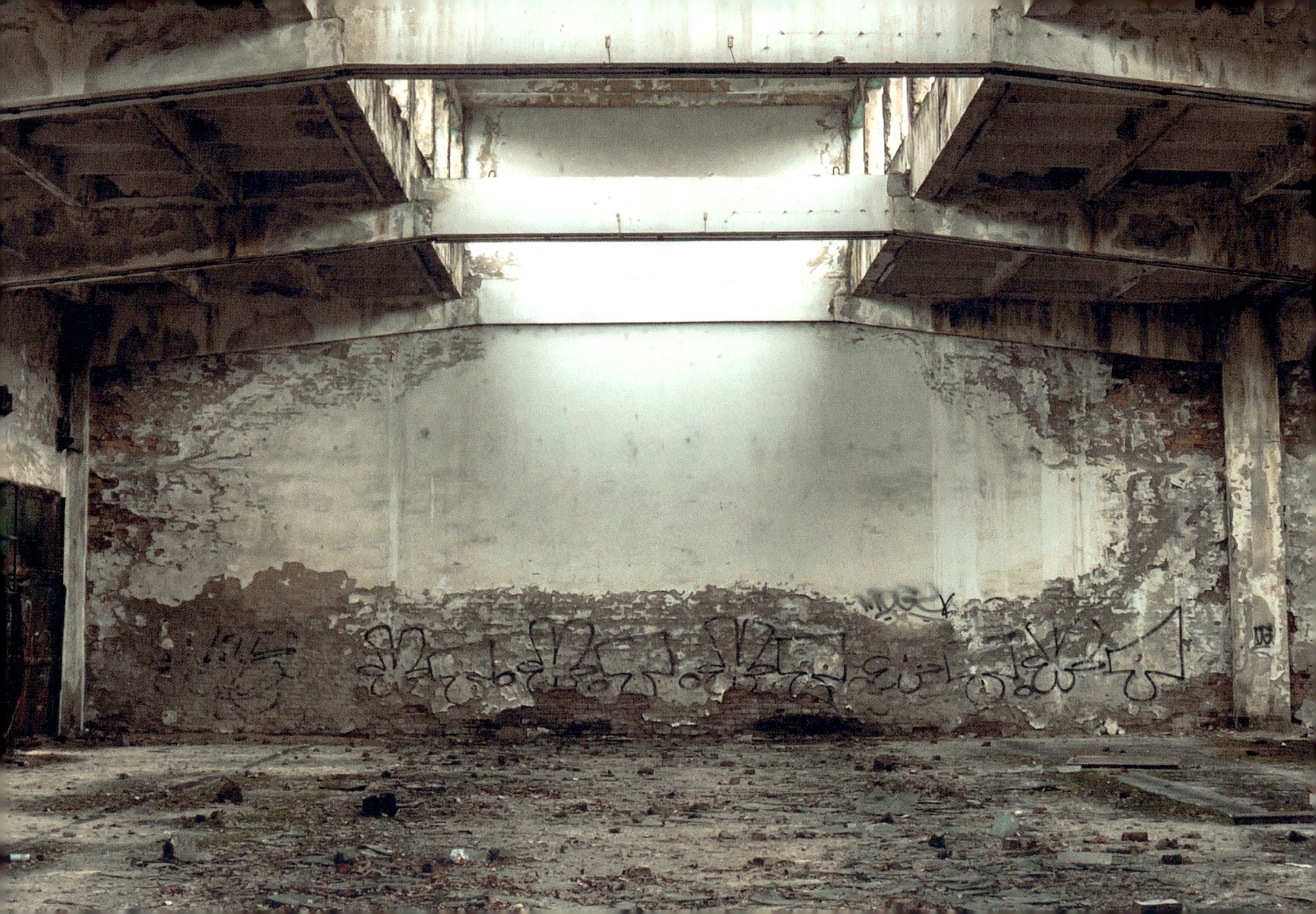

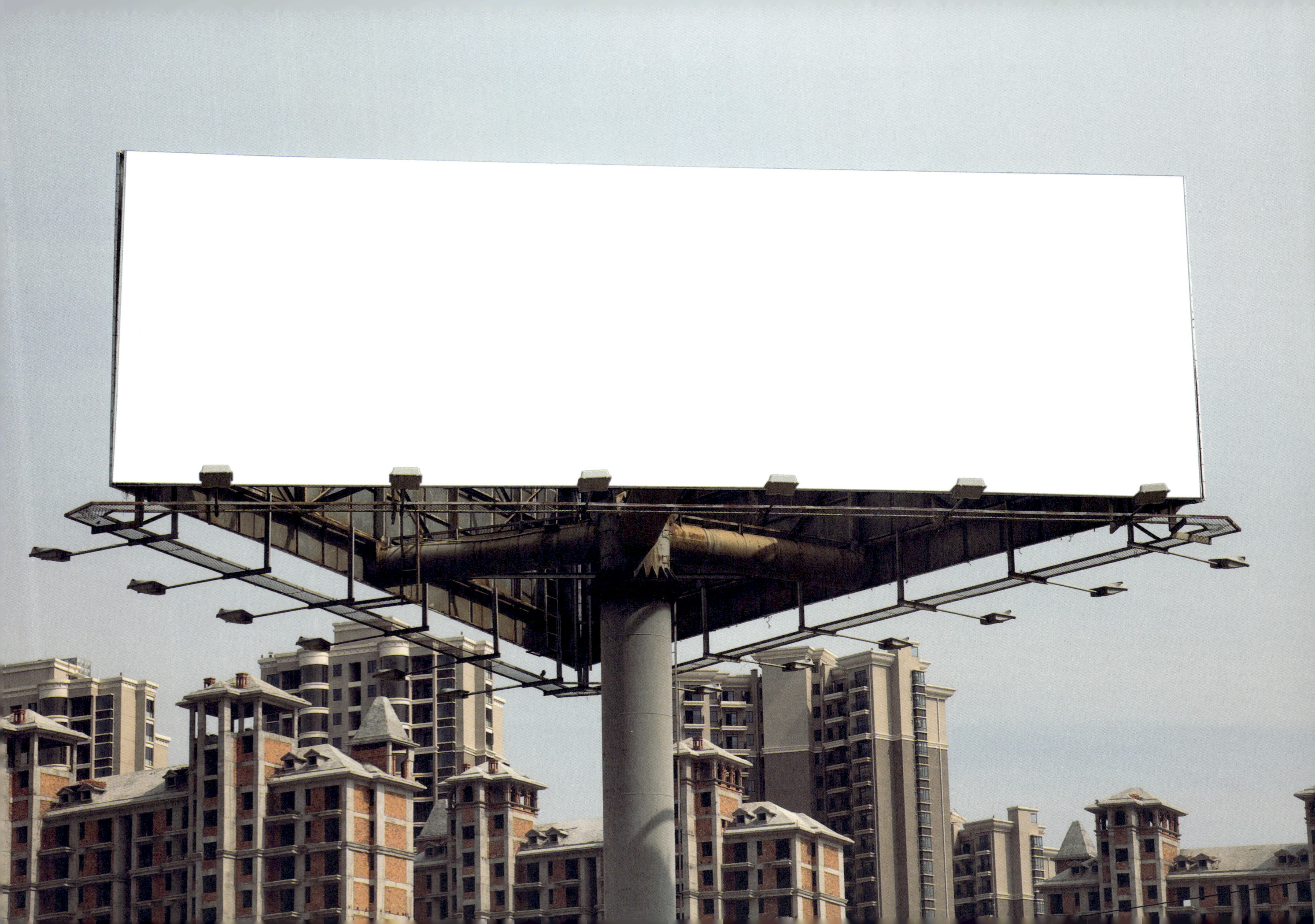

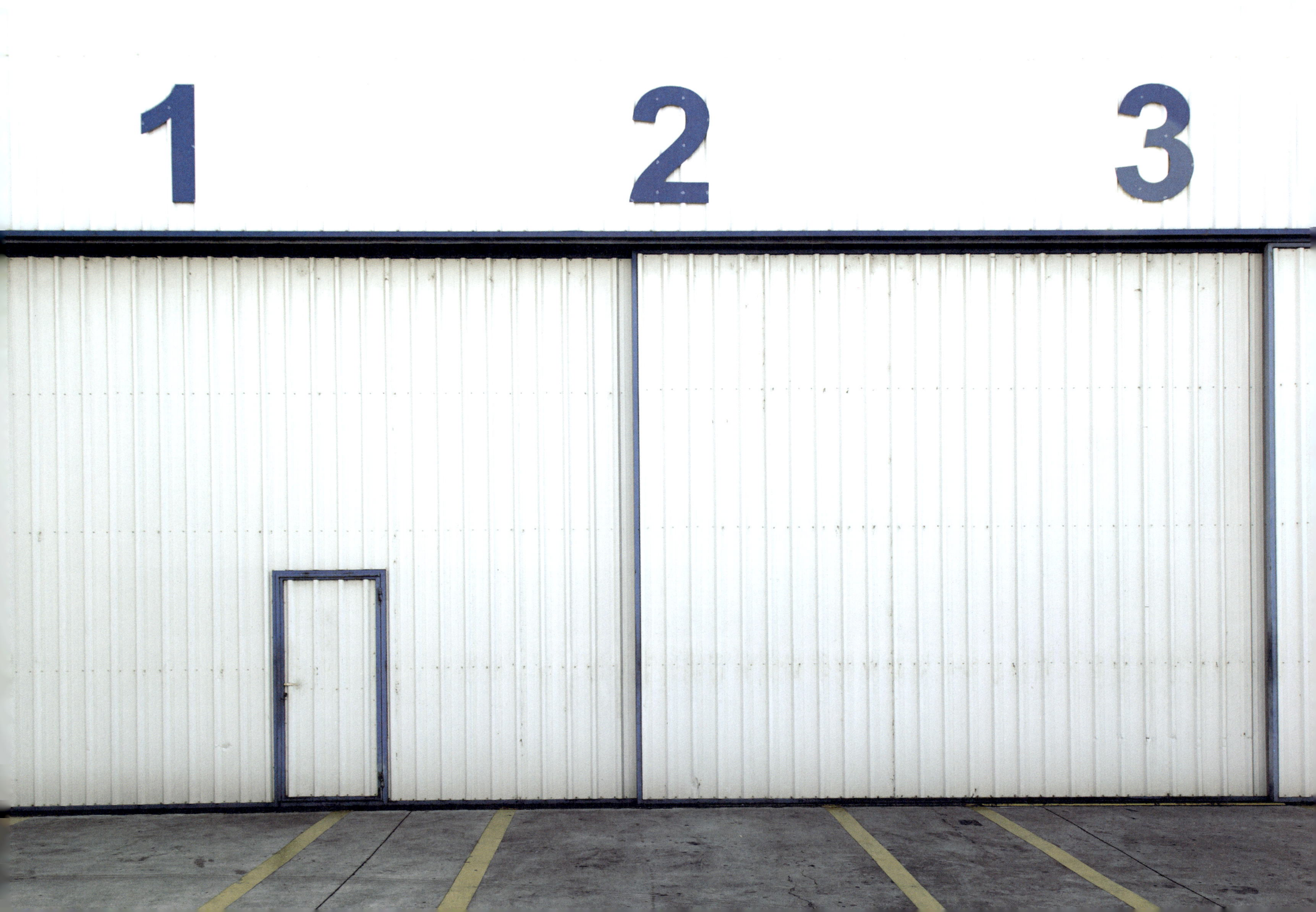

1 2 3

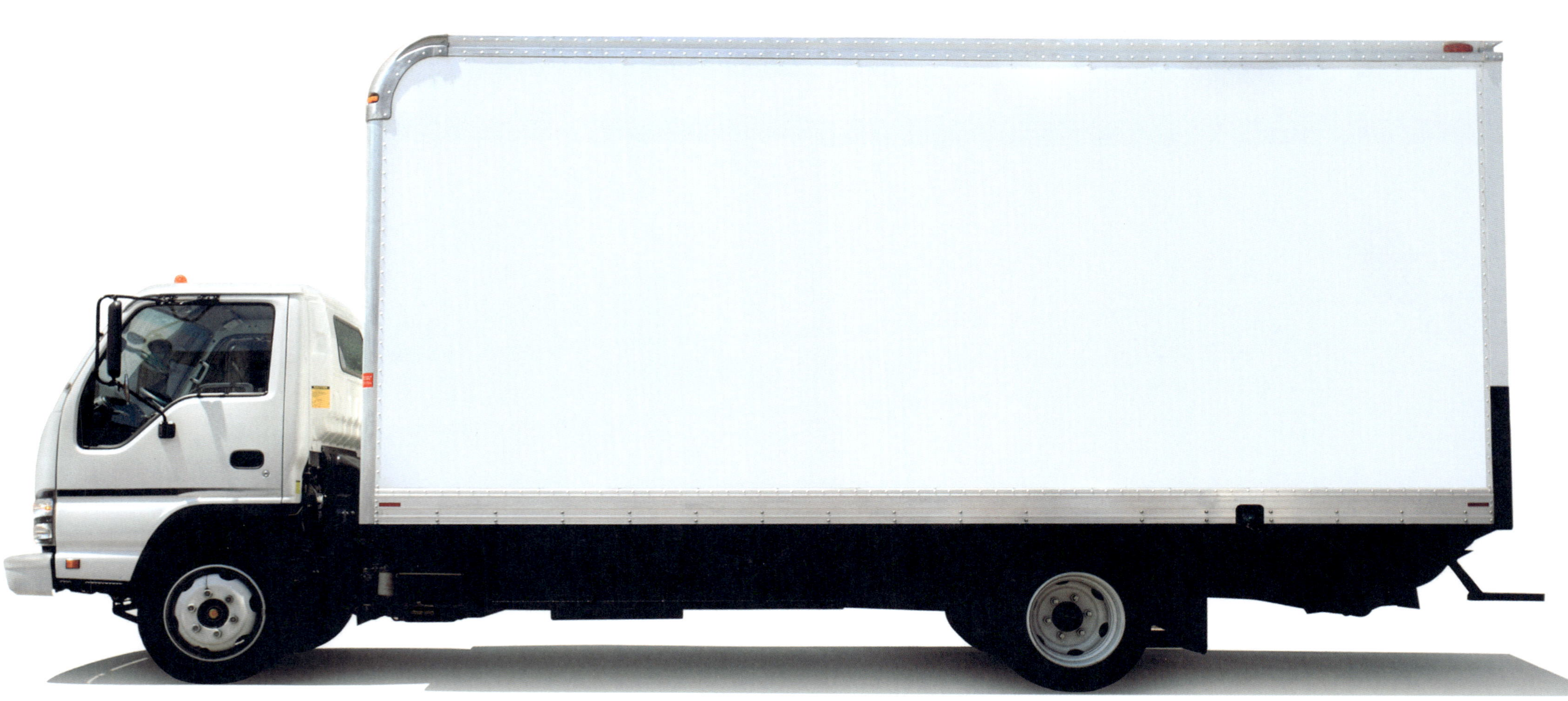

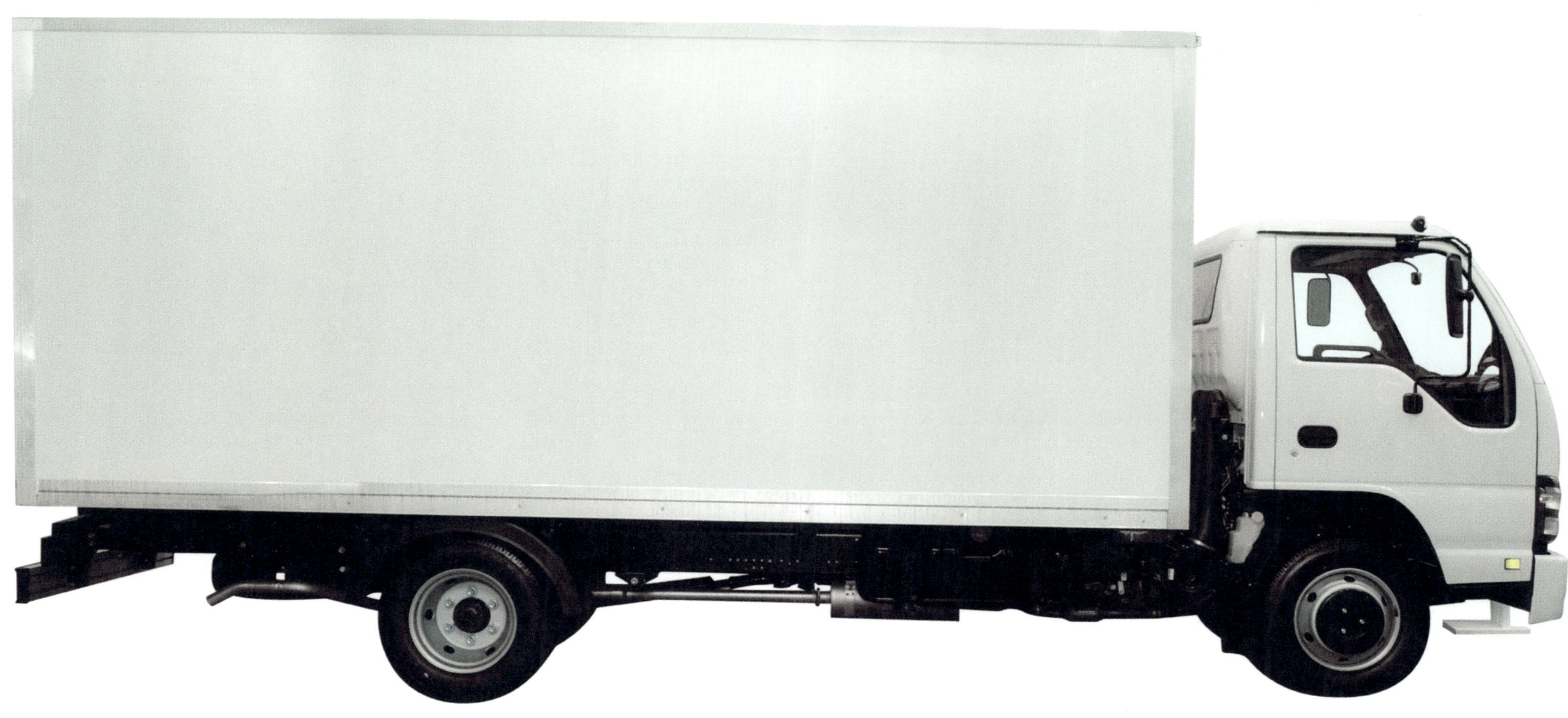

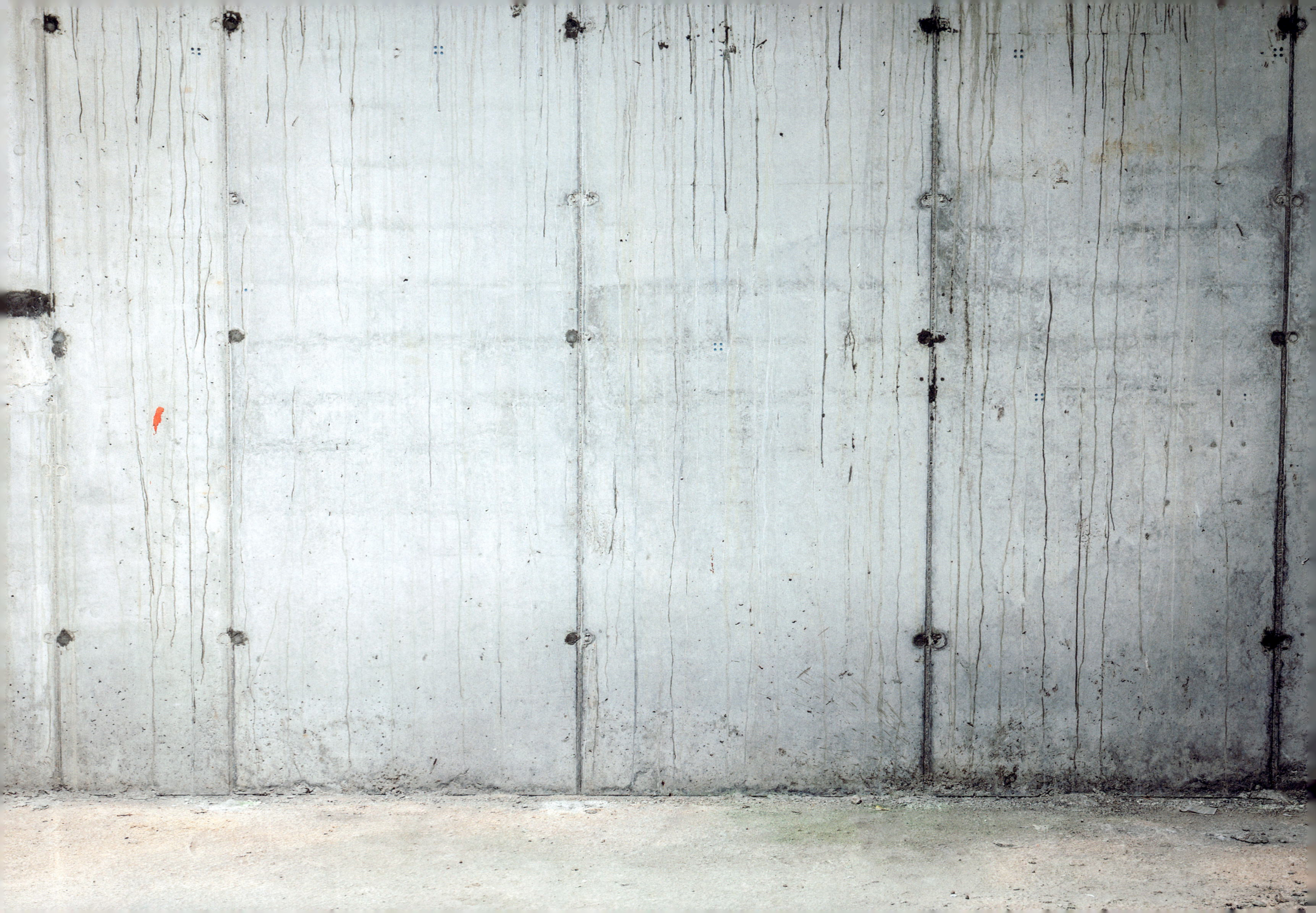

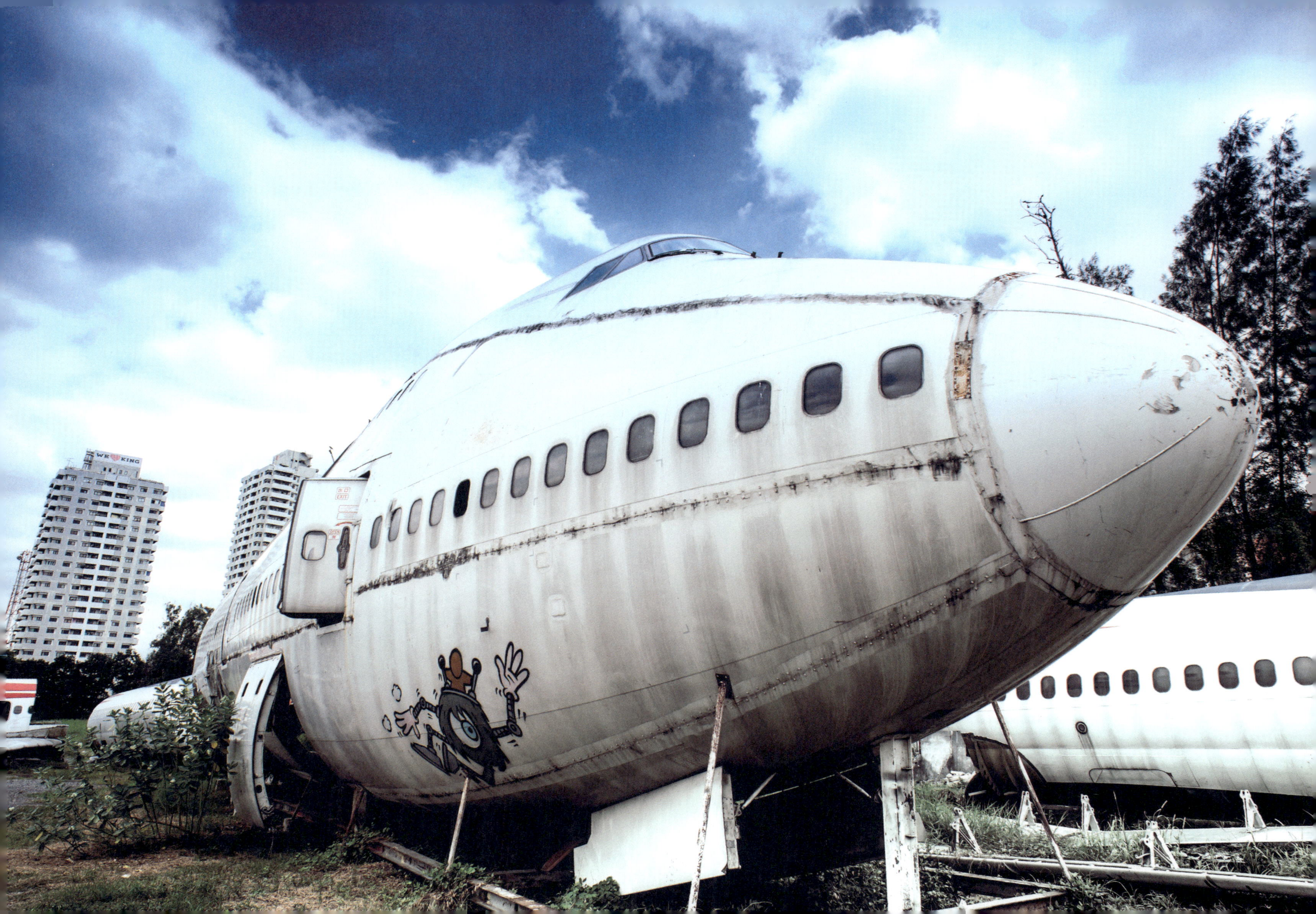

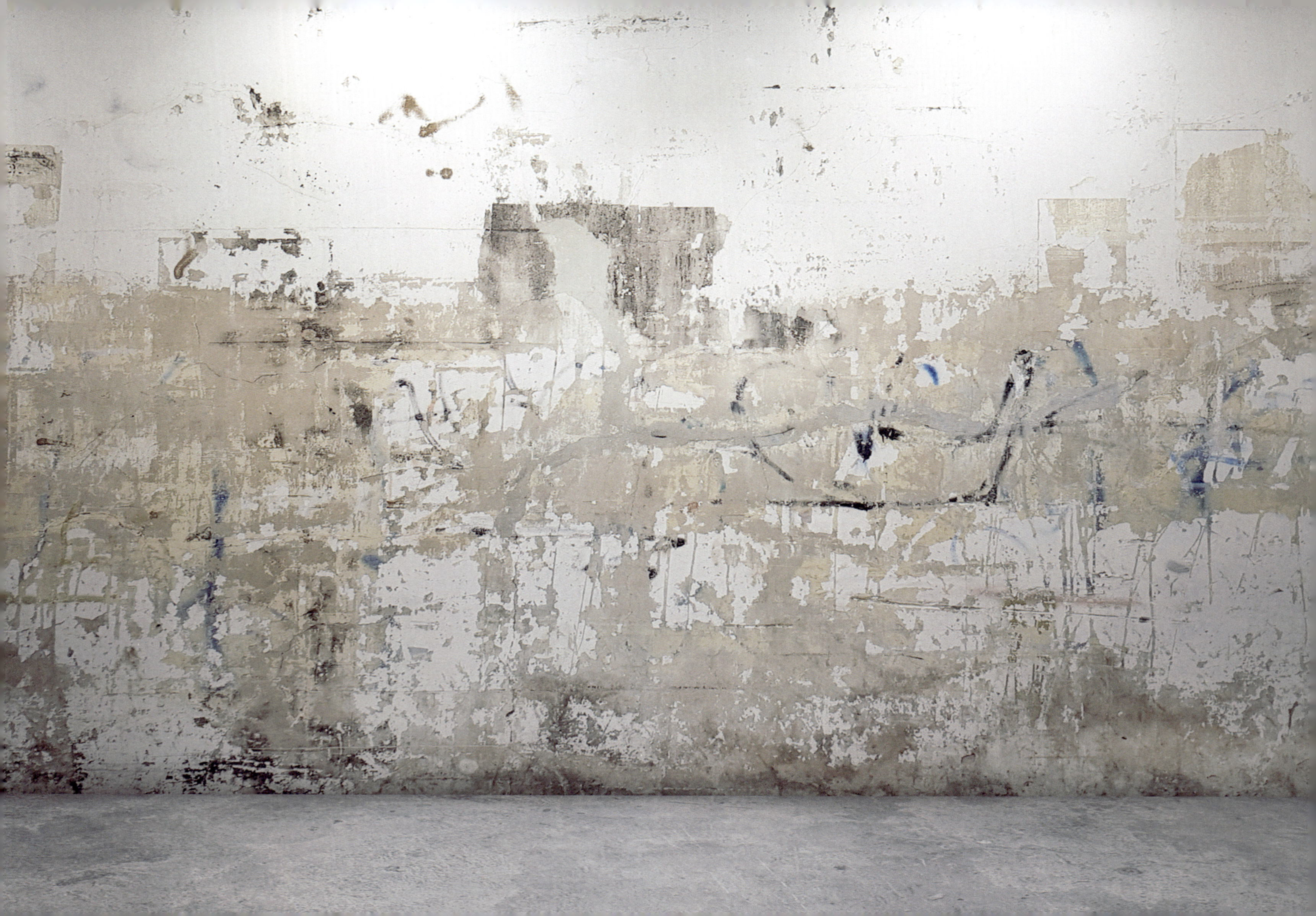

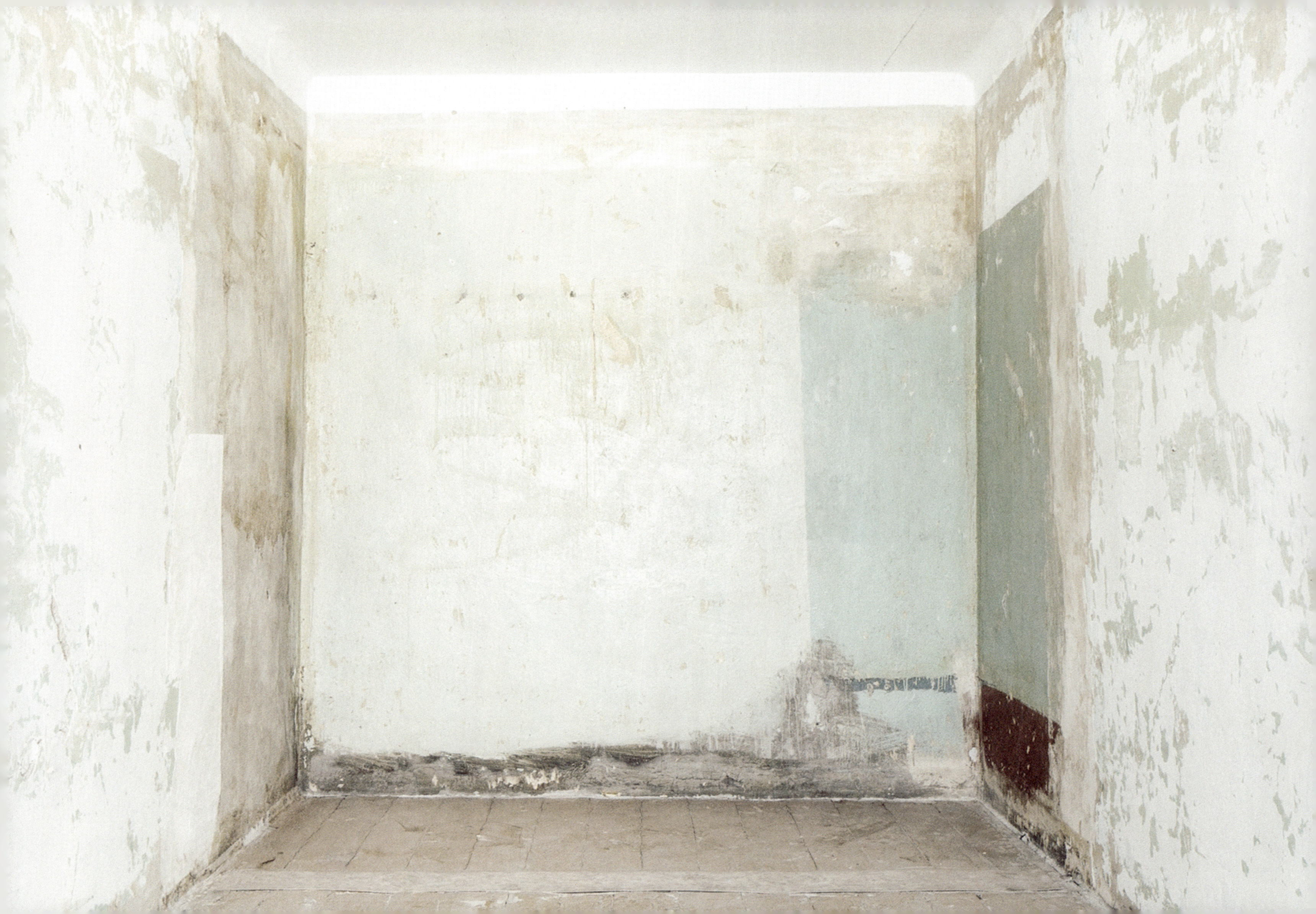

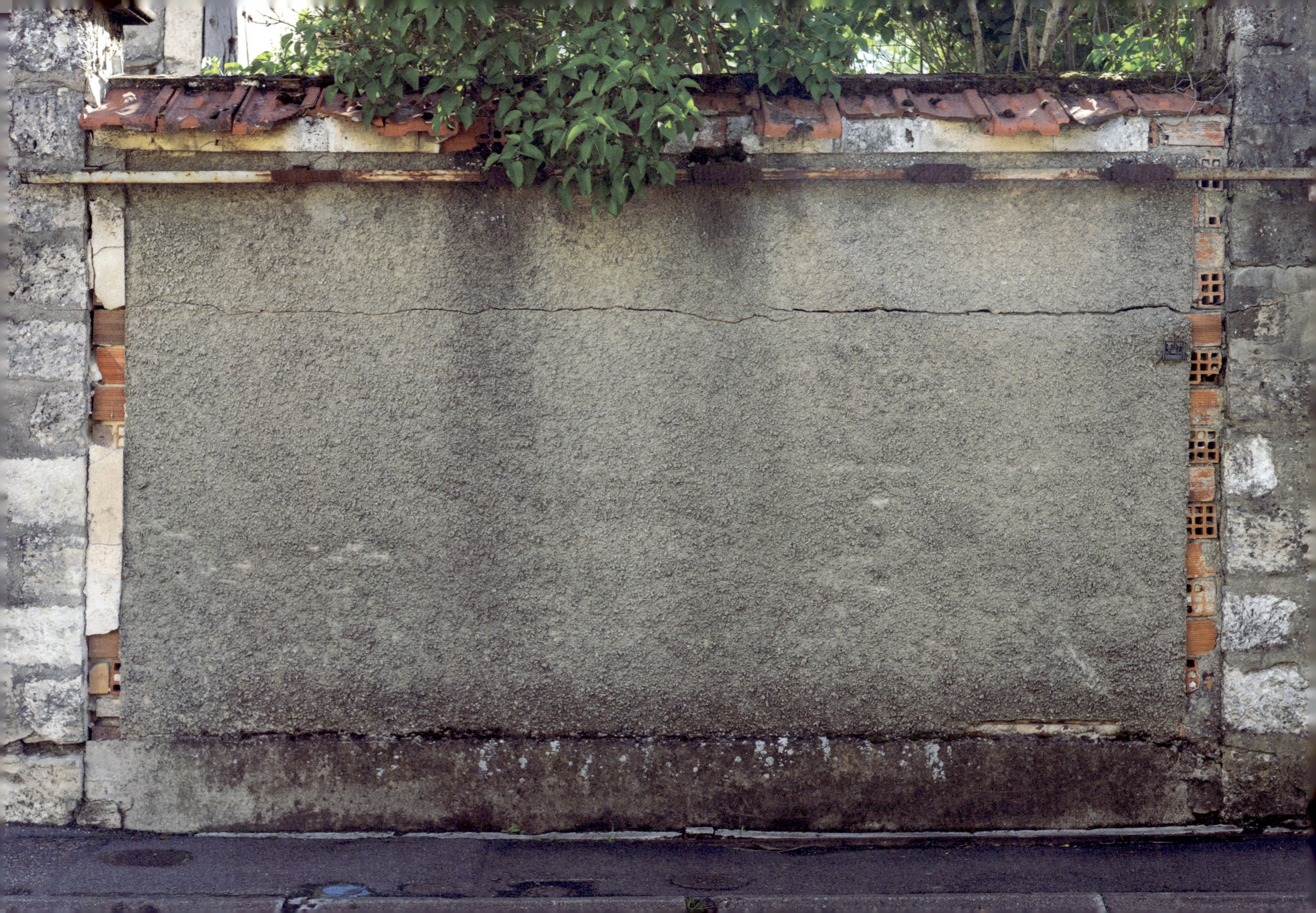

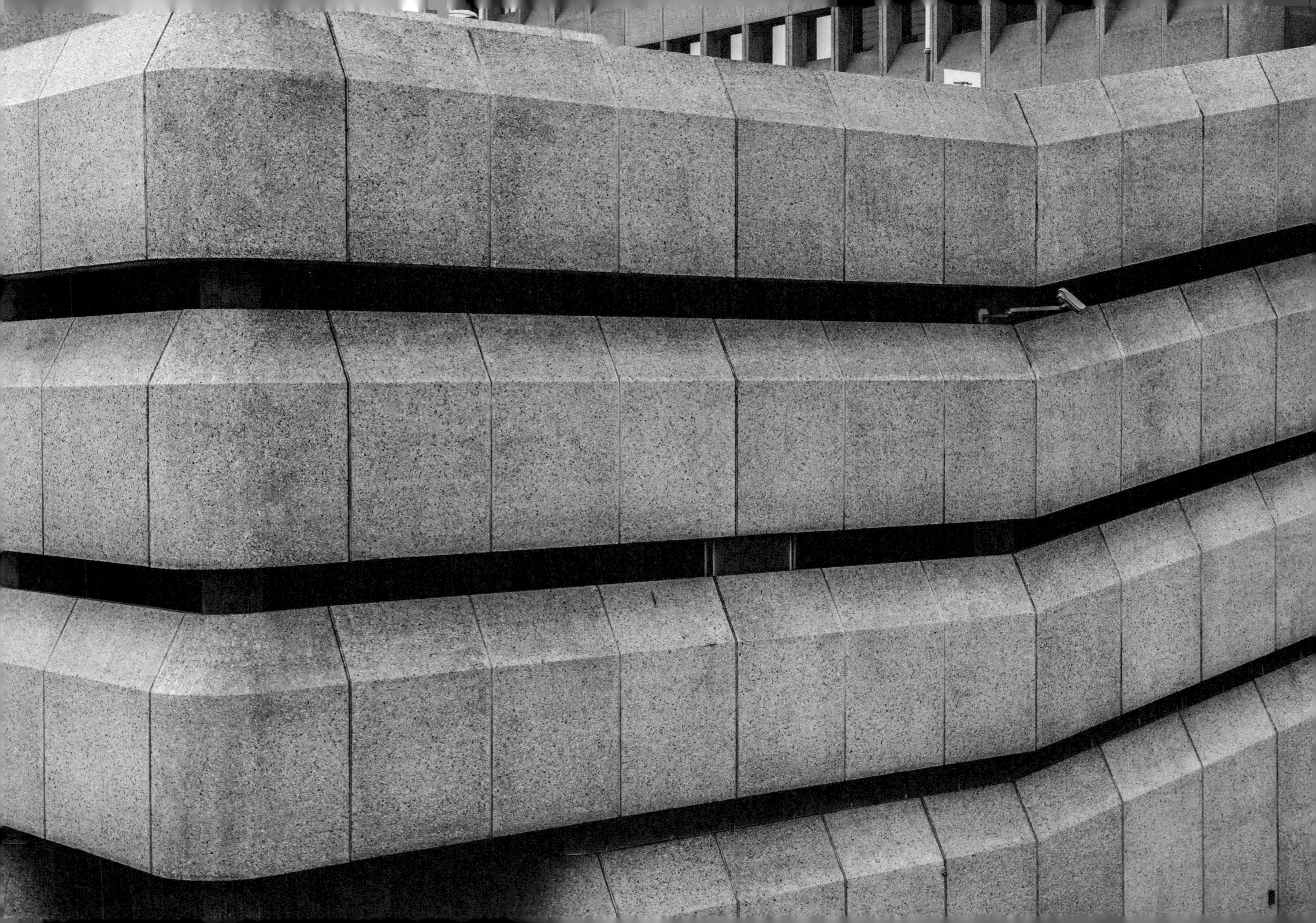

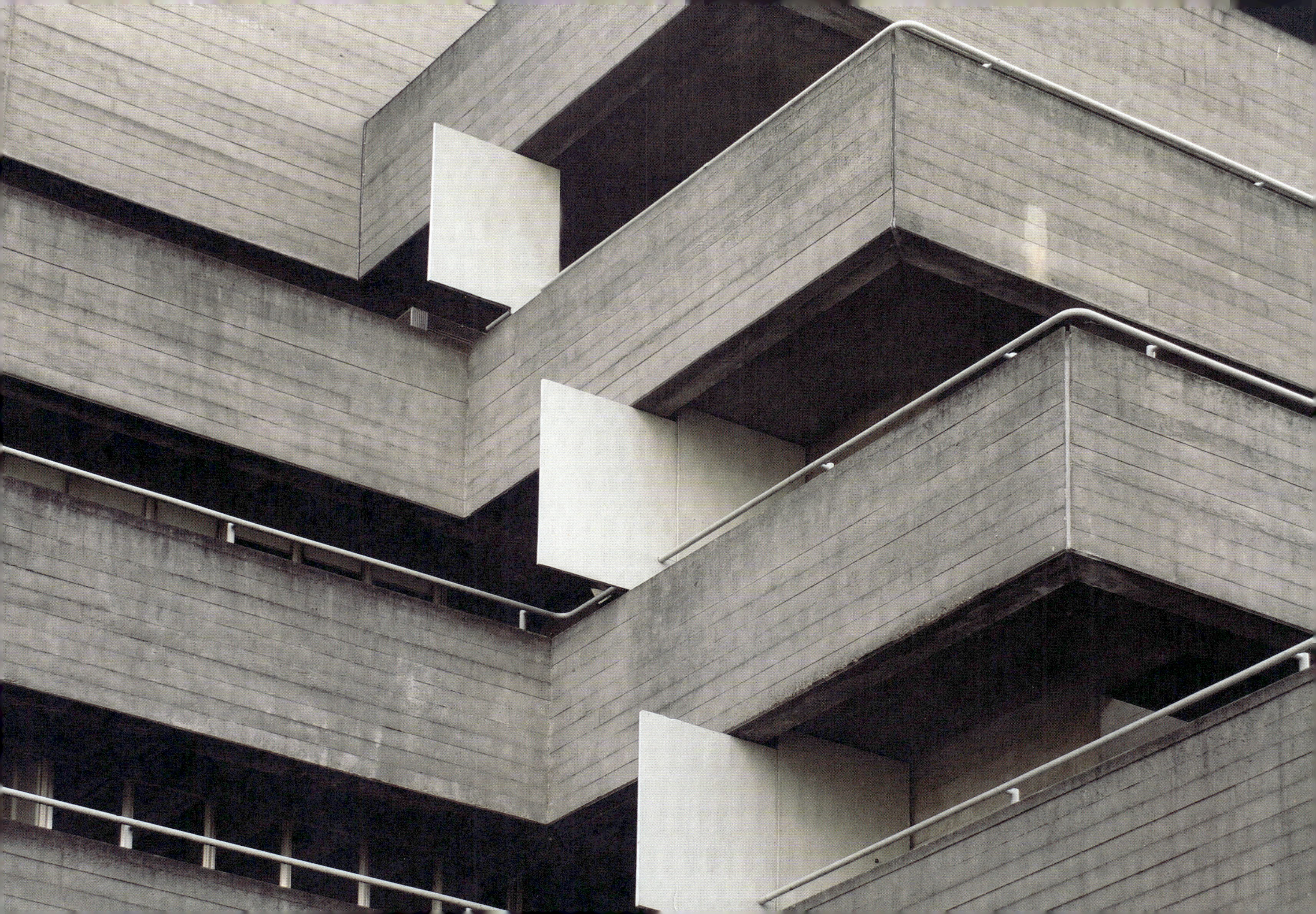

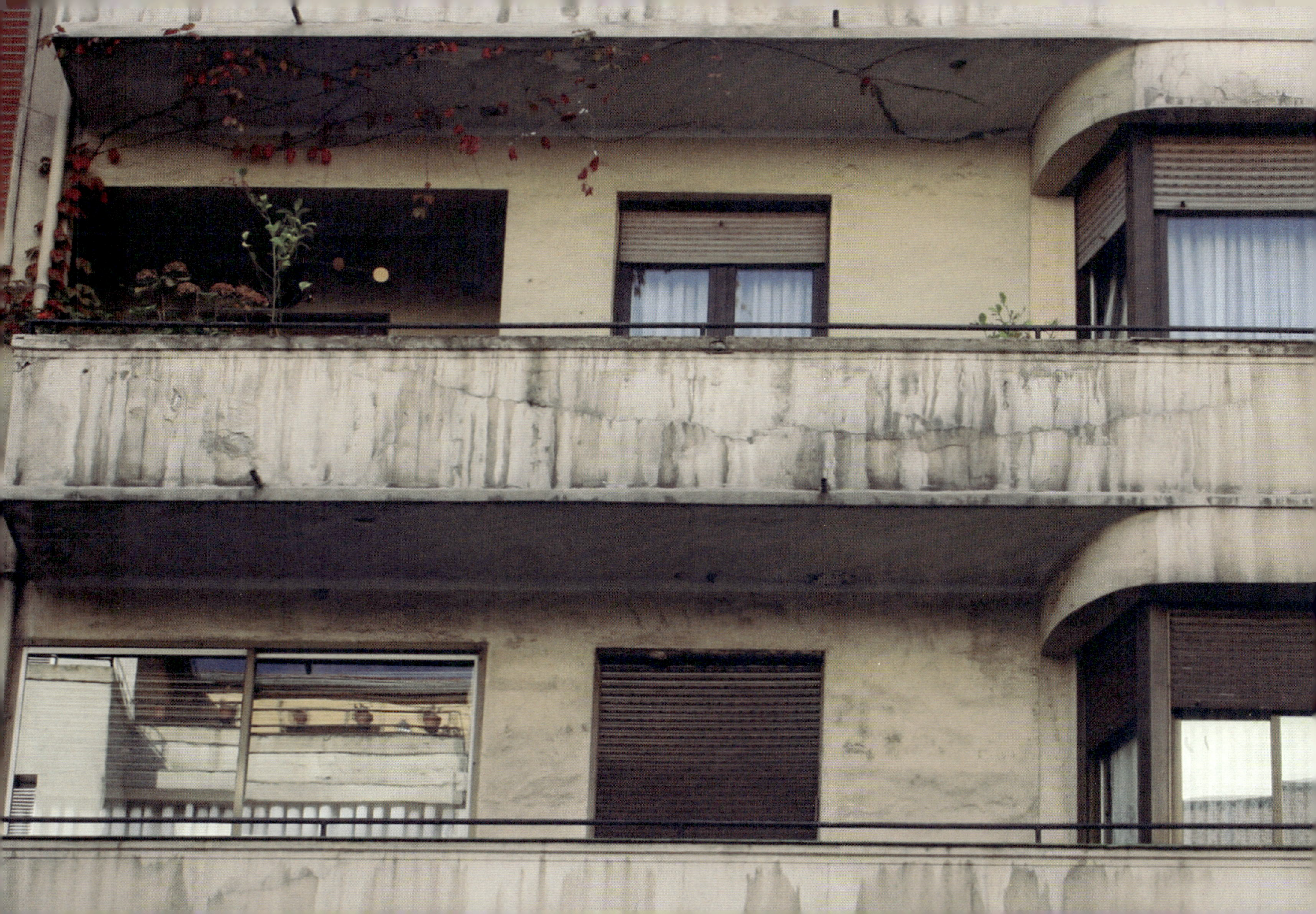

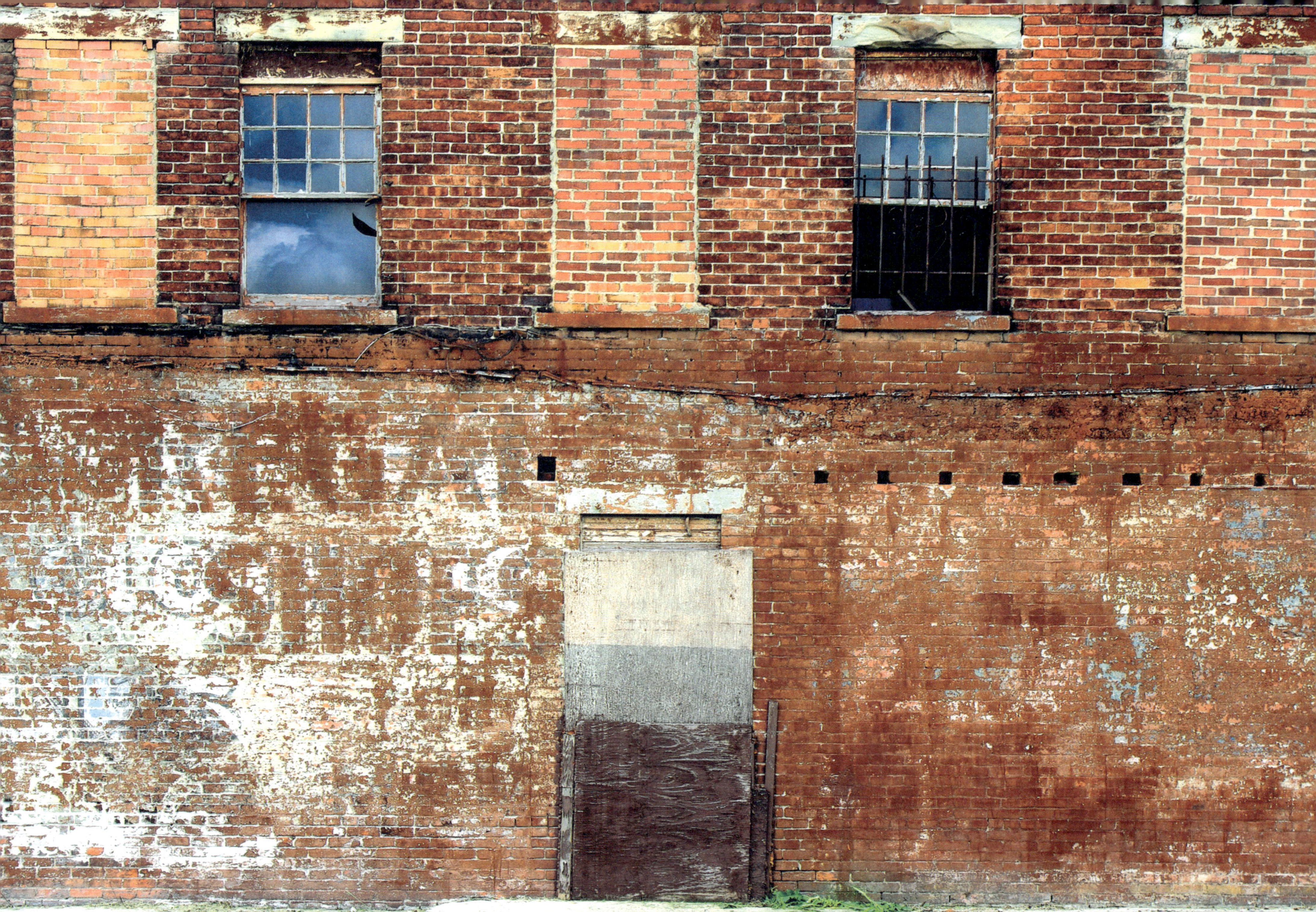

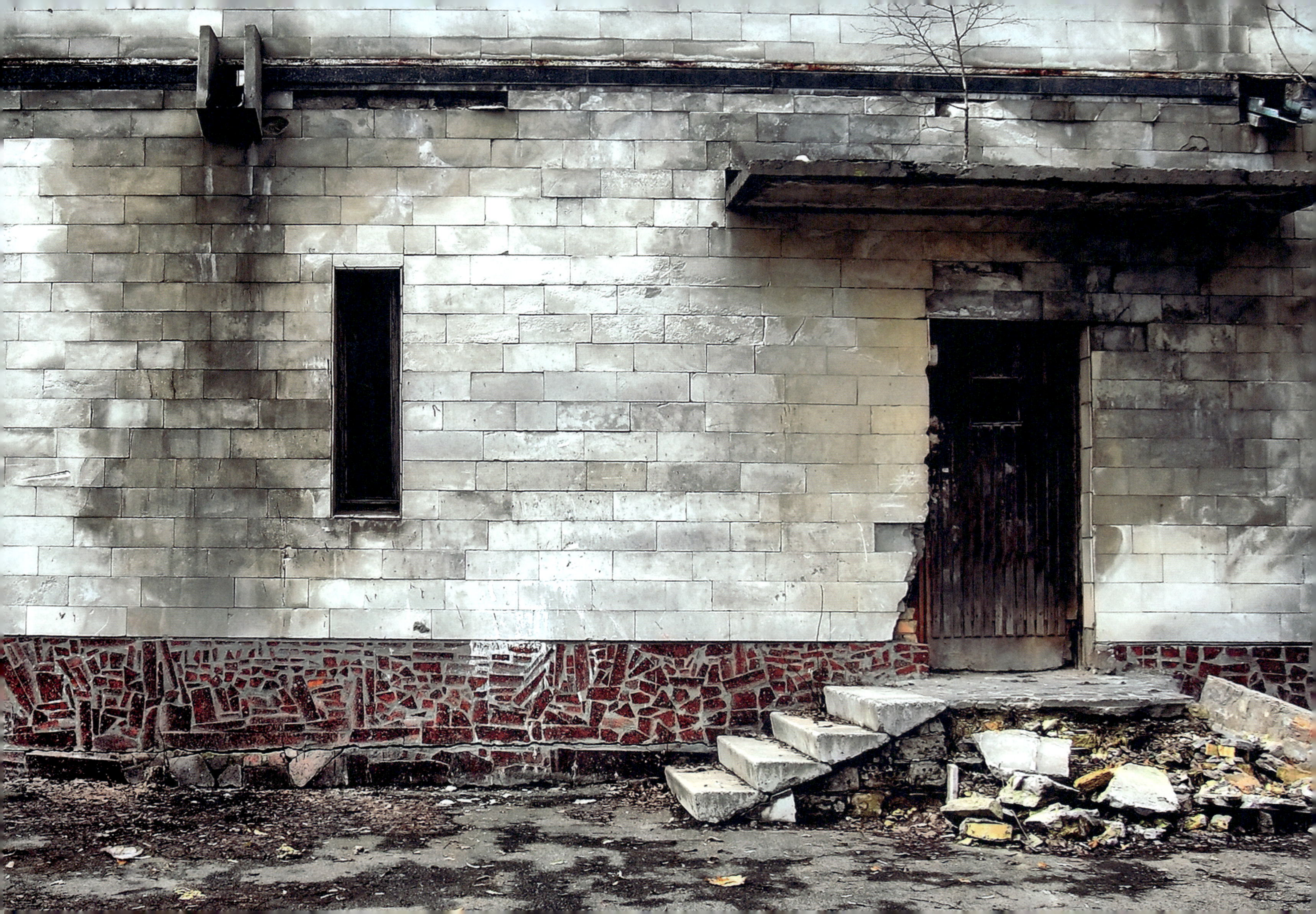

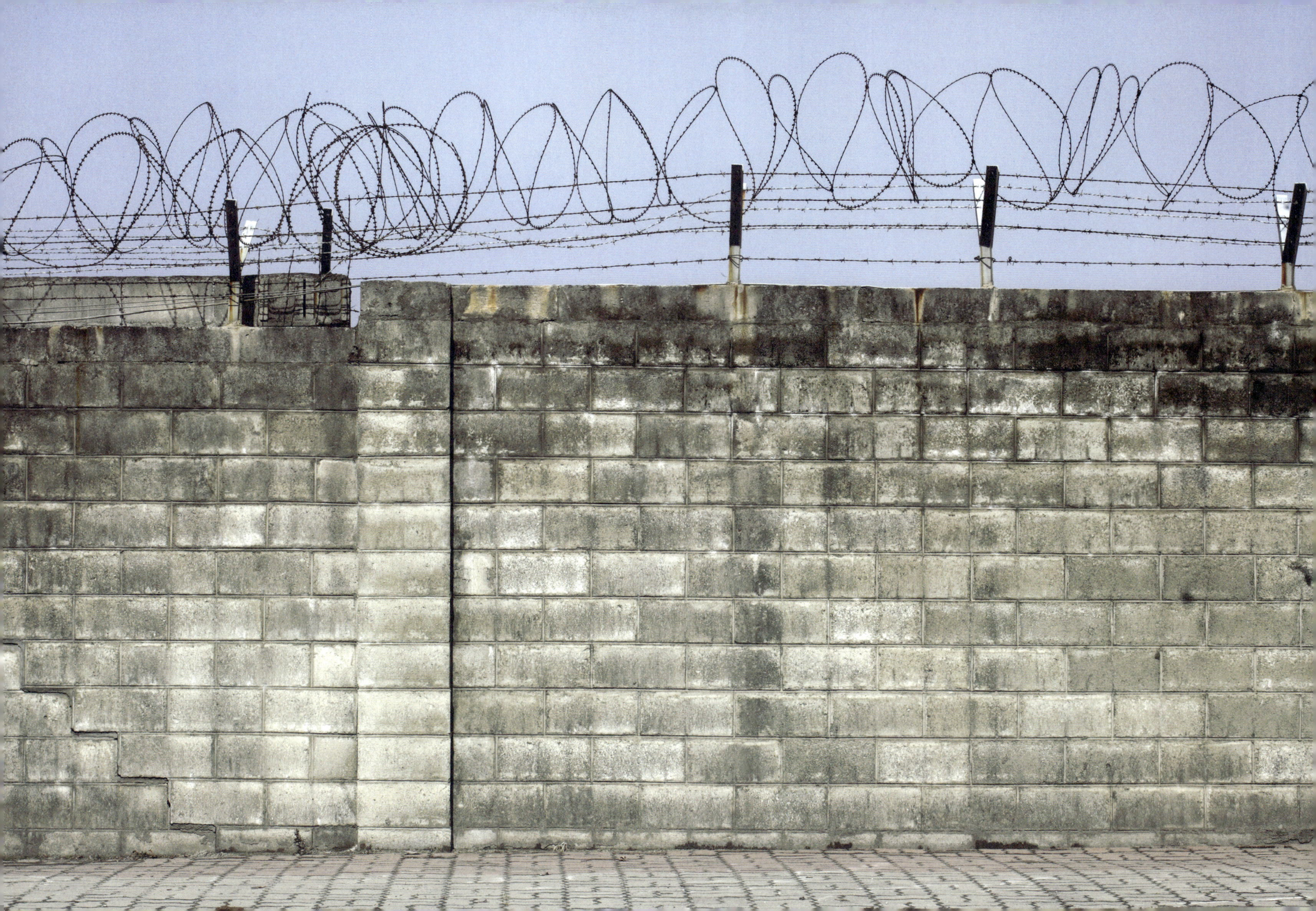

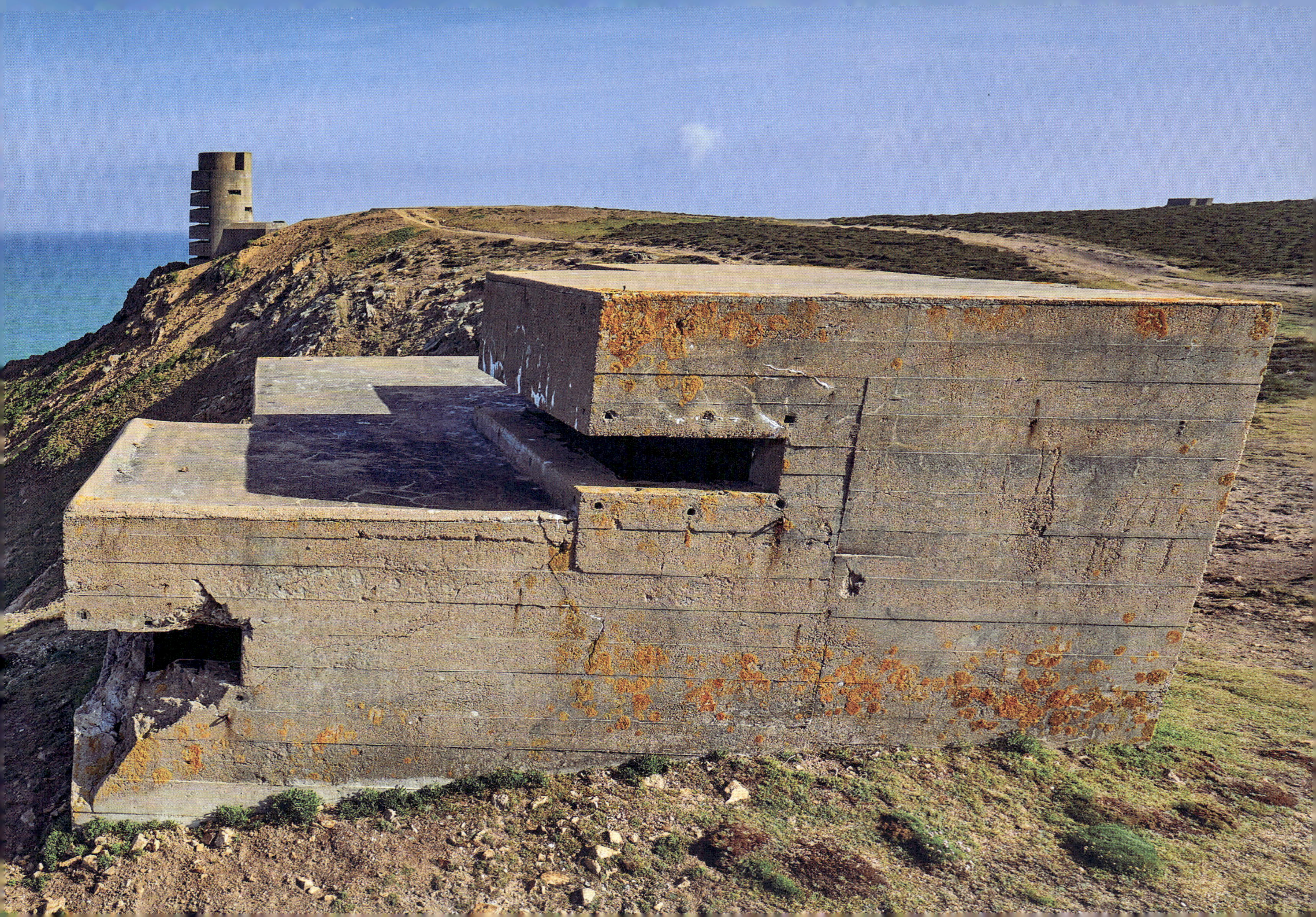

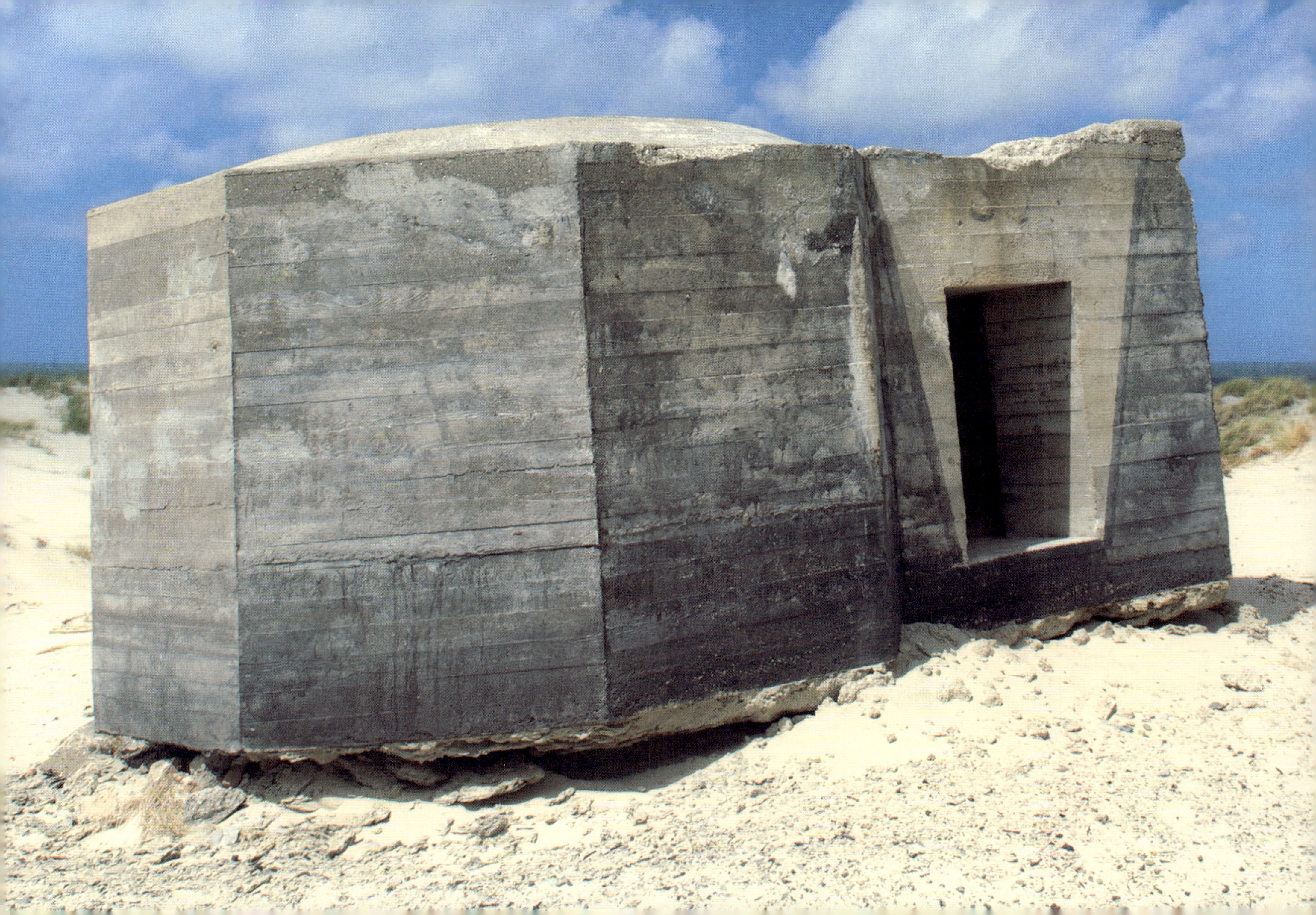

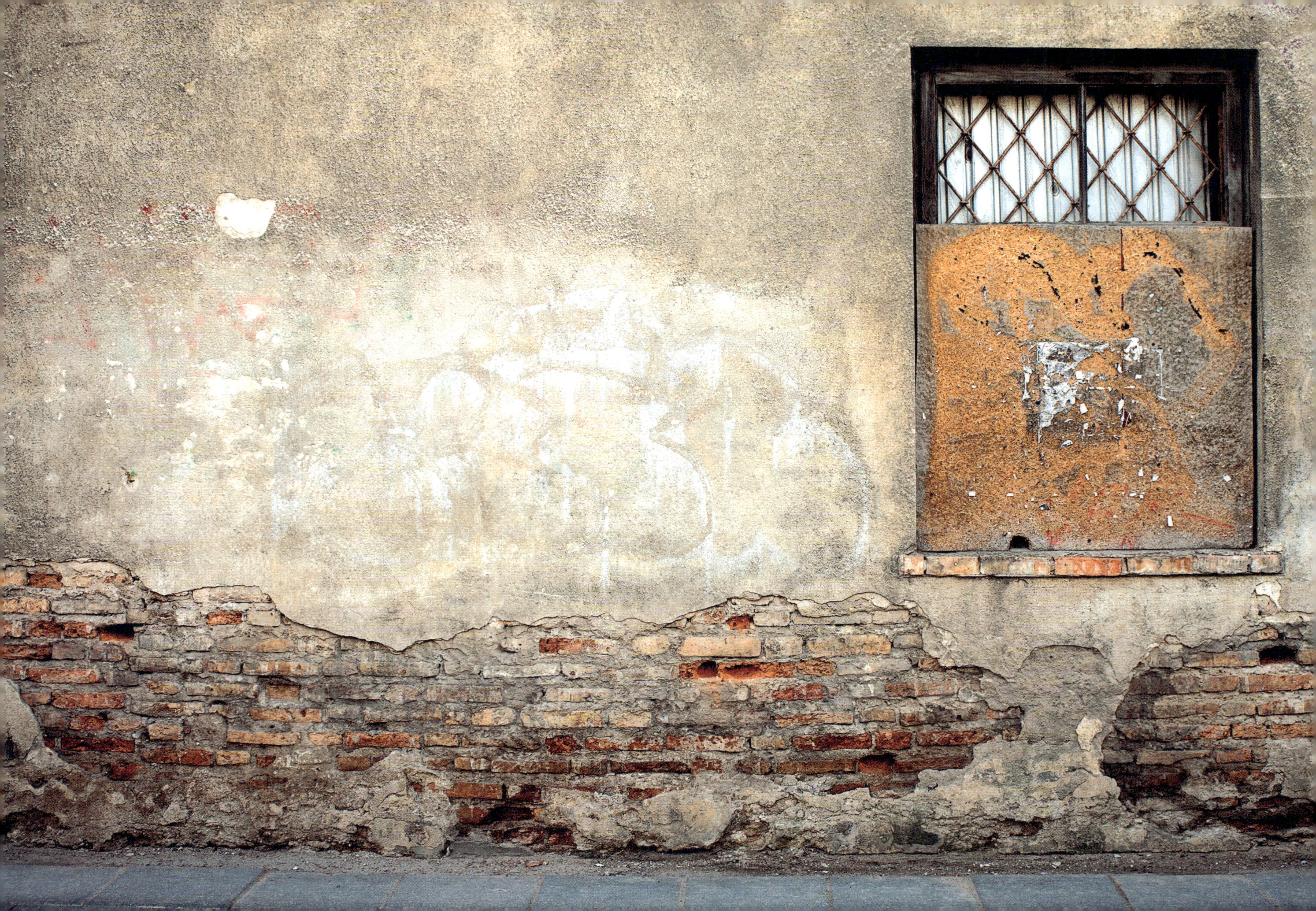

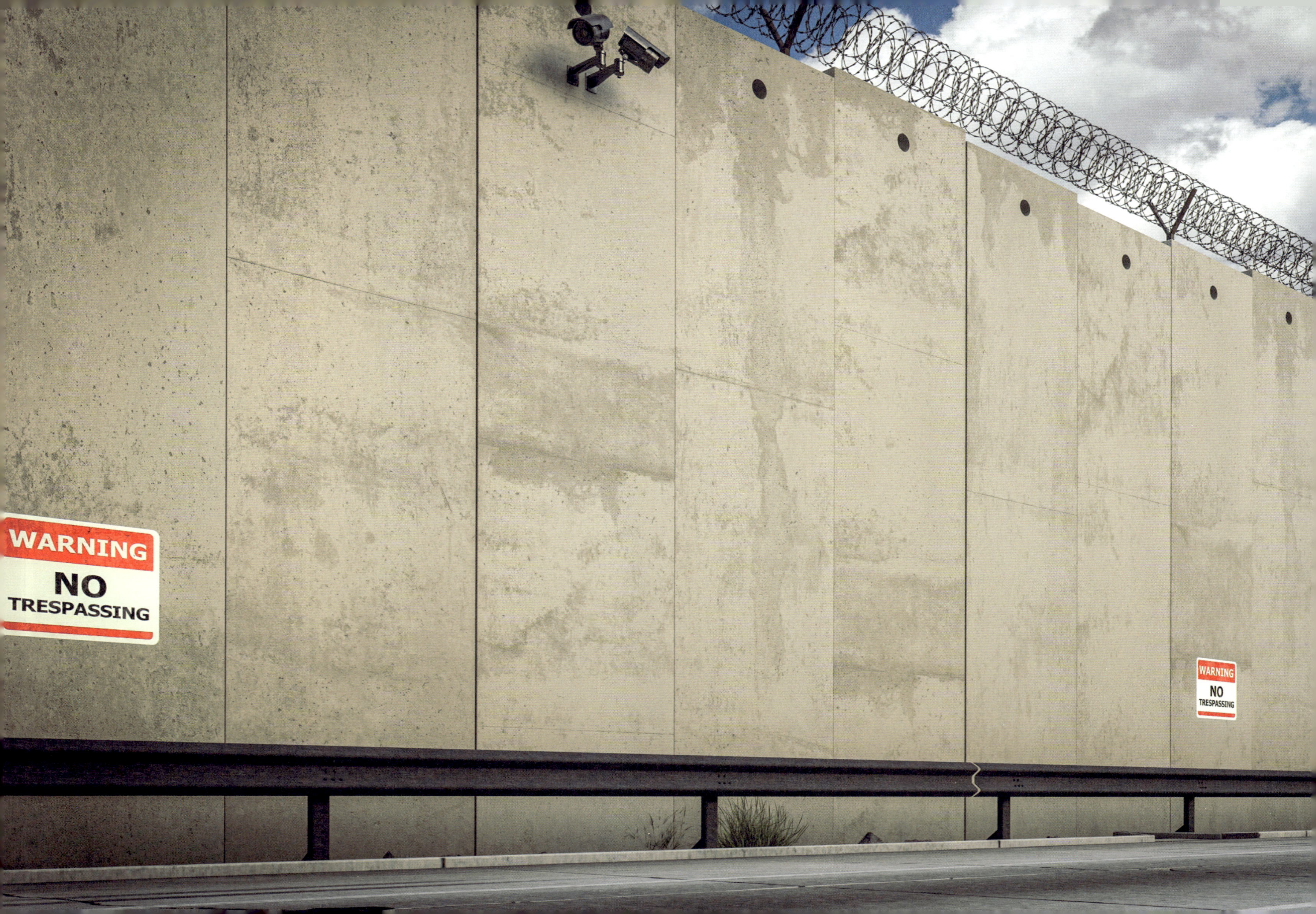
WARNING
NO
TRESPASSING
WARNING
NO
TRESPASSING

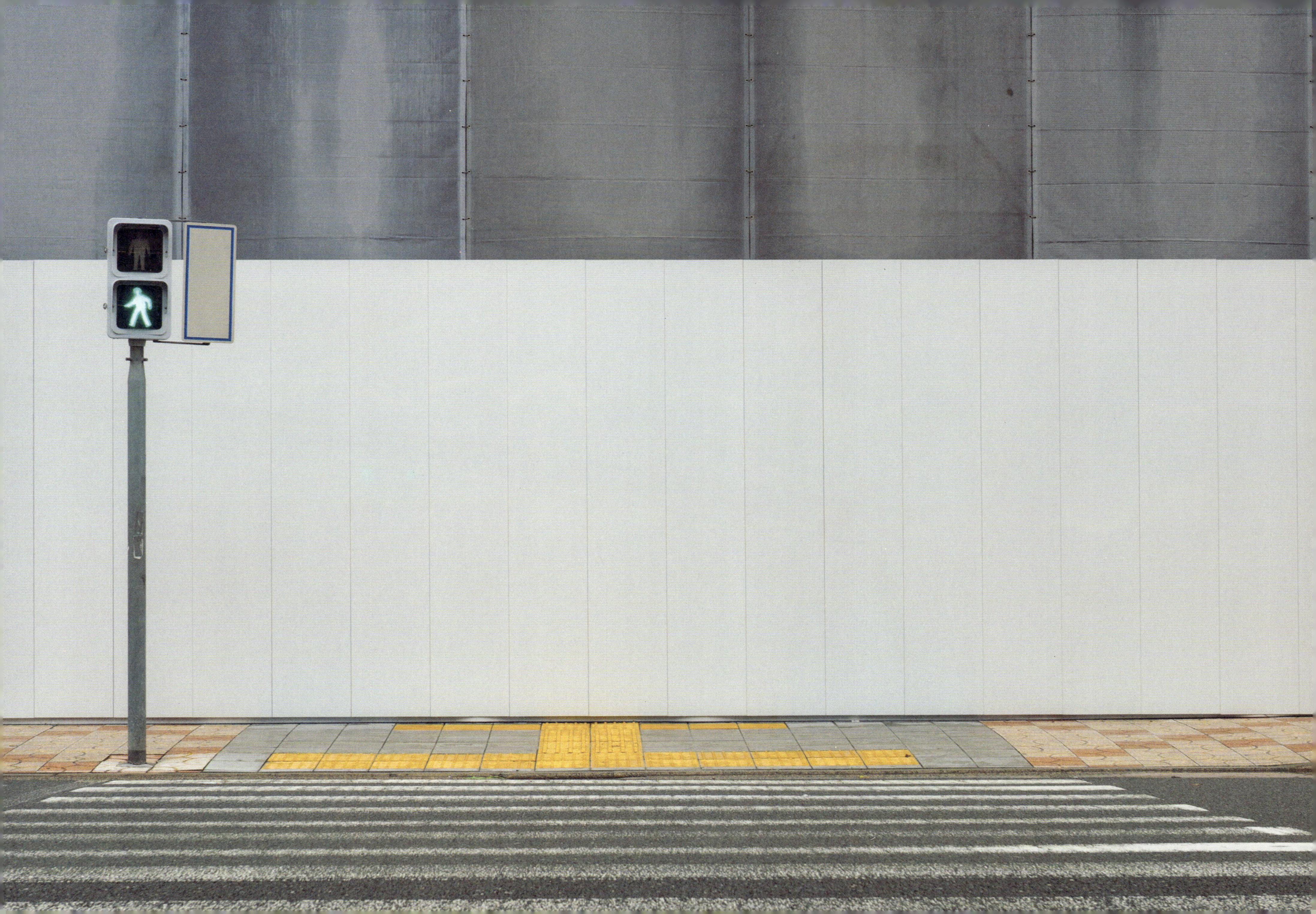

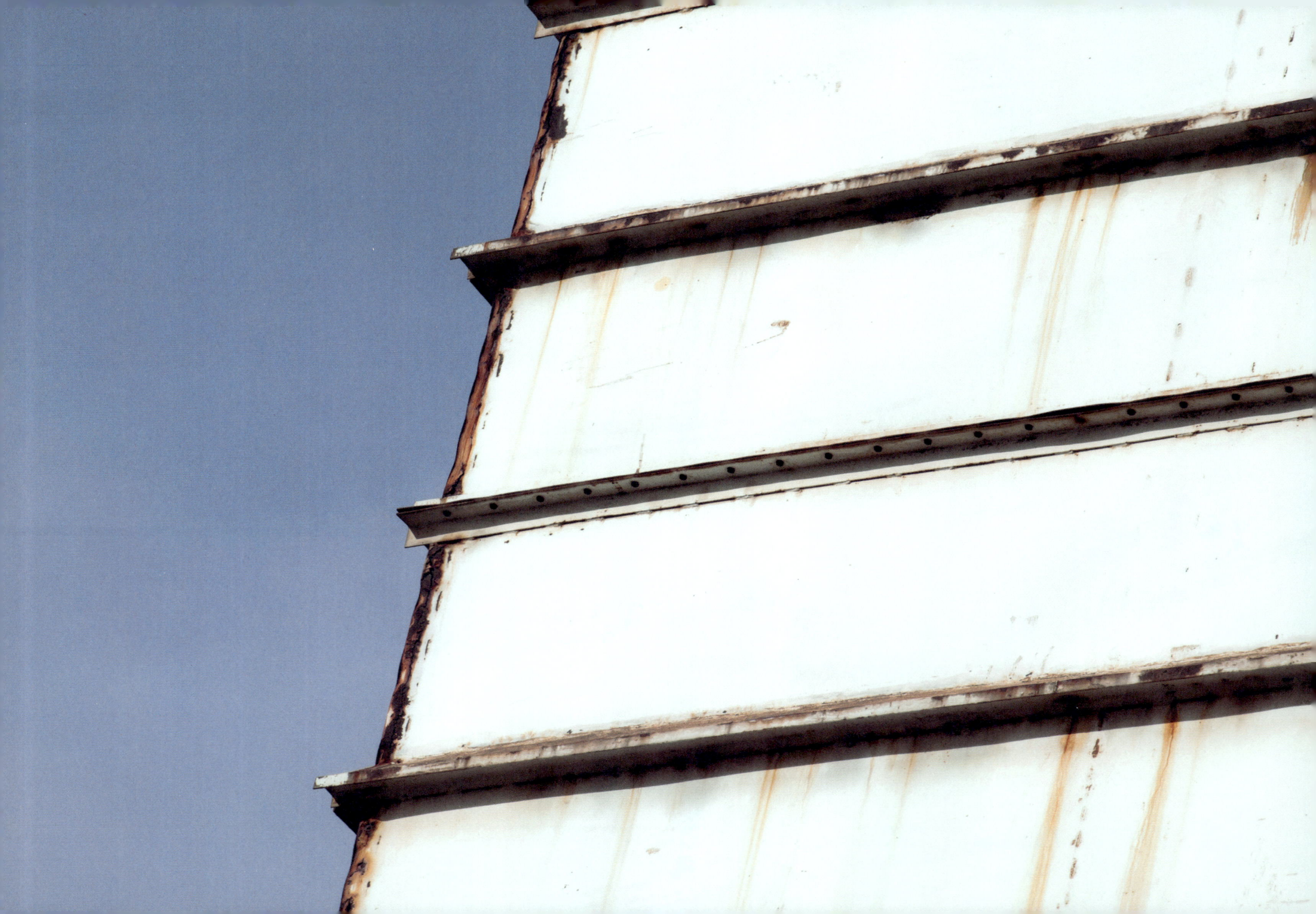

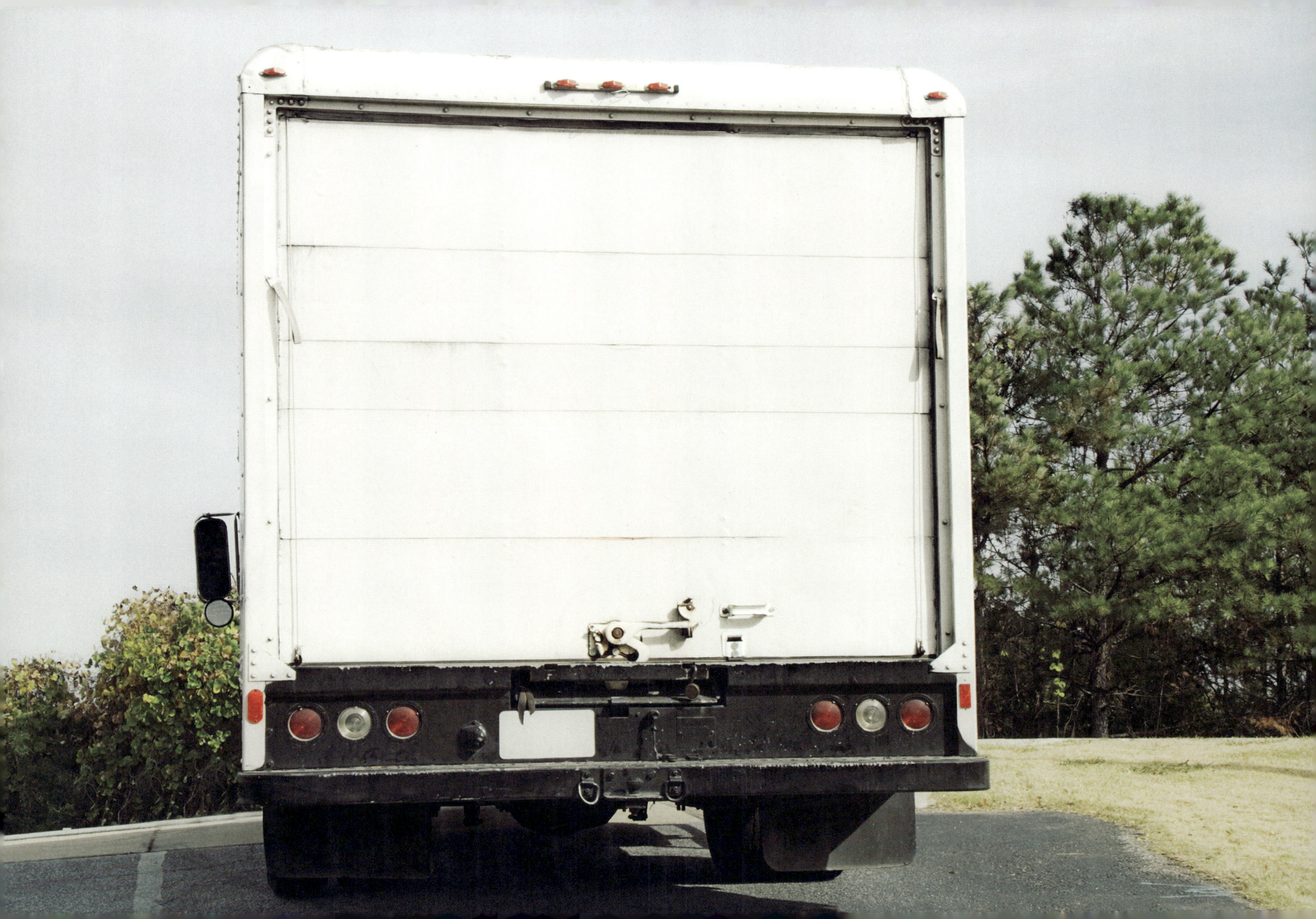

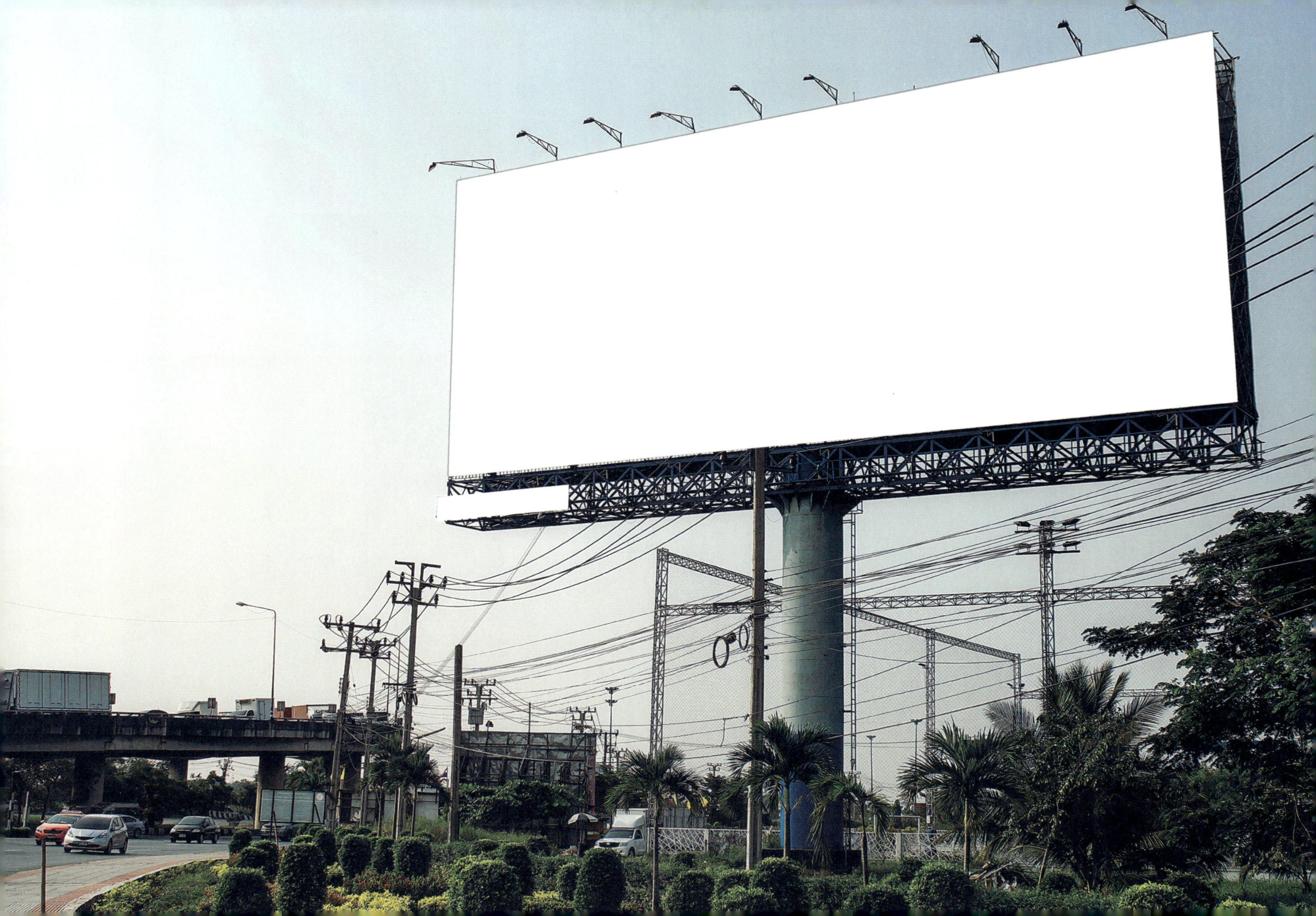

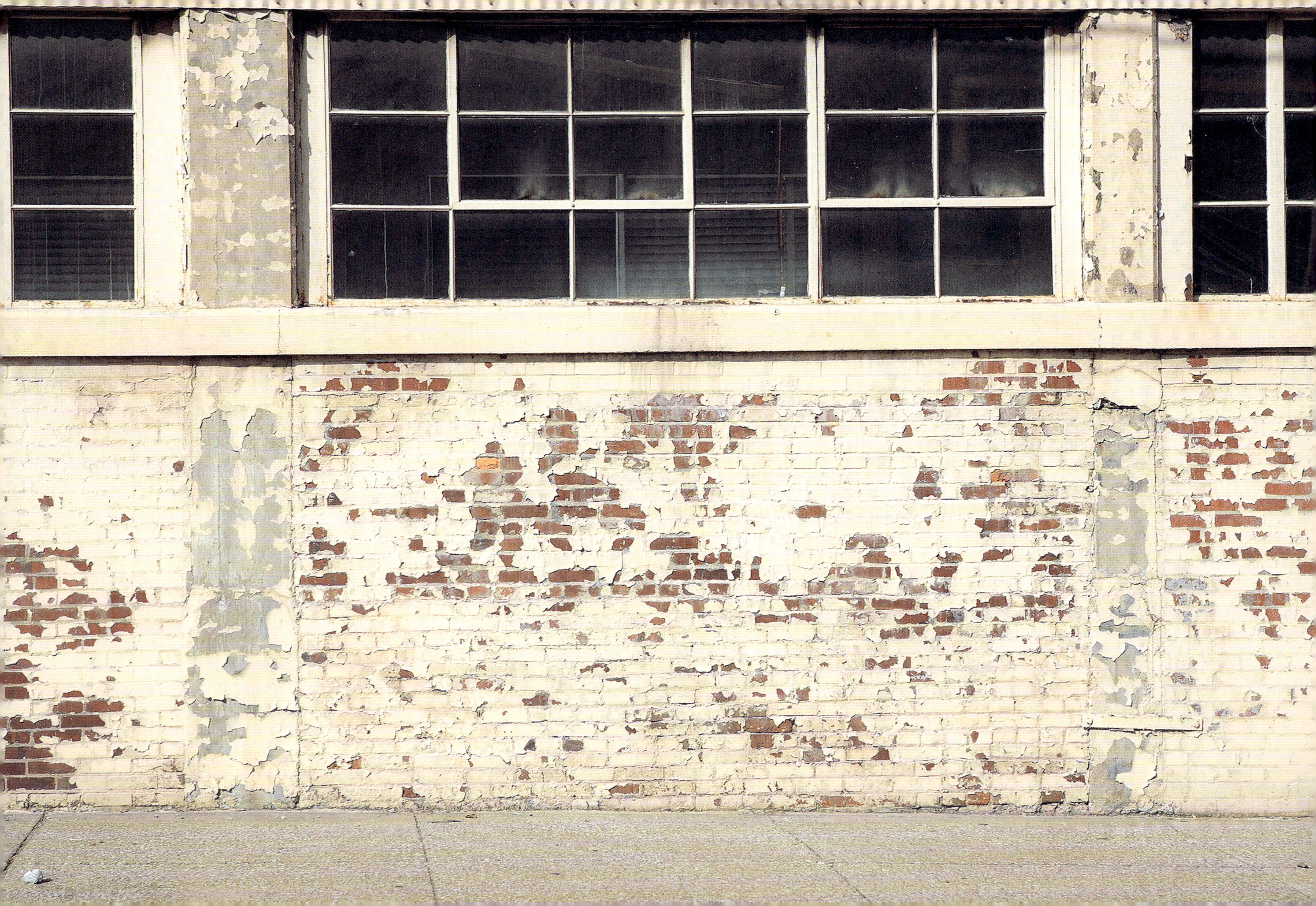

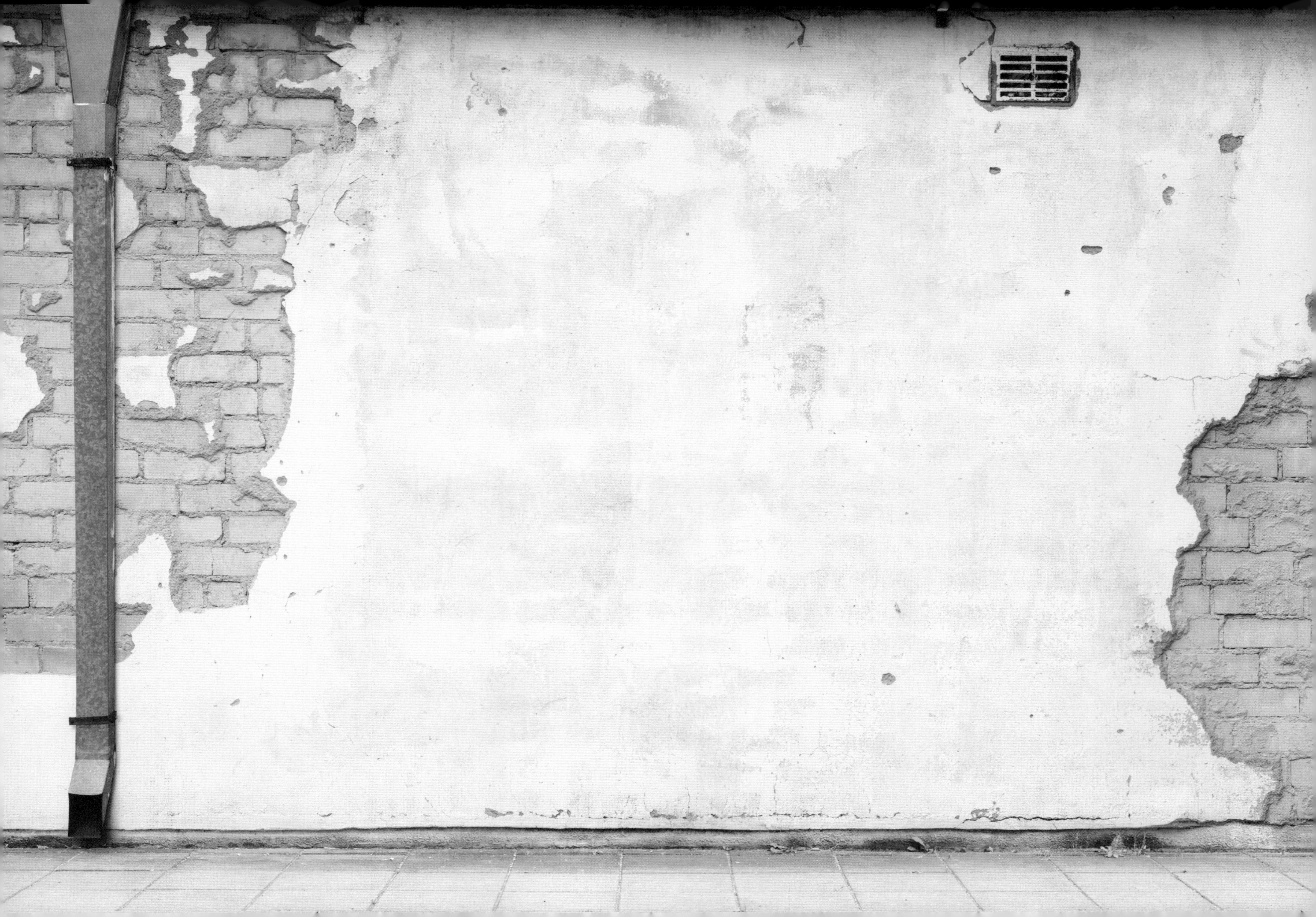

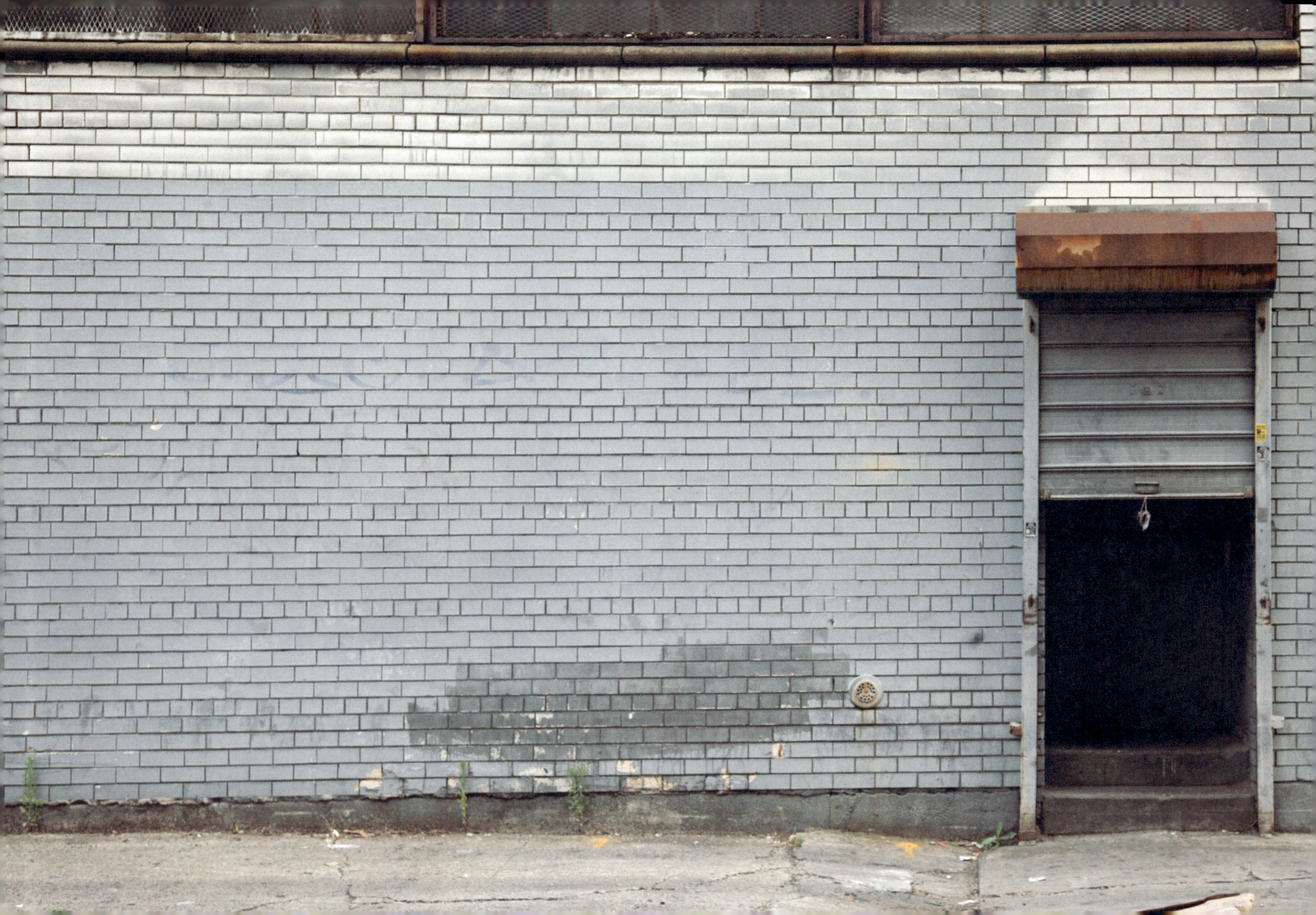

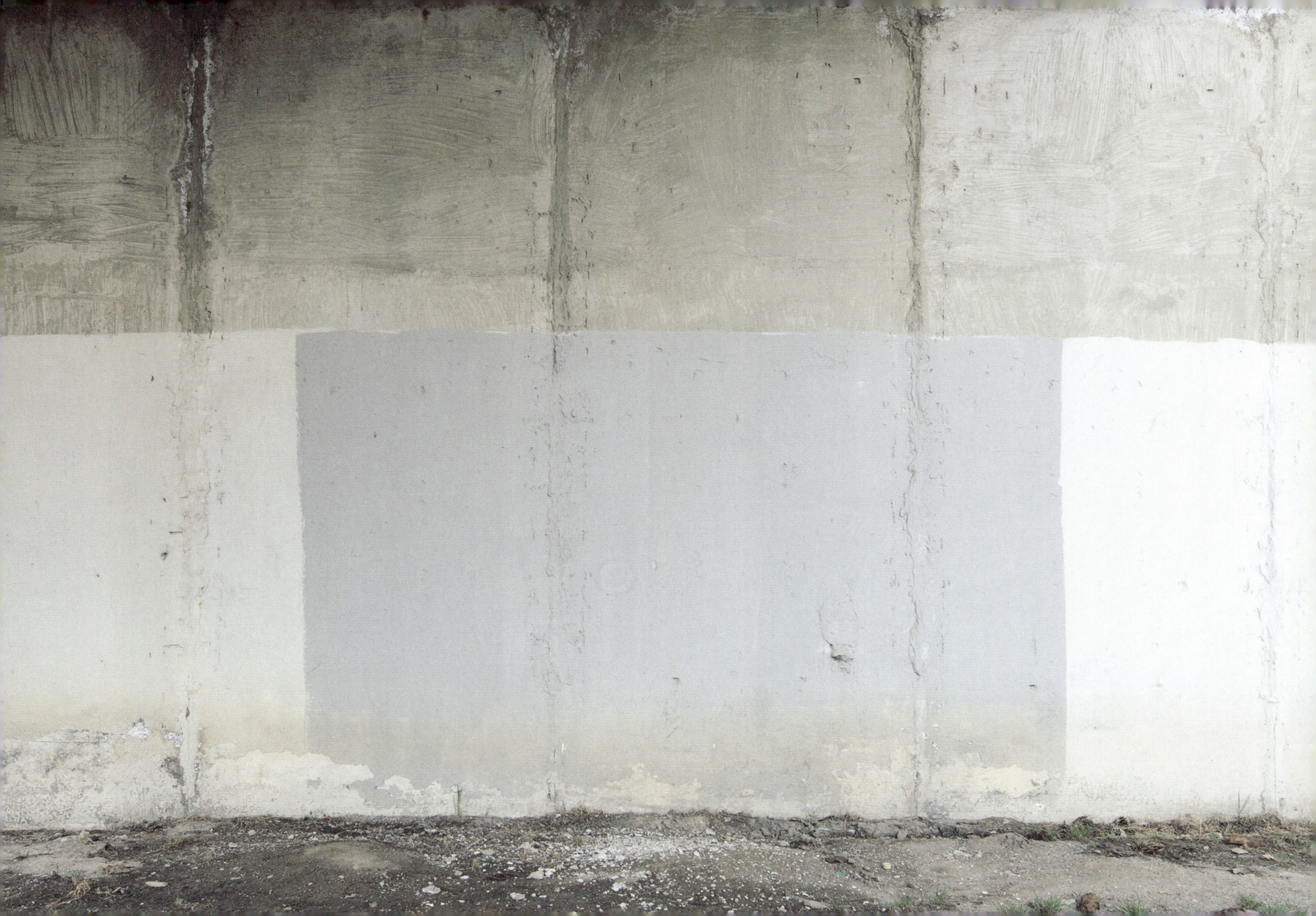

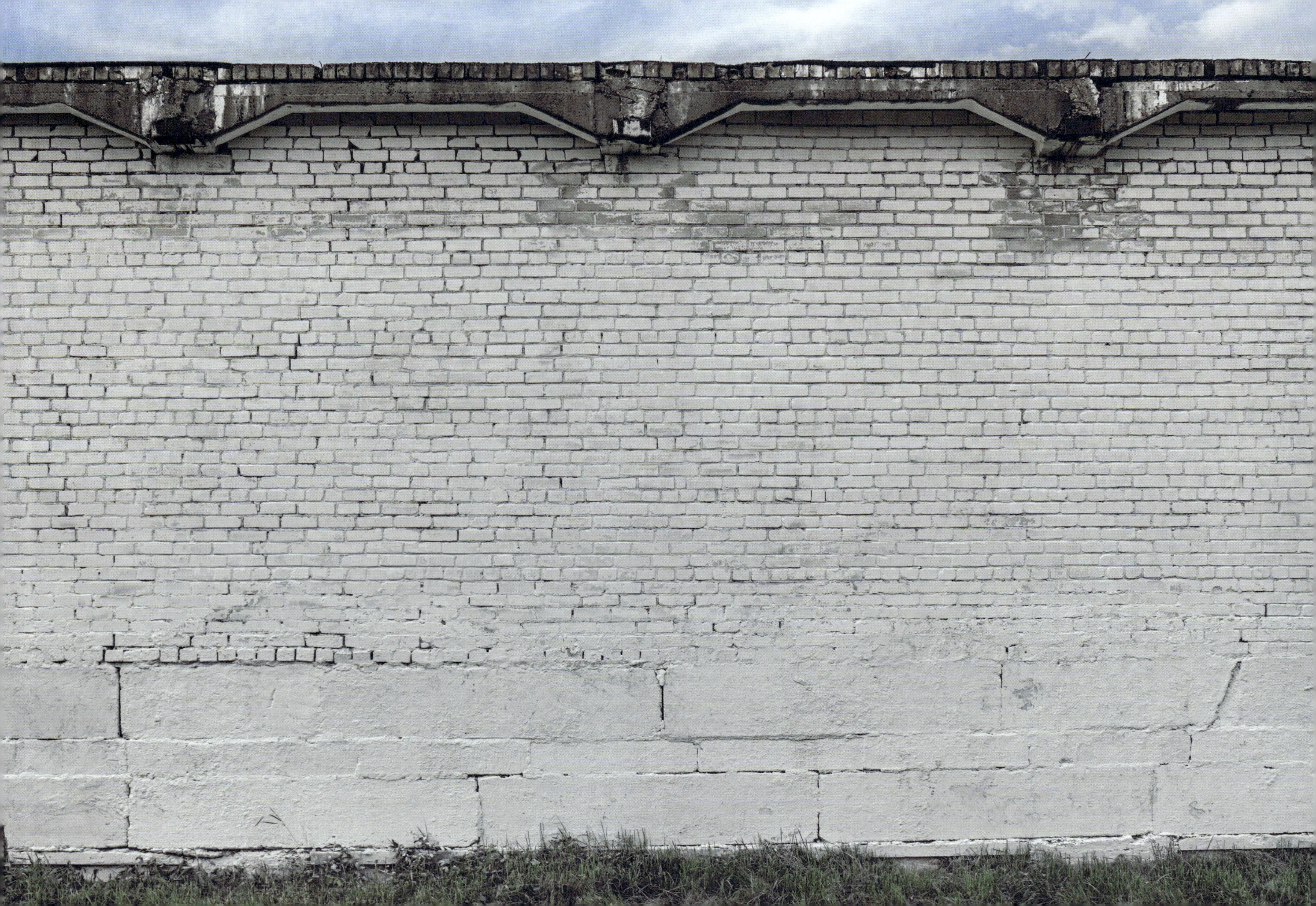

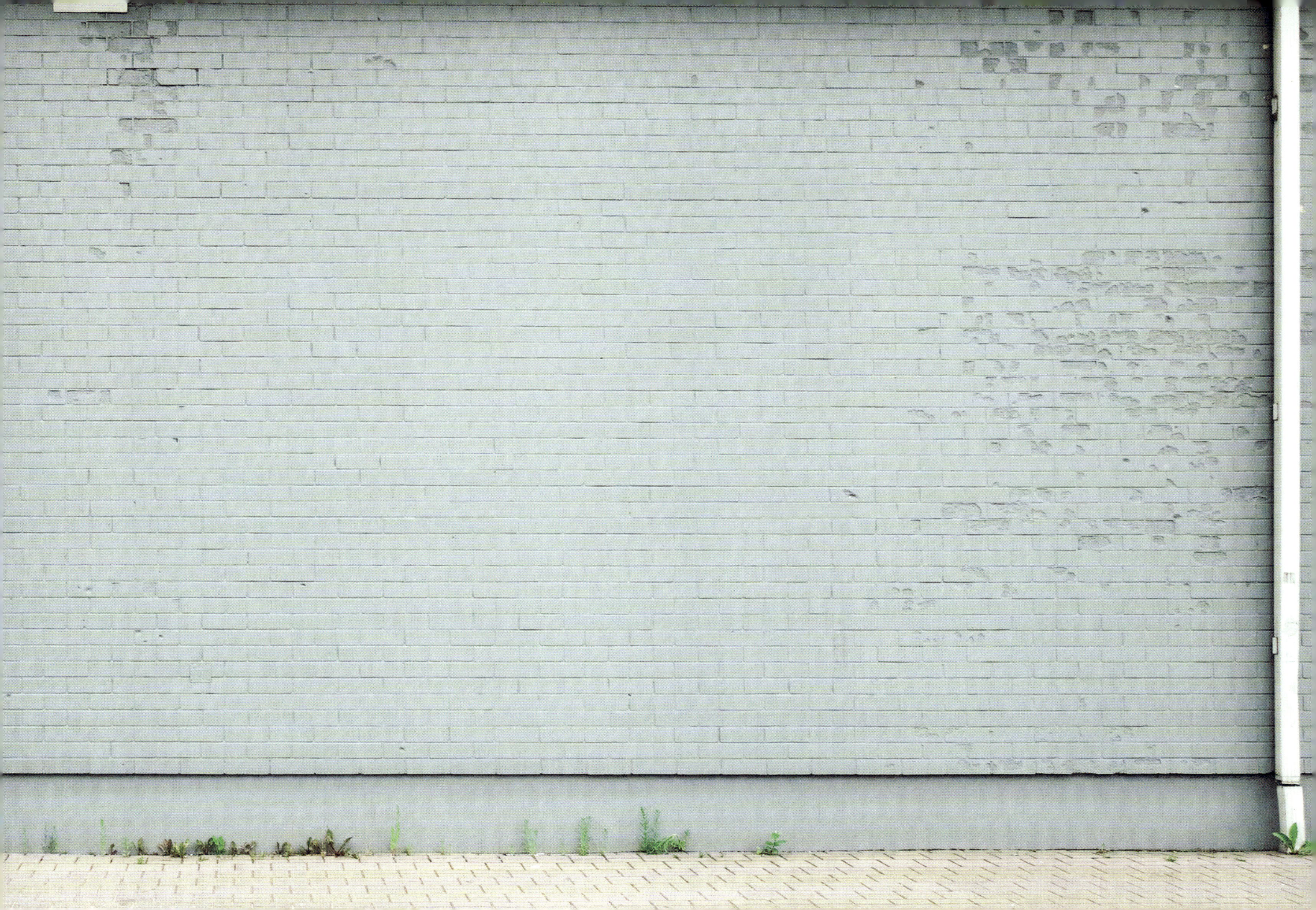

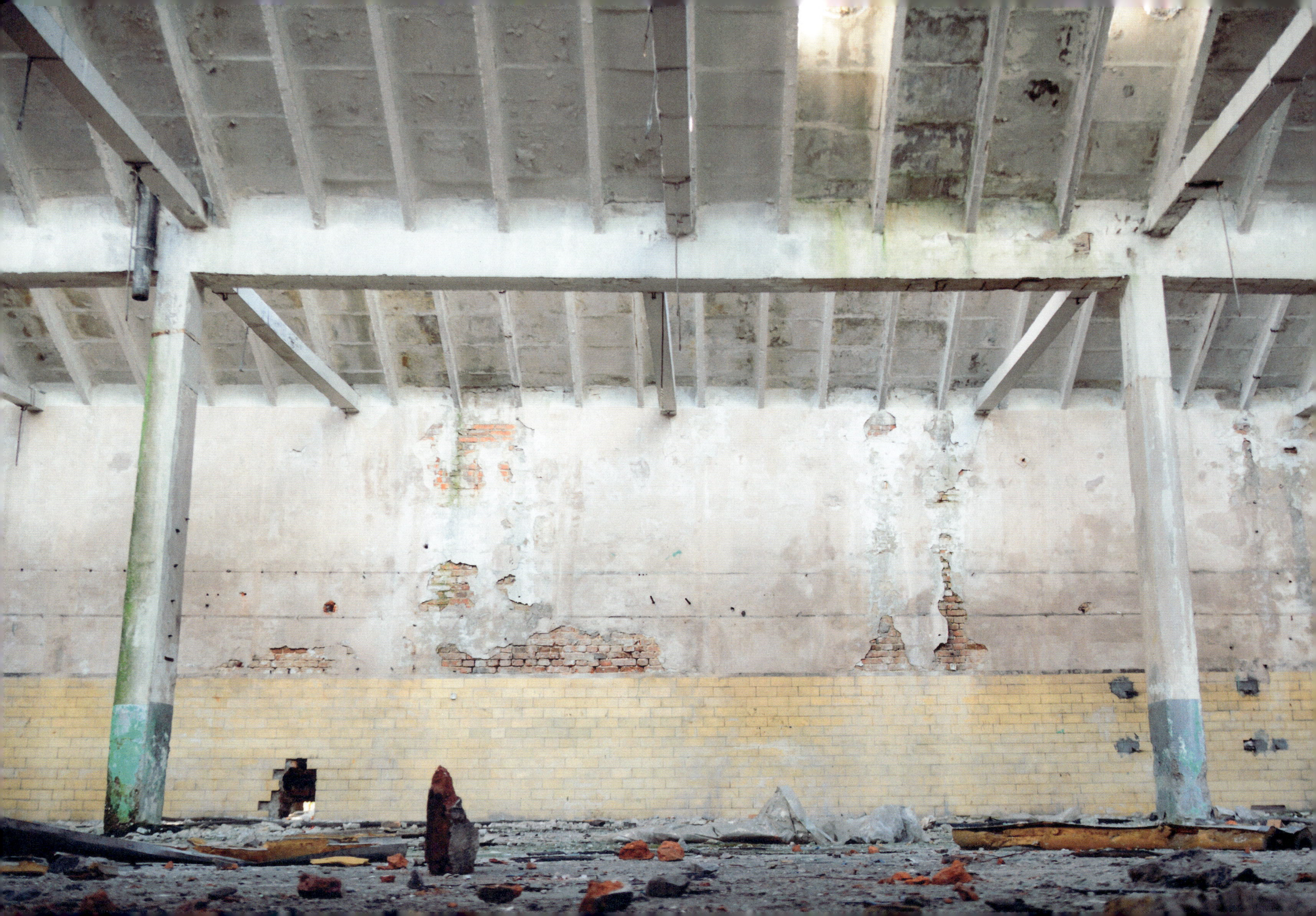

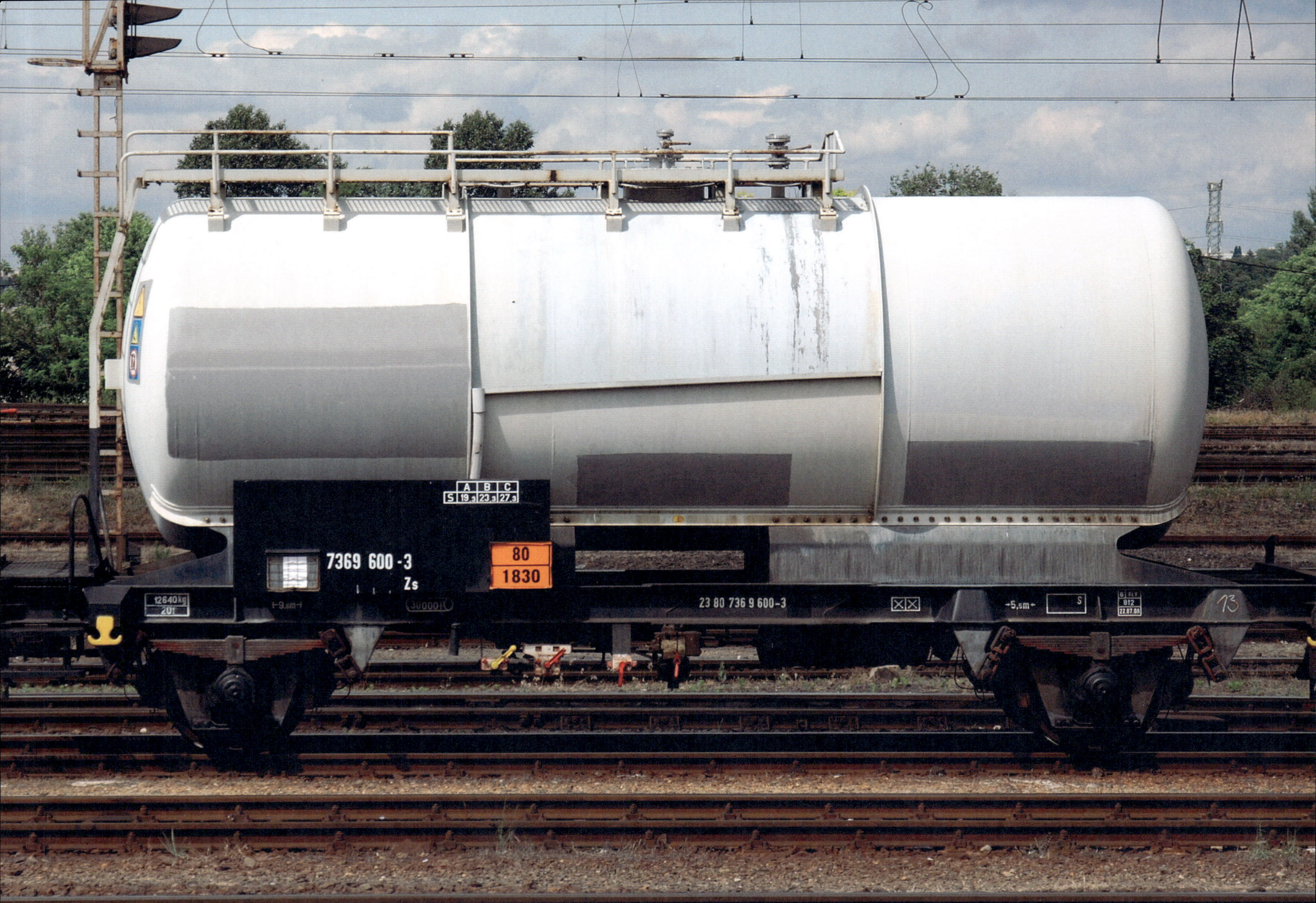

A B C
S 19.3 23.3 27.3
7369 600-3
Zs
80
1830
12640 kg
20 t
23 80 736 9 600-3
S

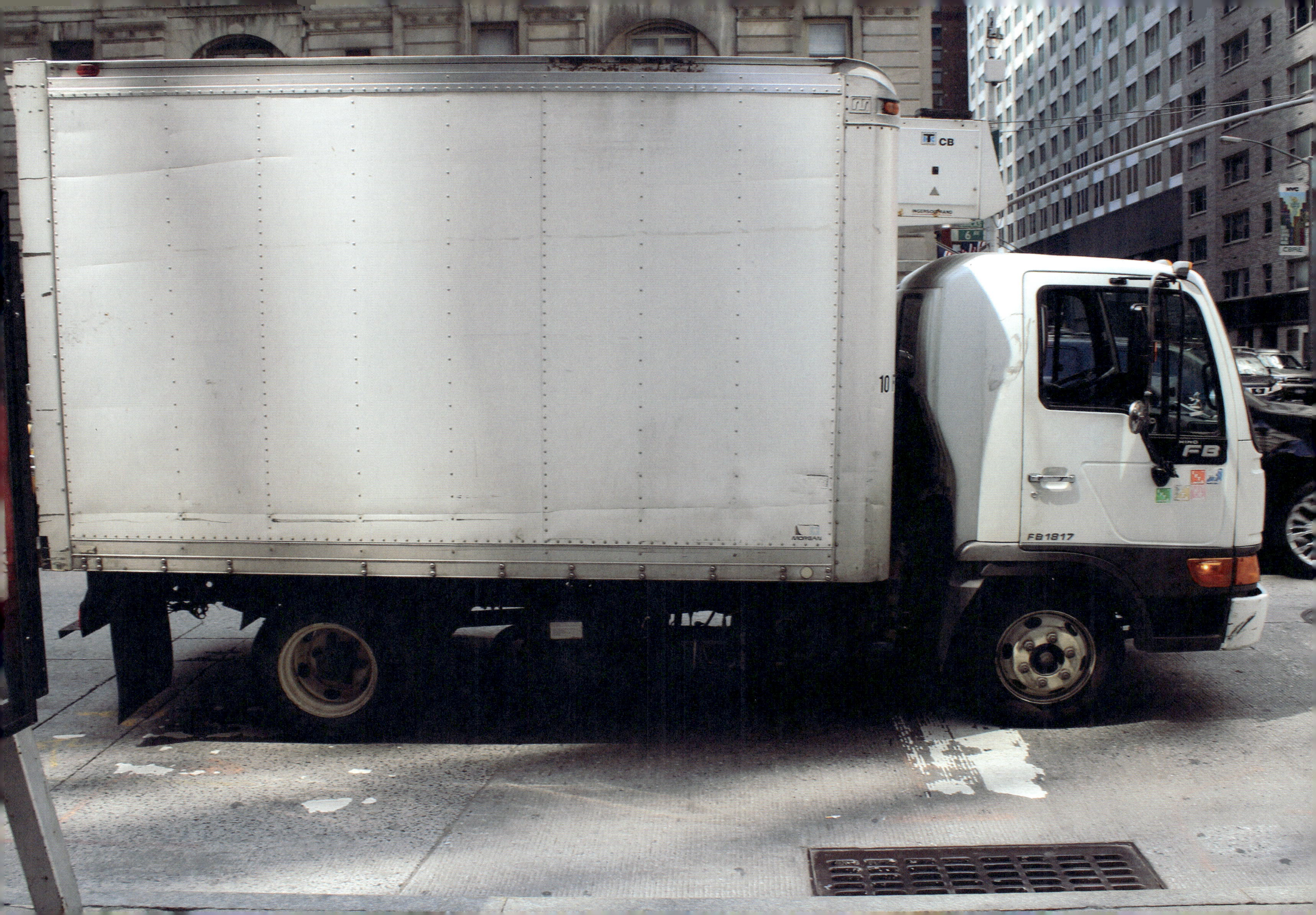

CB
FB
FB1817
MORGAN

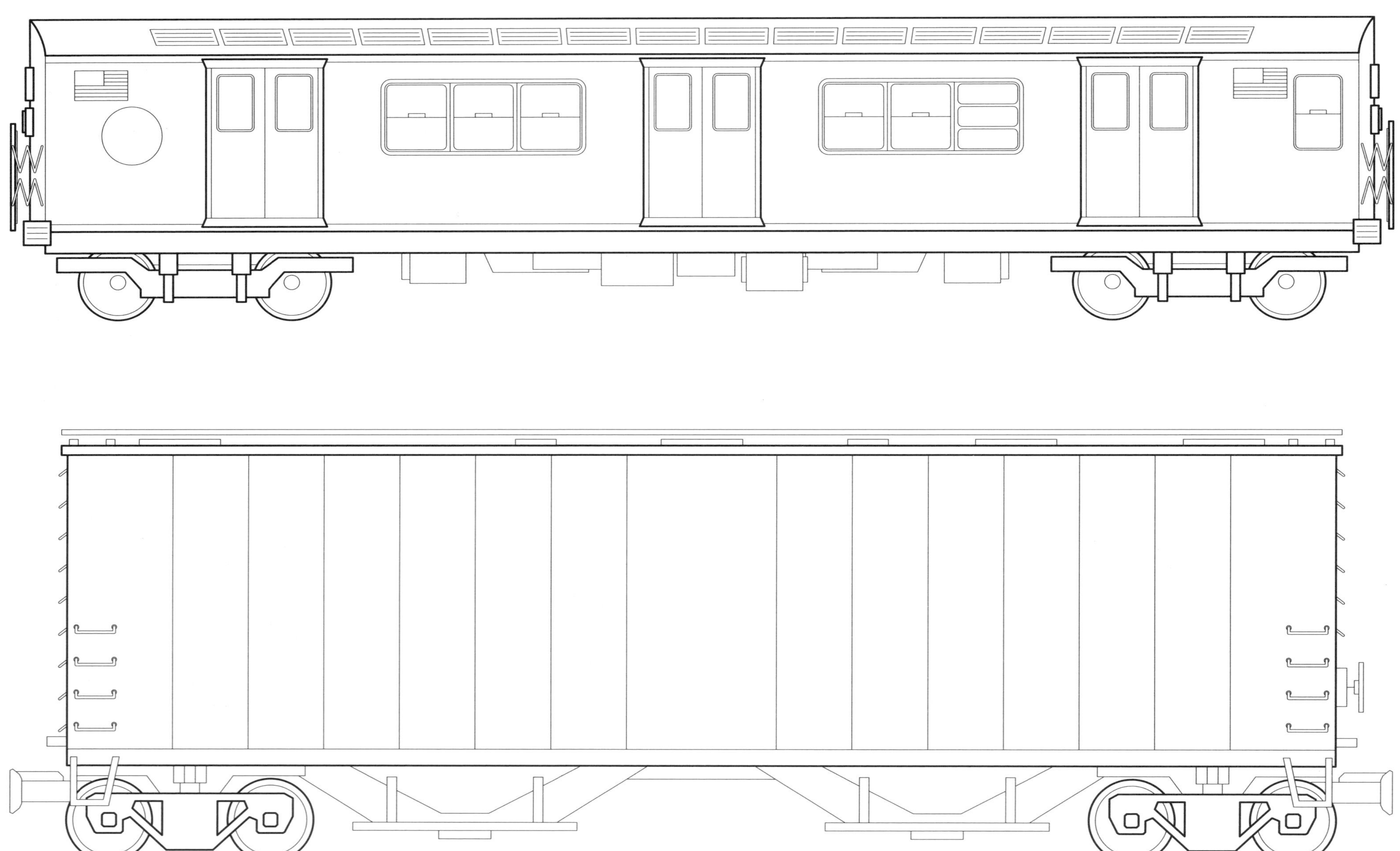

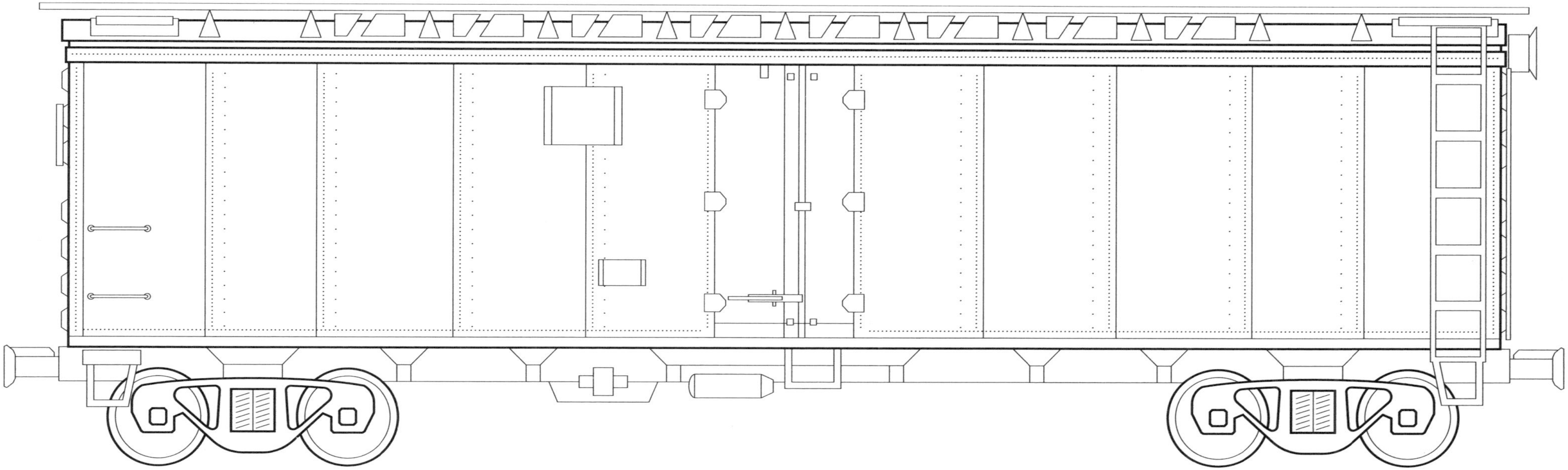

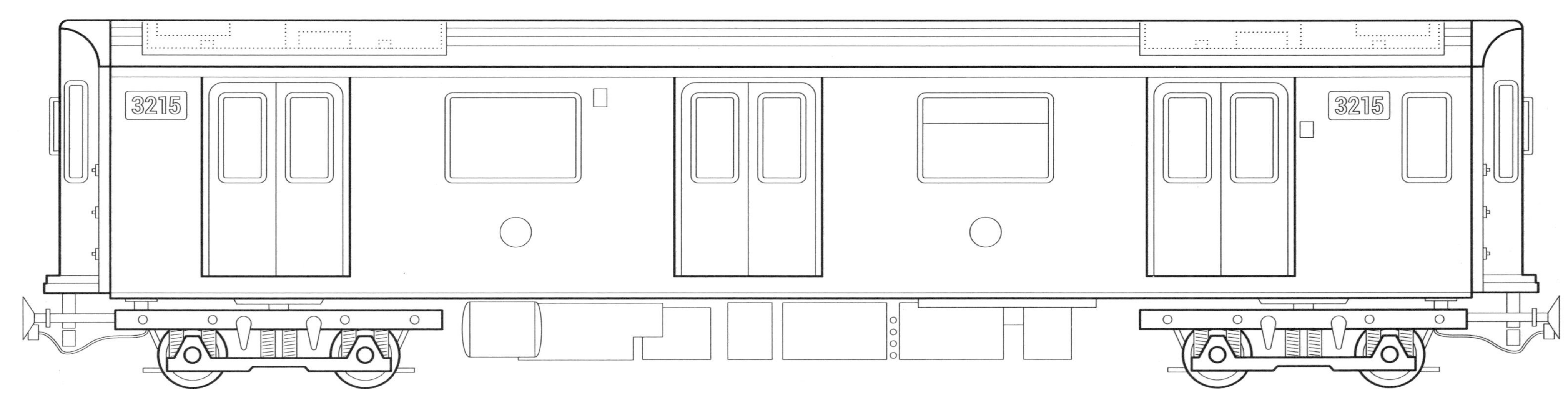

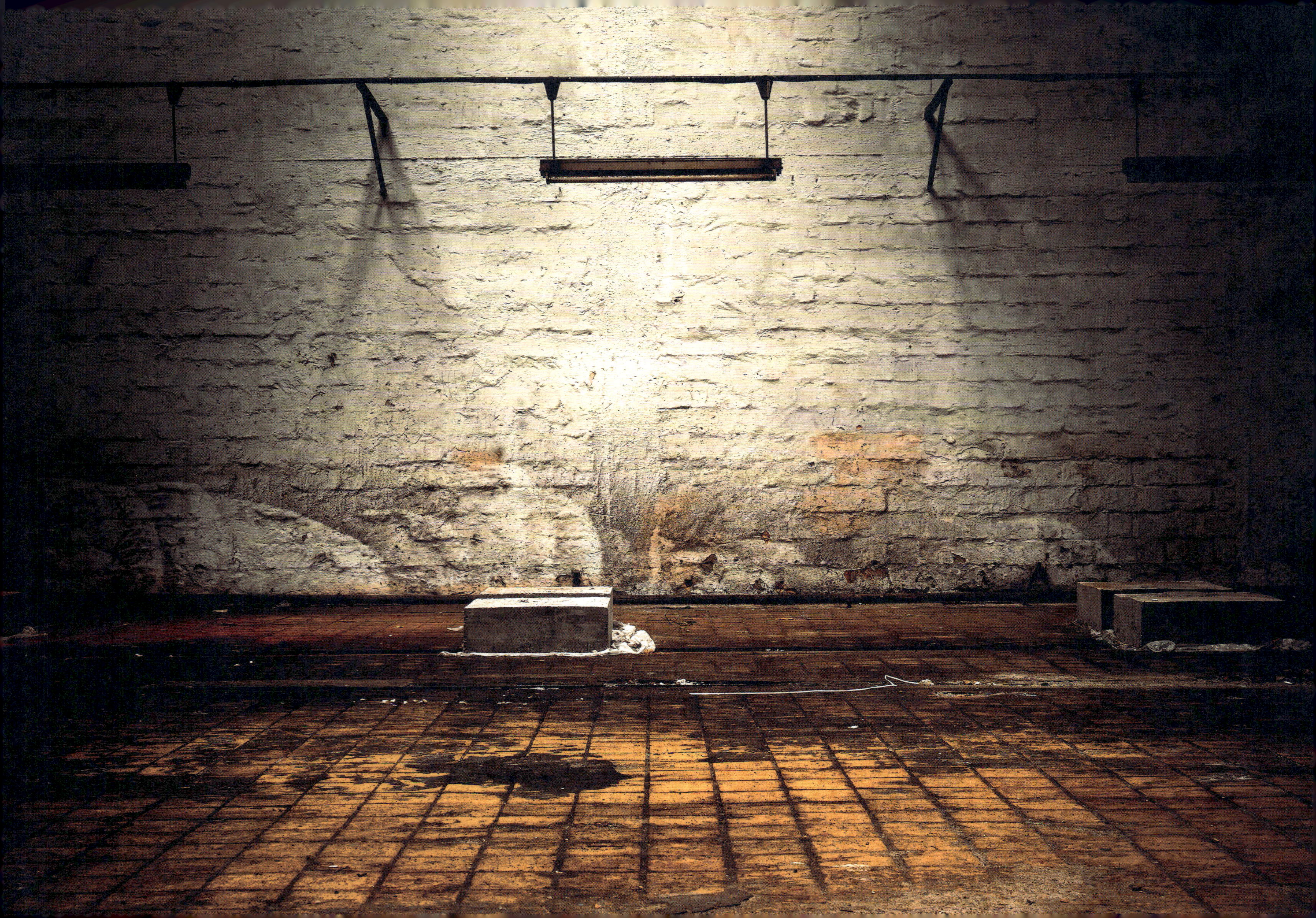

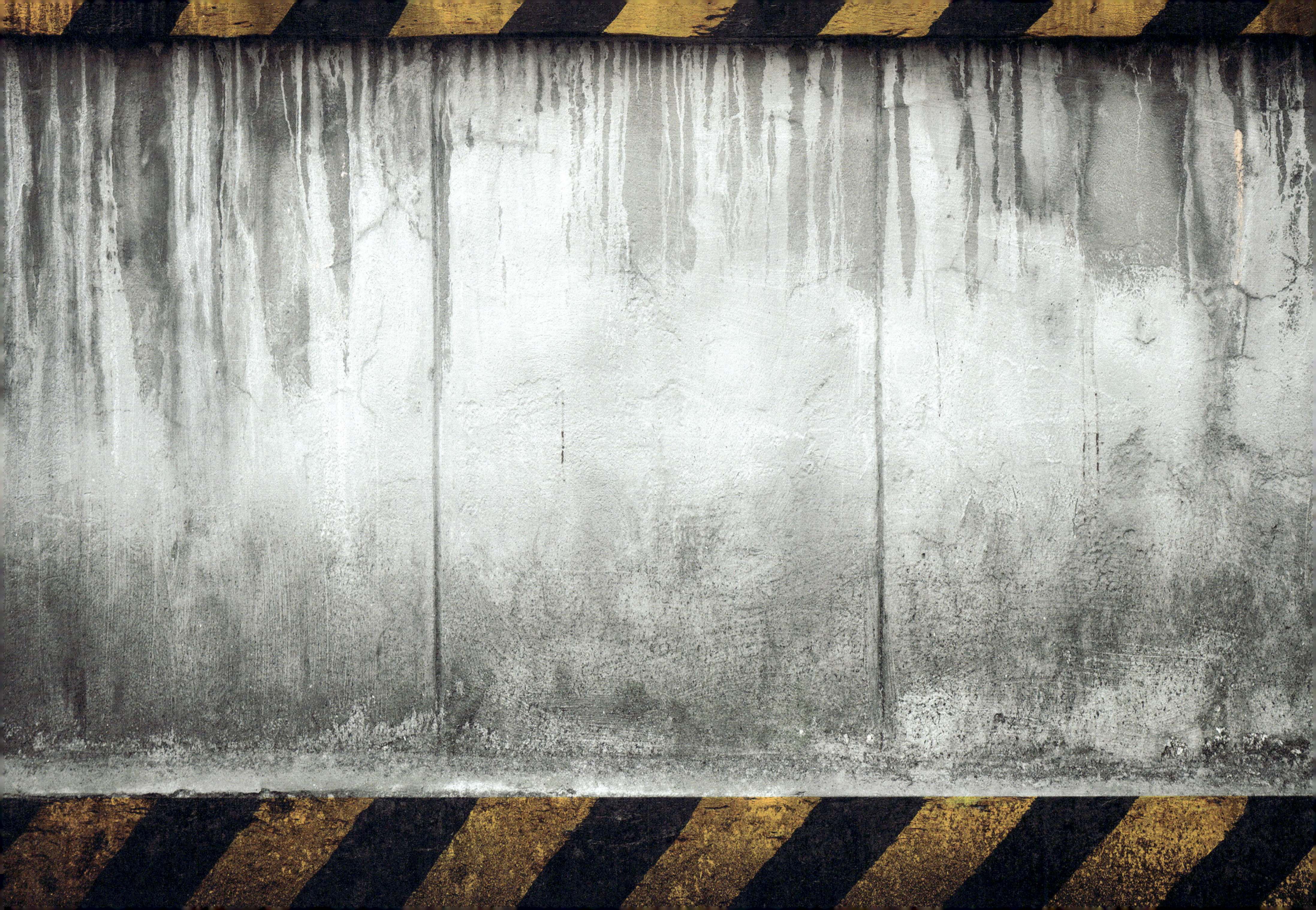

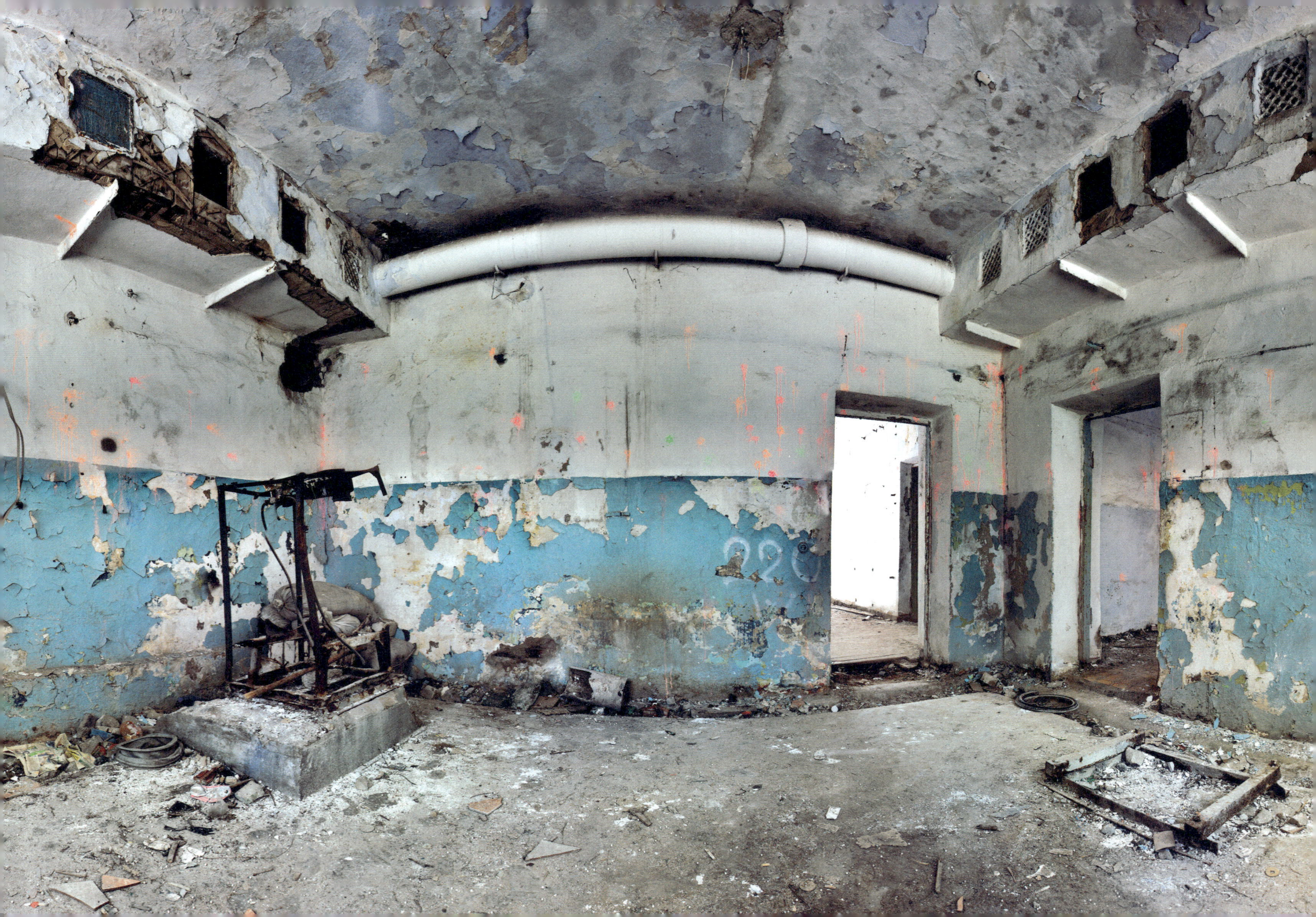

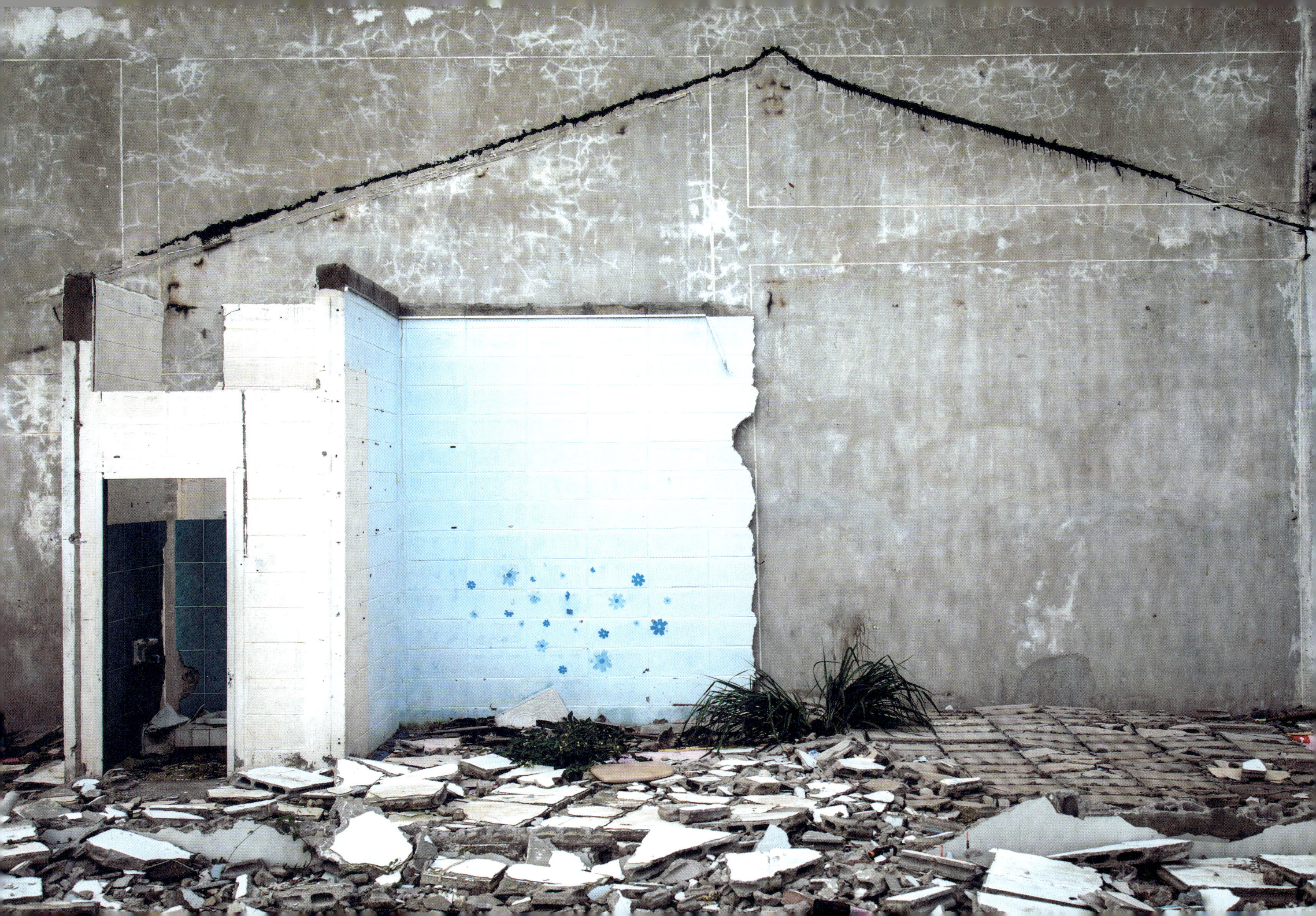

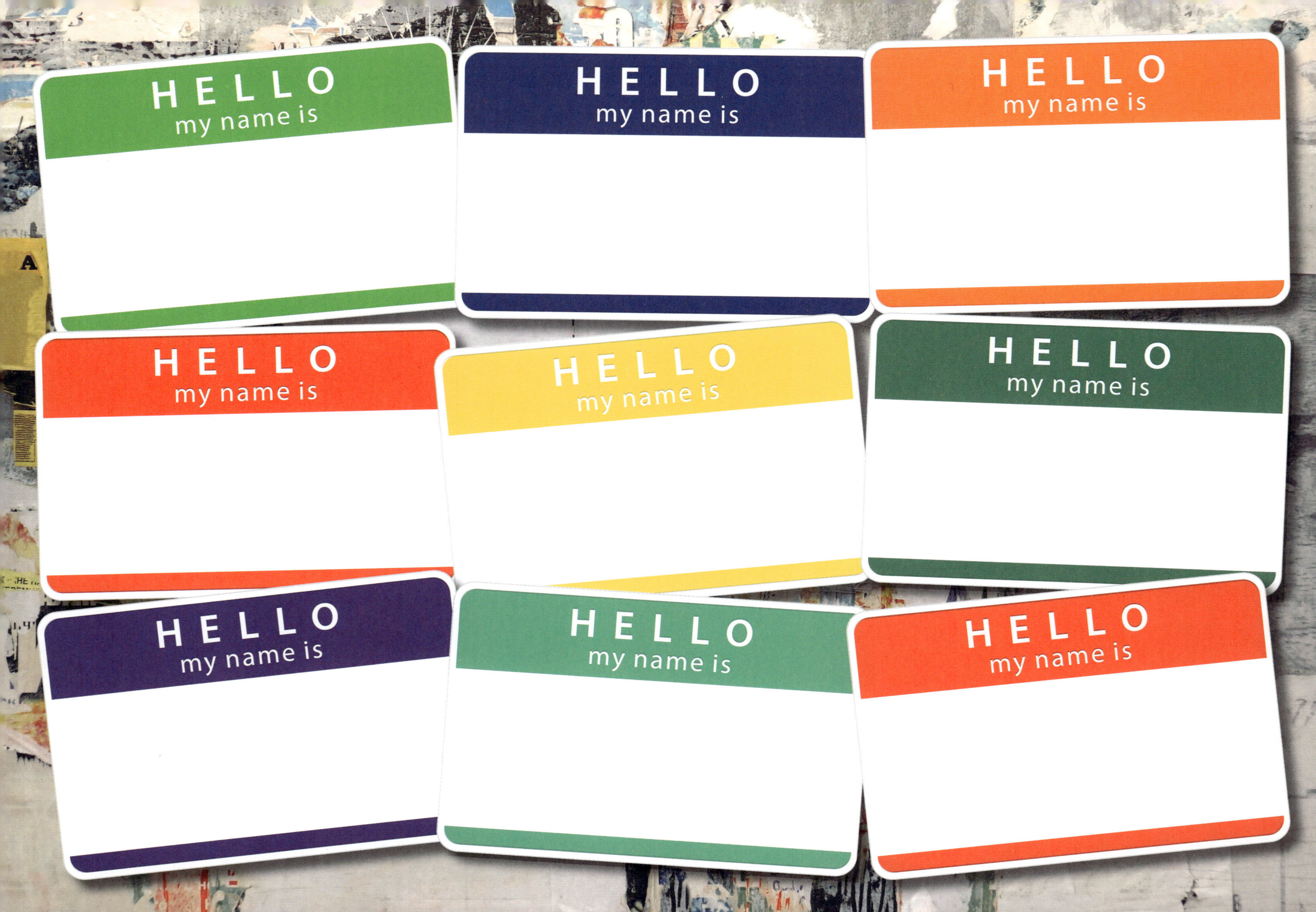
HELLO
my name is
HELLO
my name is
HELLO
my name is
HELLO
my name is
HELLO
my name is
HELLO
my name is
HELLO
my name is
HELLO
my name is
HELLO
my name is

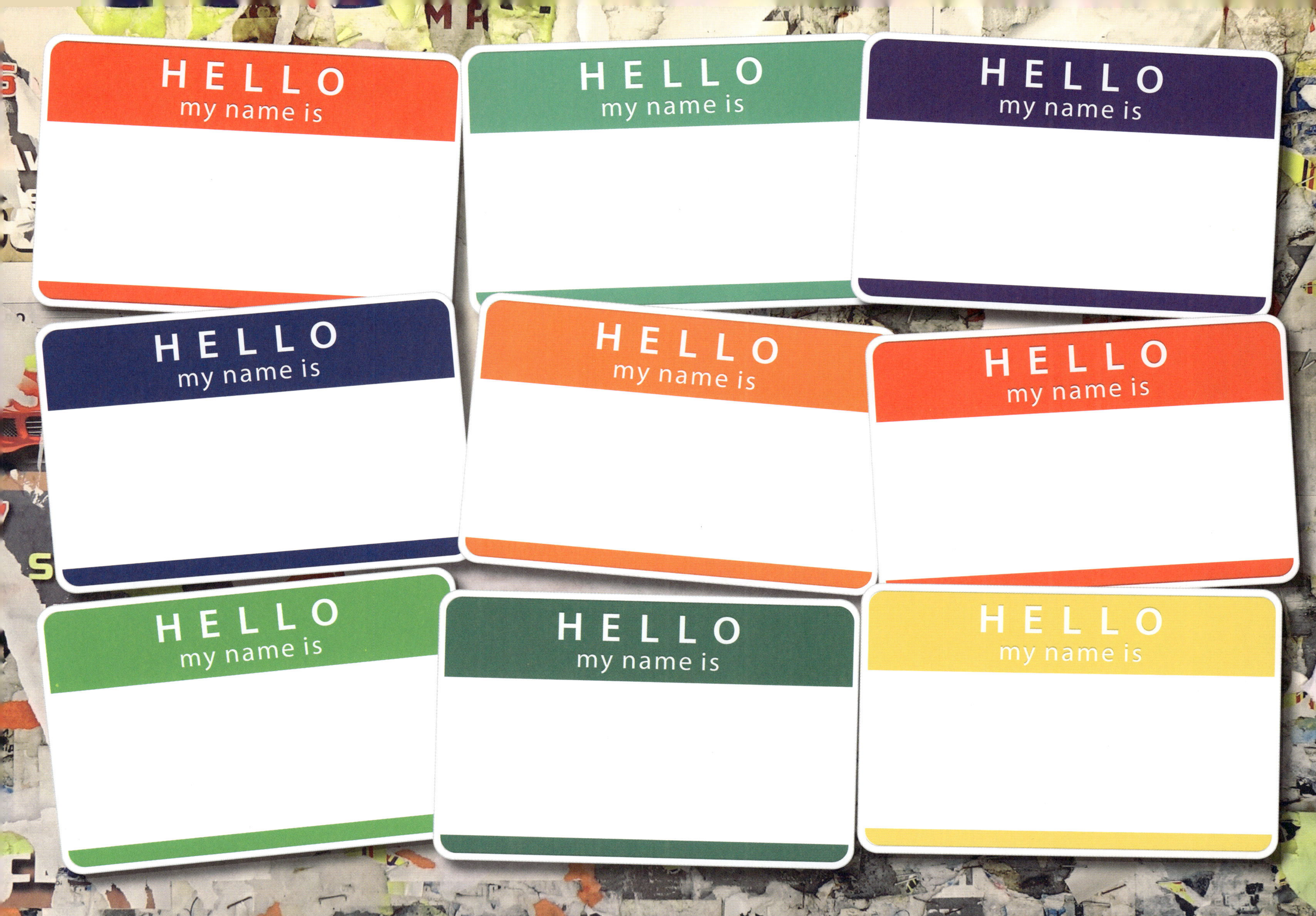

HELLO
my name is
HELLO
my name is
HELLO
my name is
HELLO
my name is
HELLO
my name is
HELLO
my name is
HELLO
my name is
HELLO
my name is
HELLO
my name is

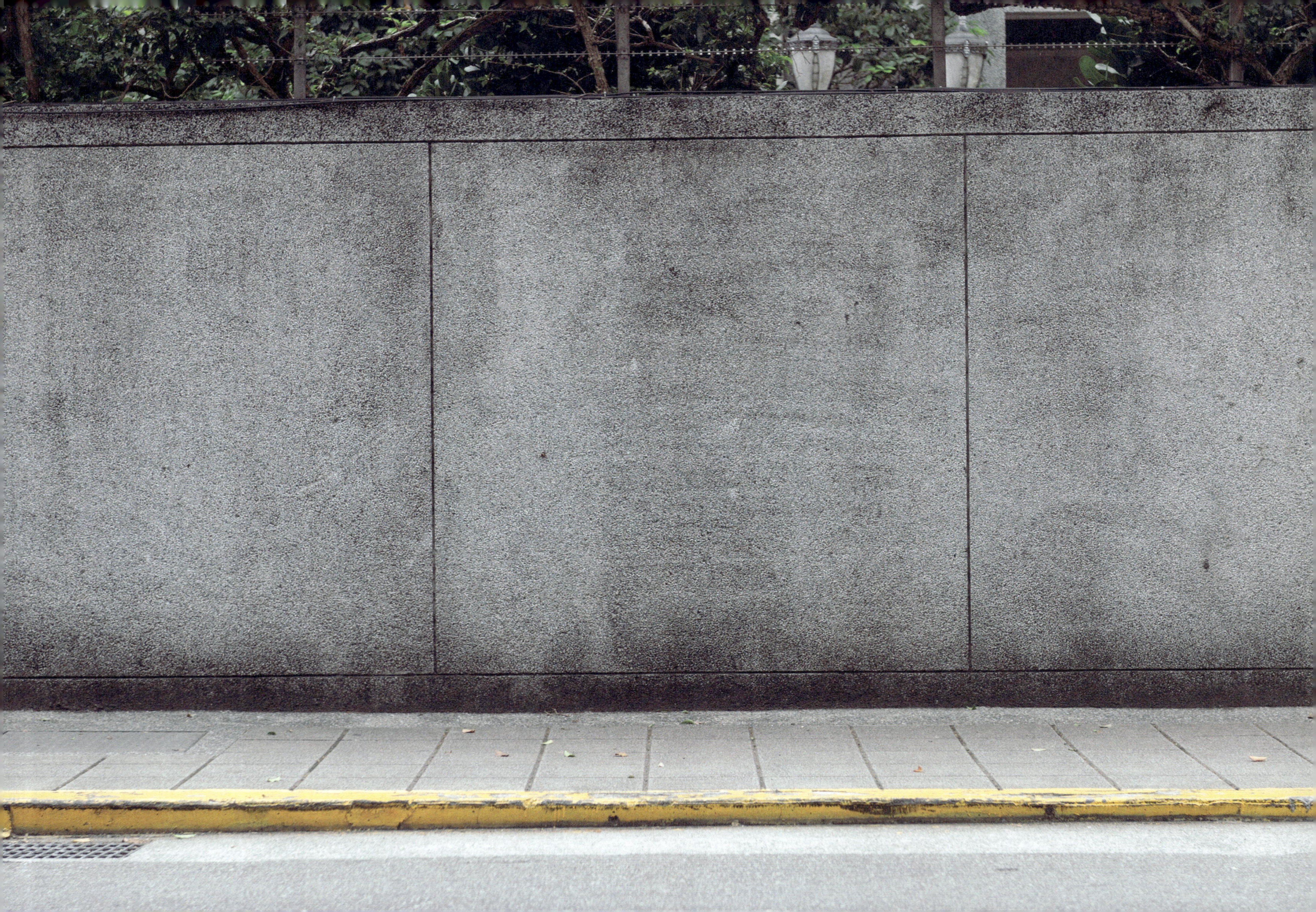

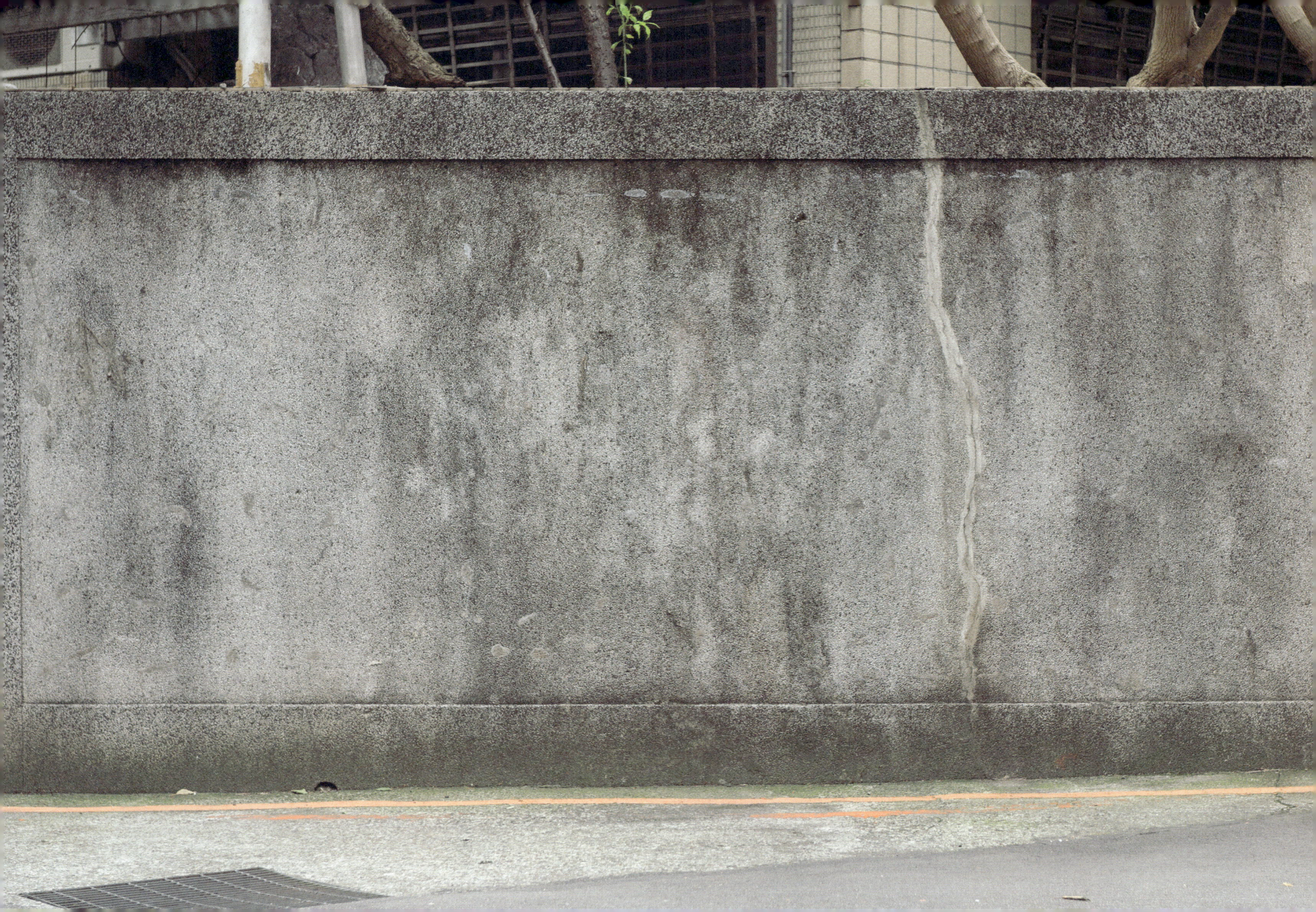

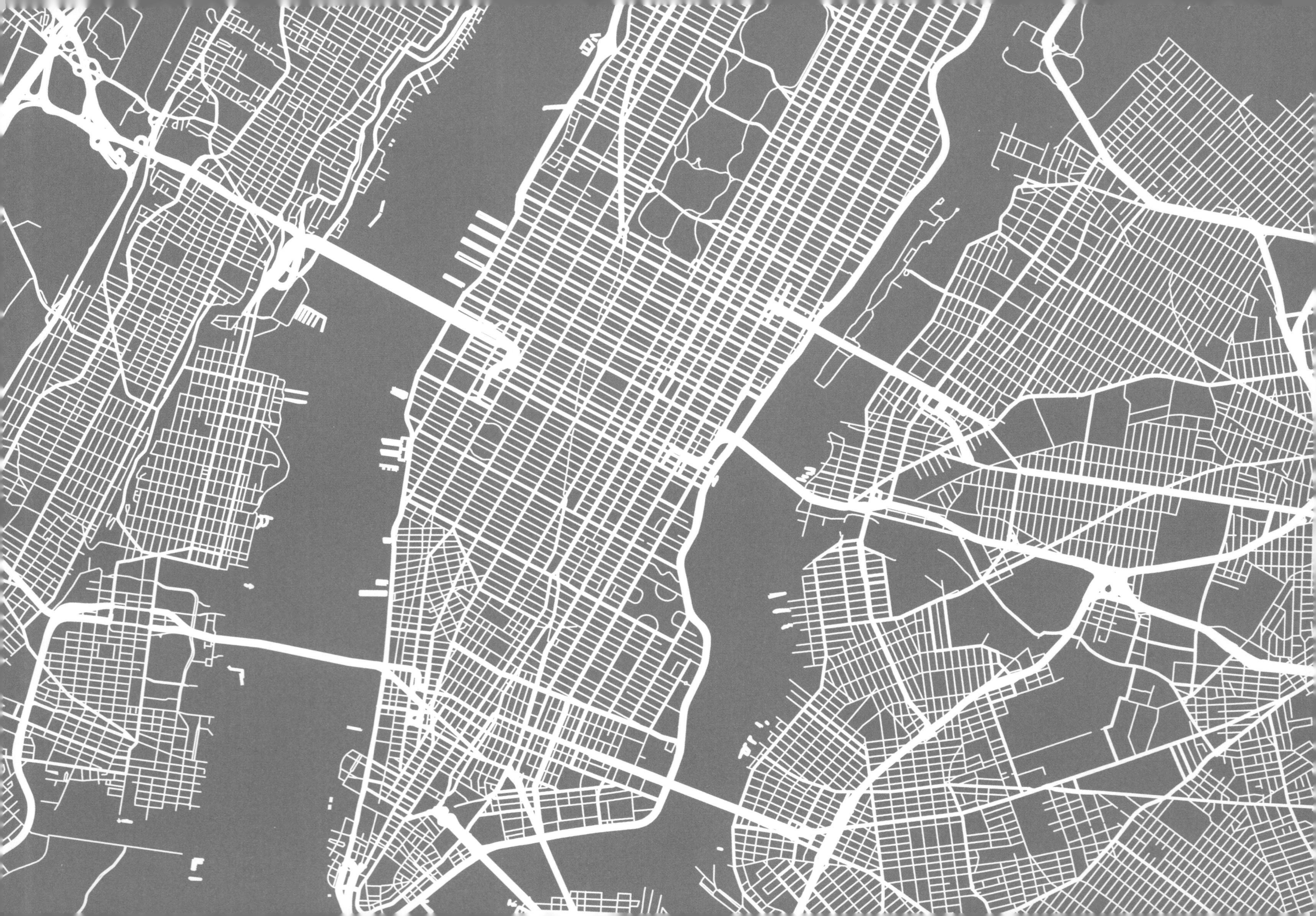

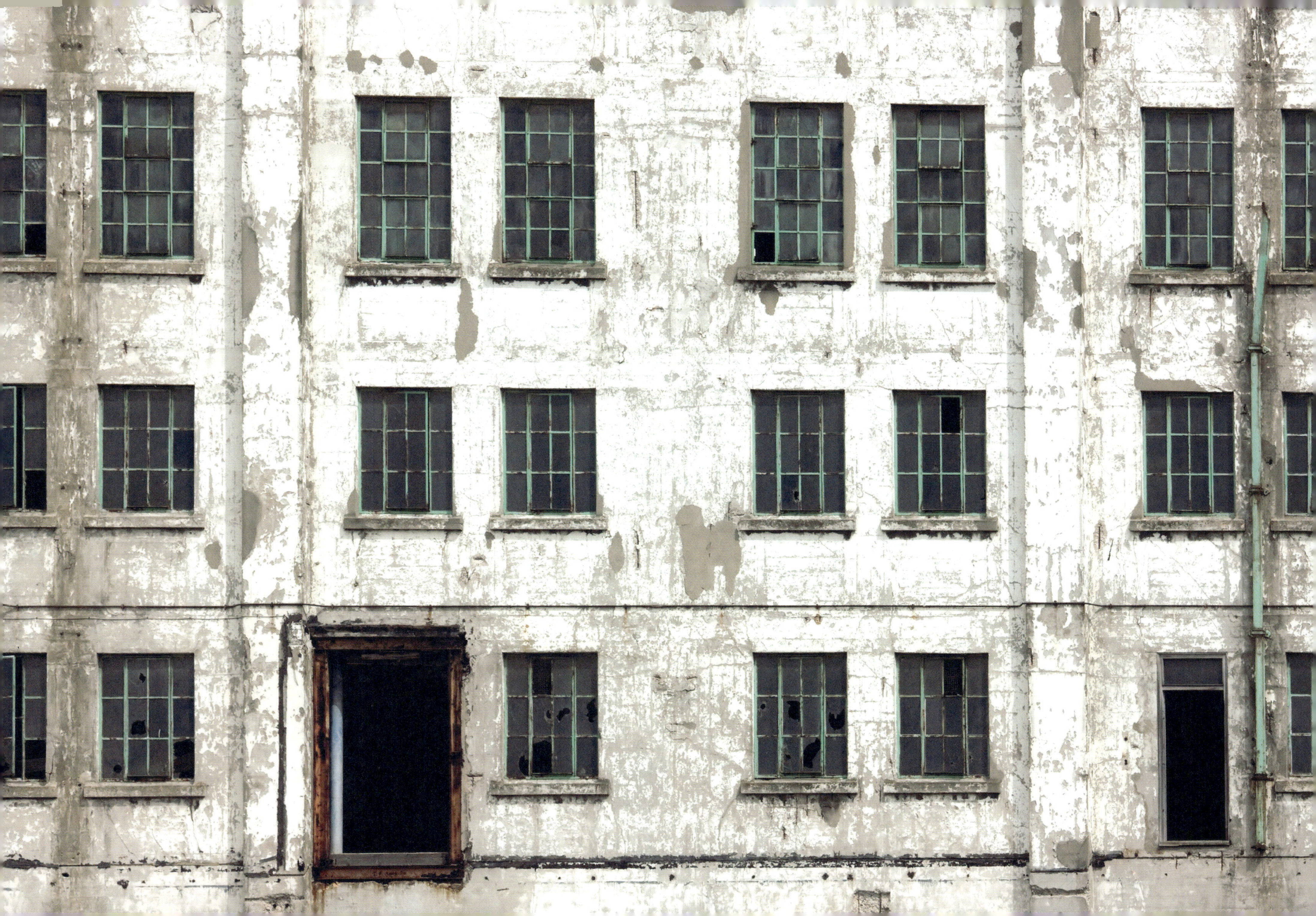

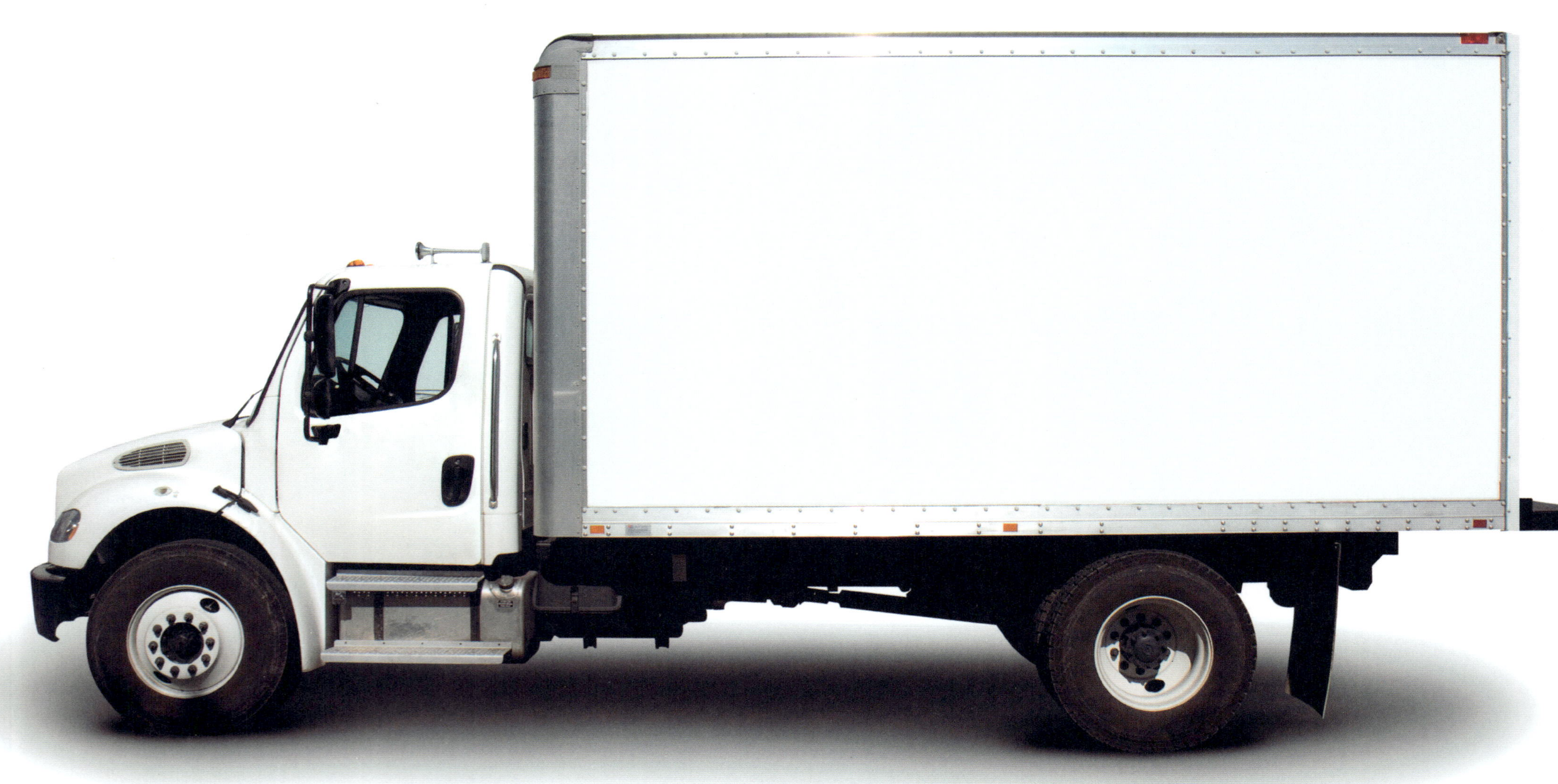

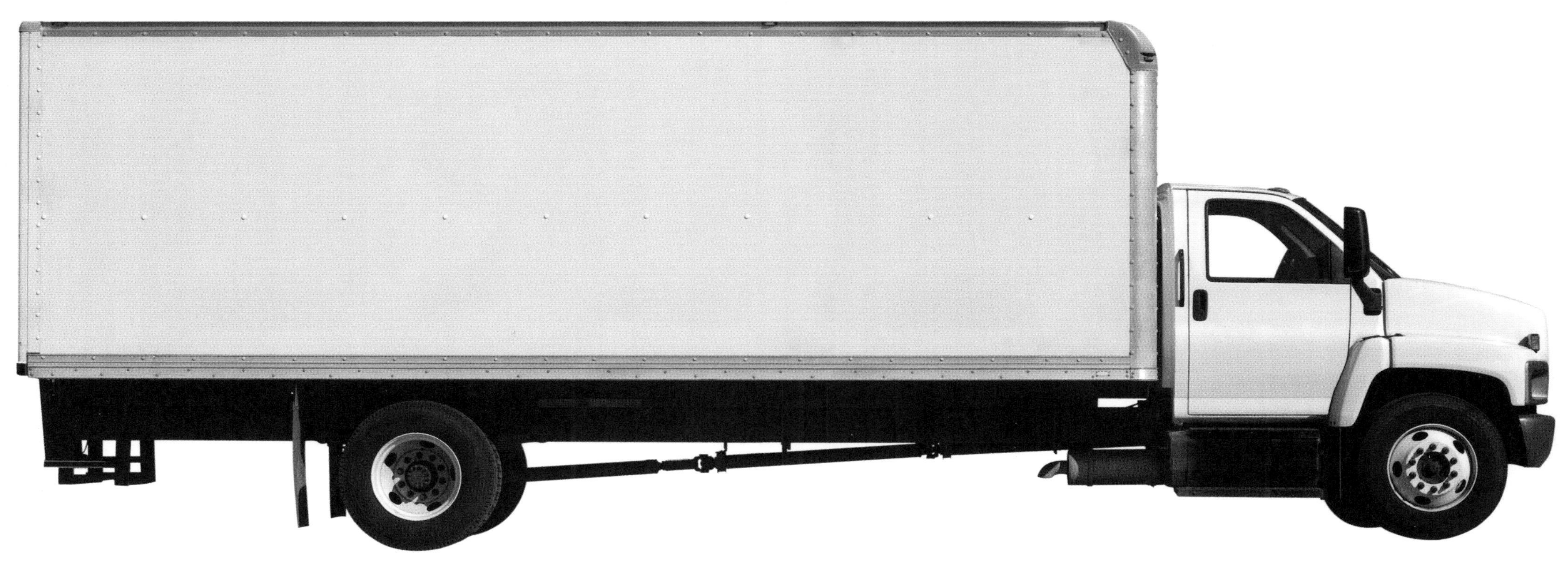

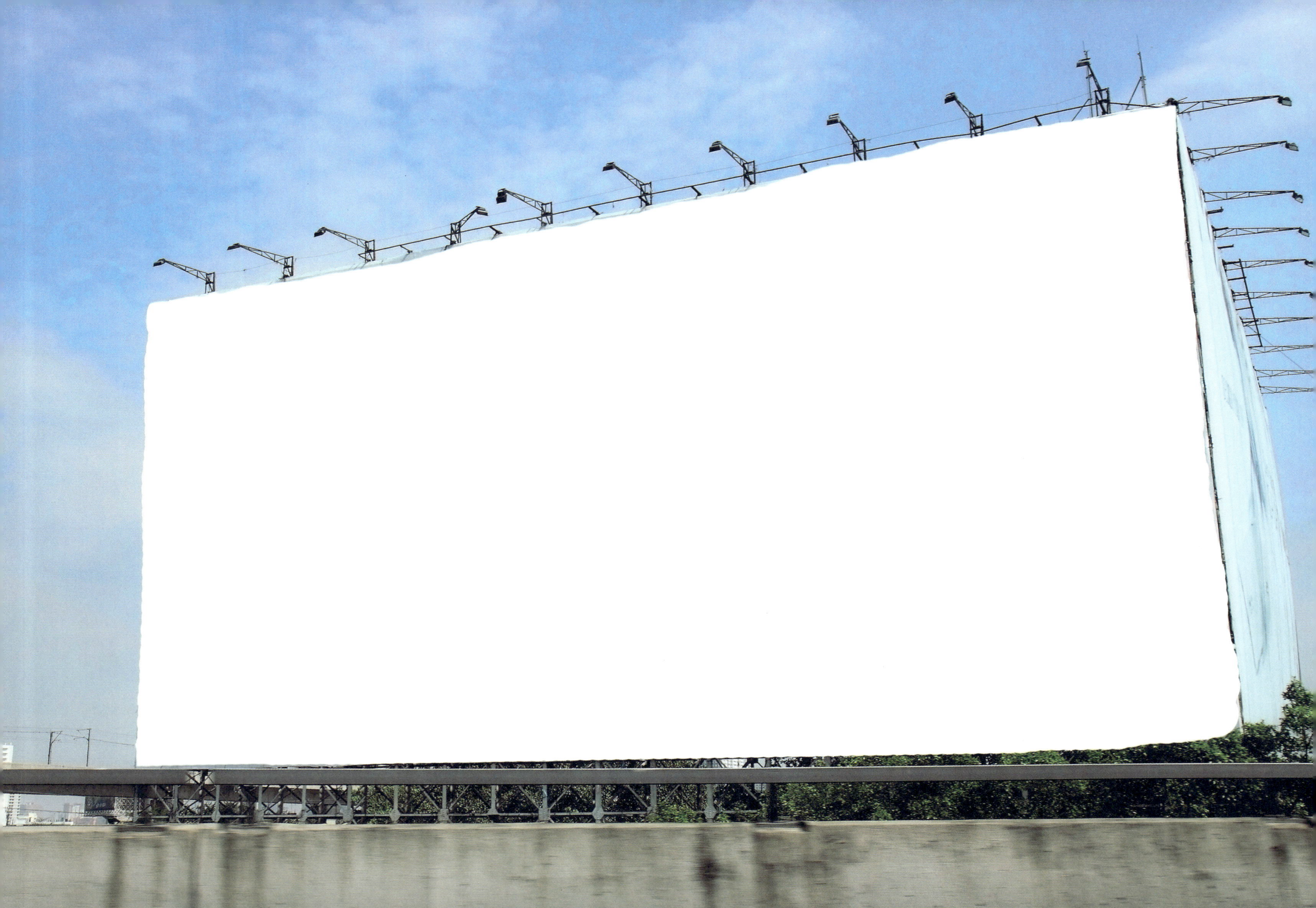

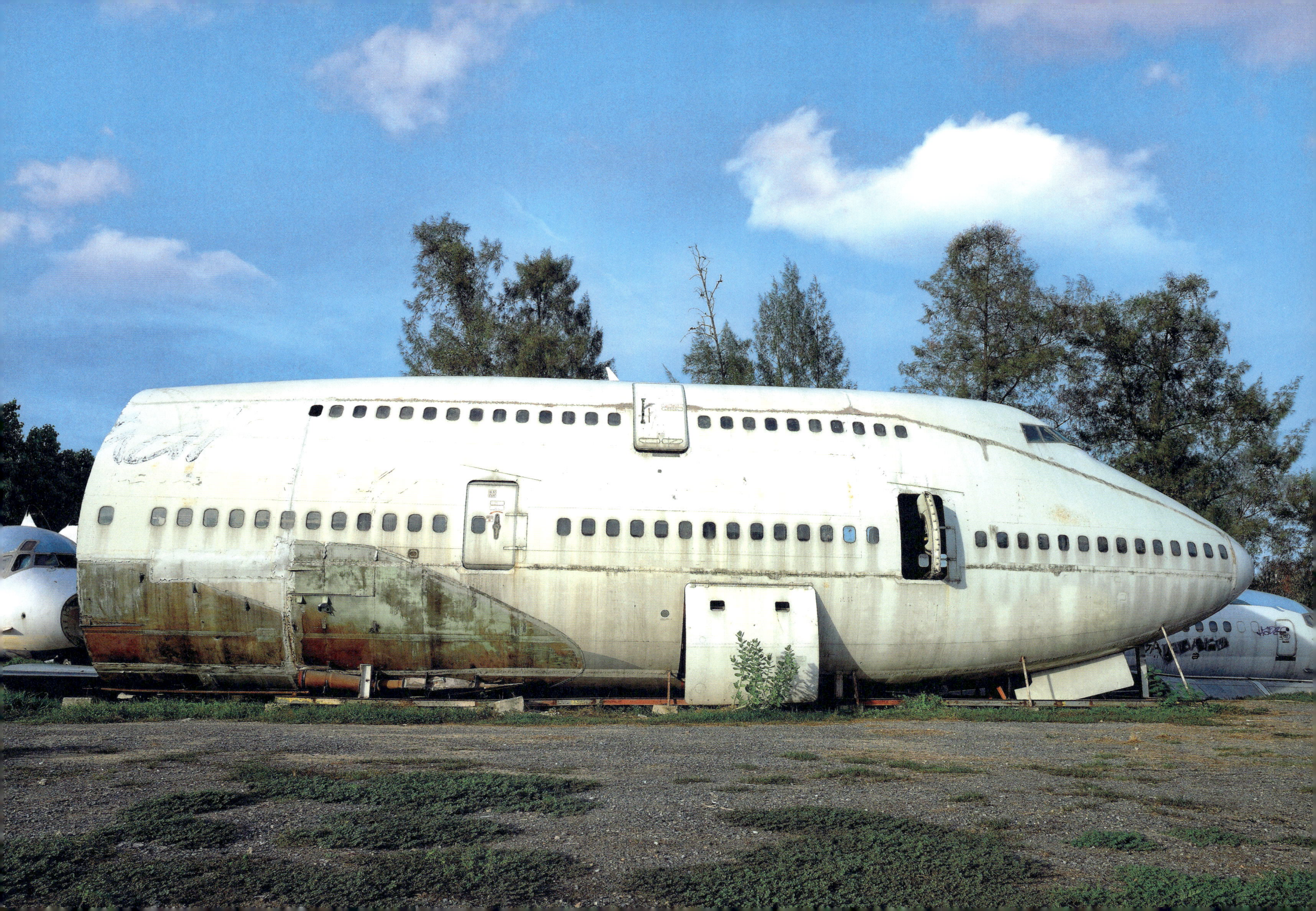

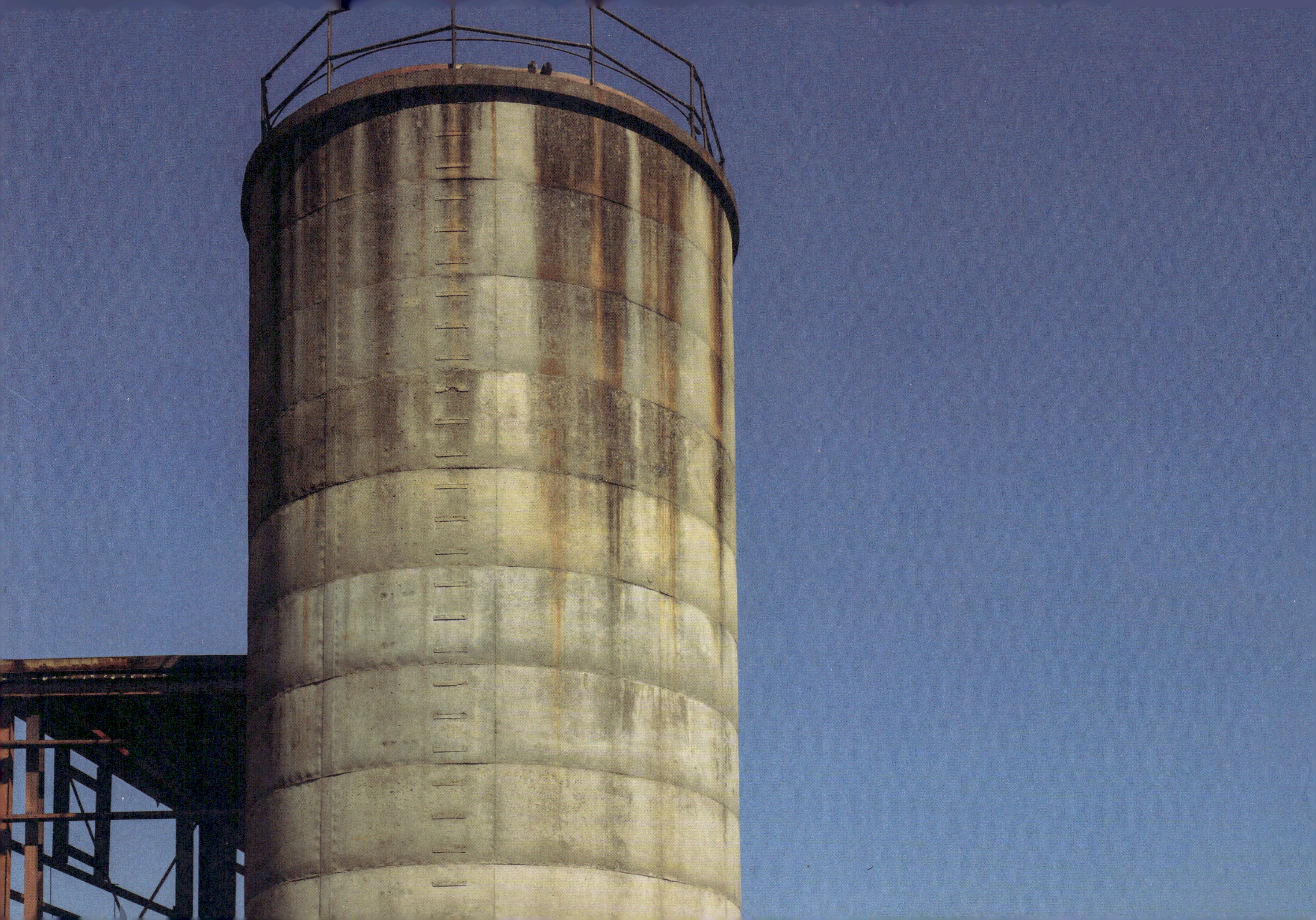

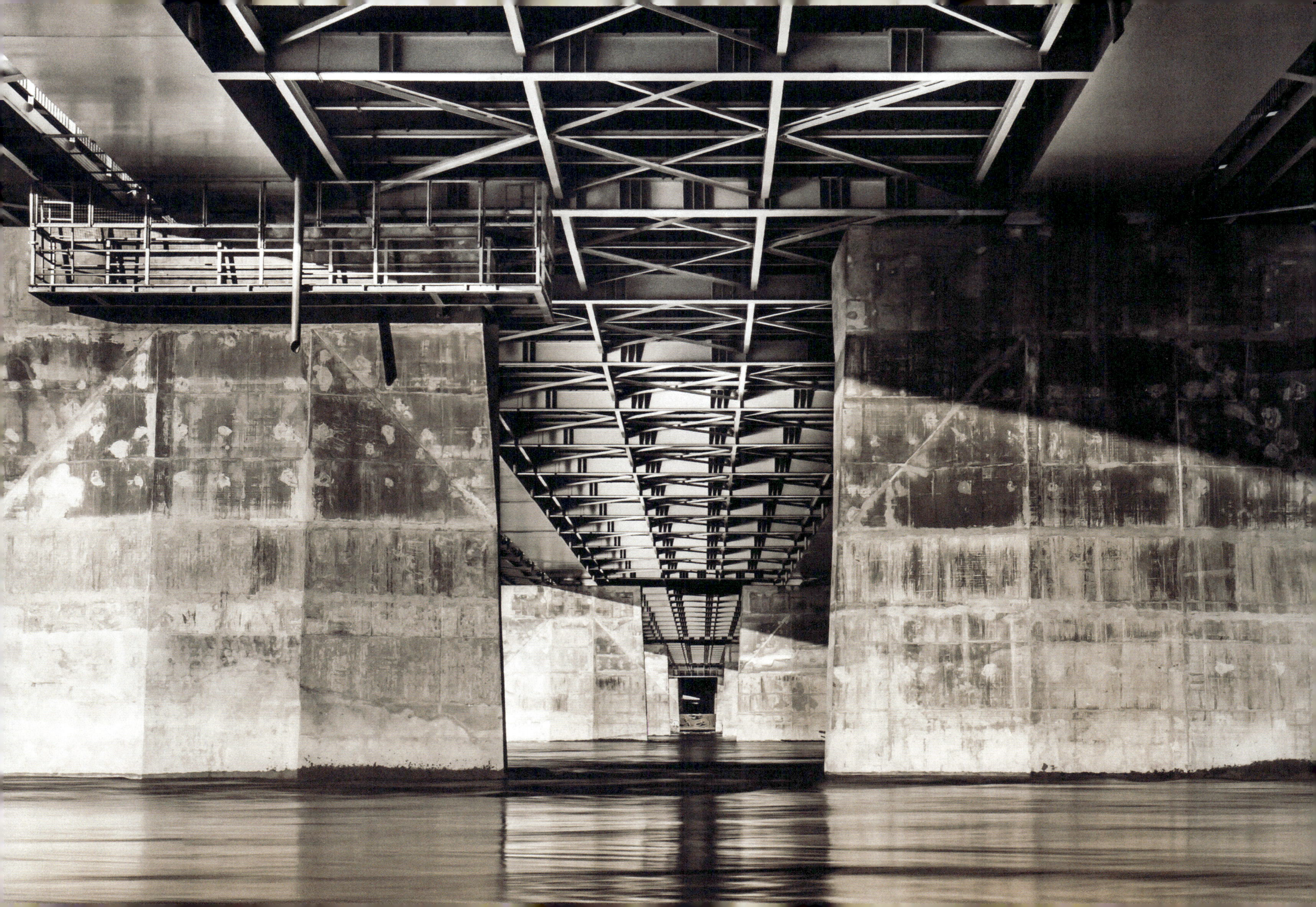

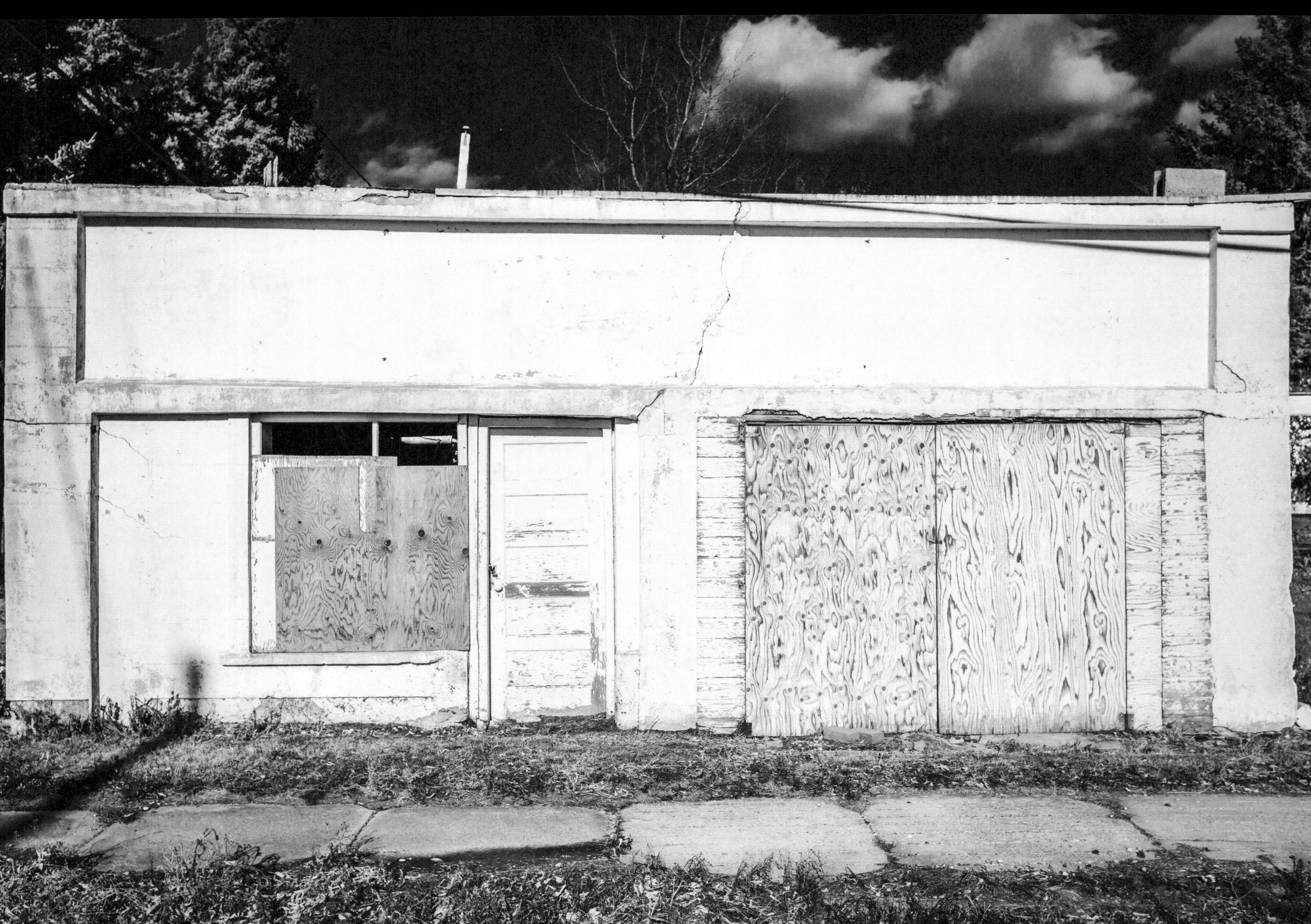

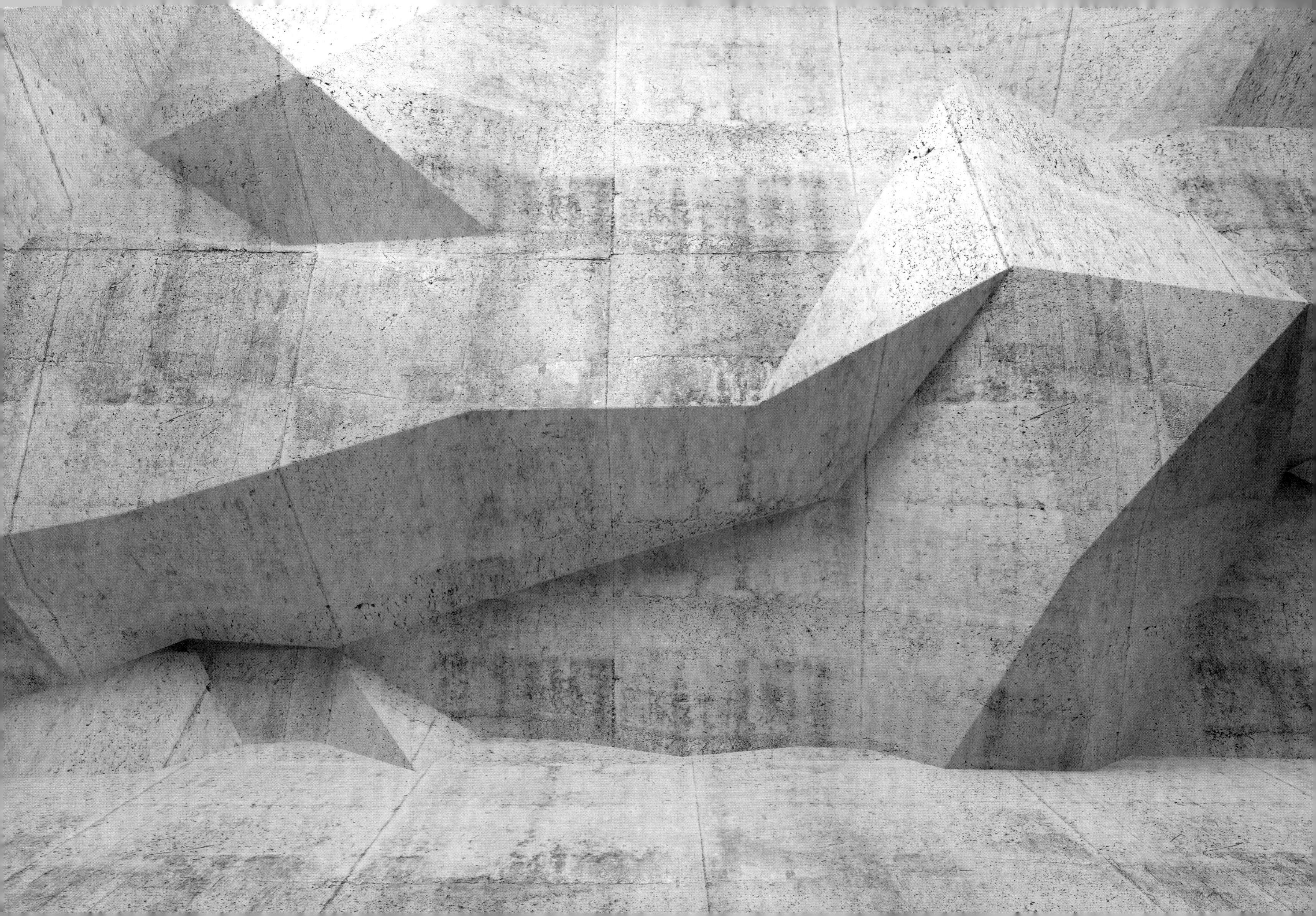

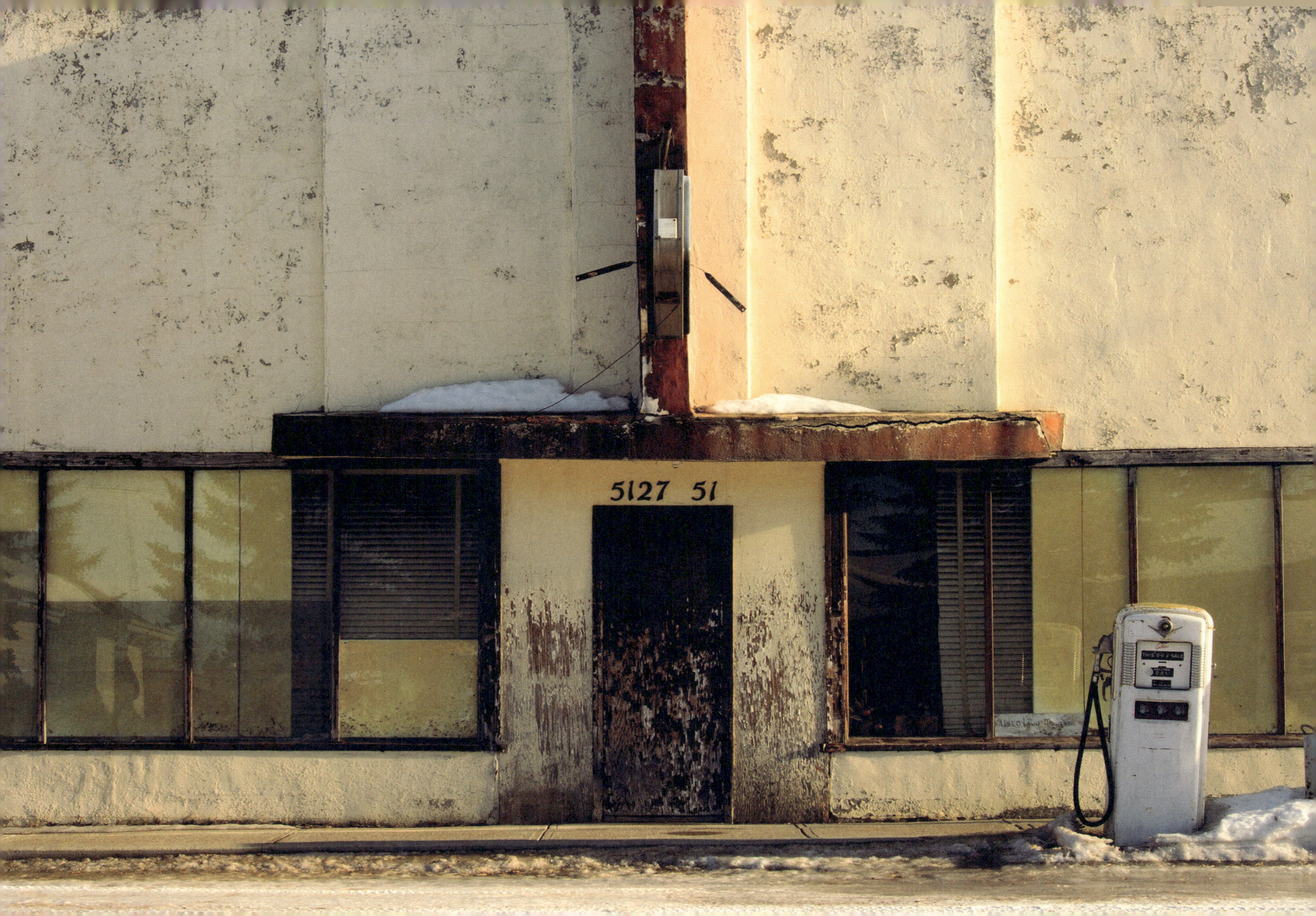
5127 51
THIS ONE 4 SALE

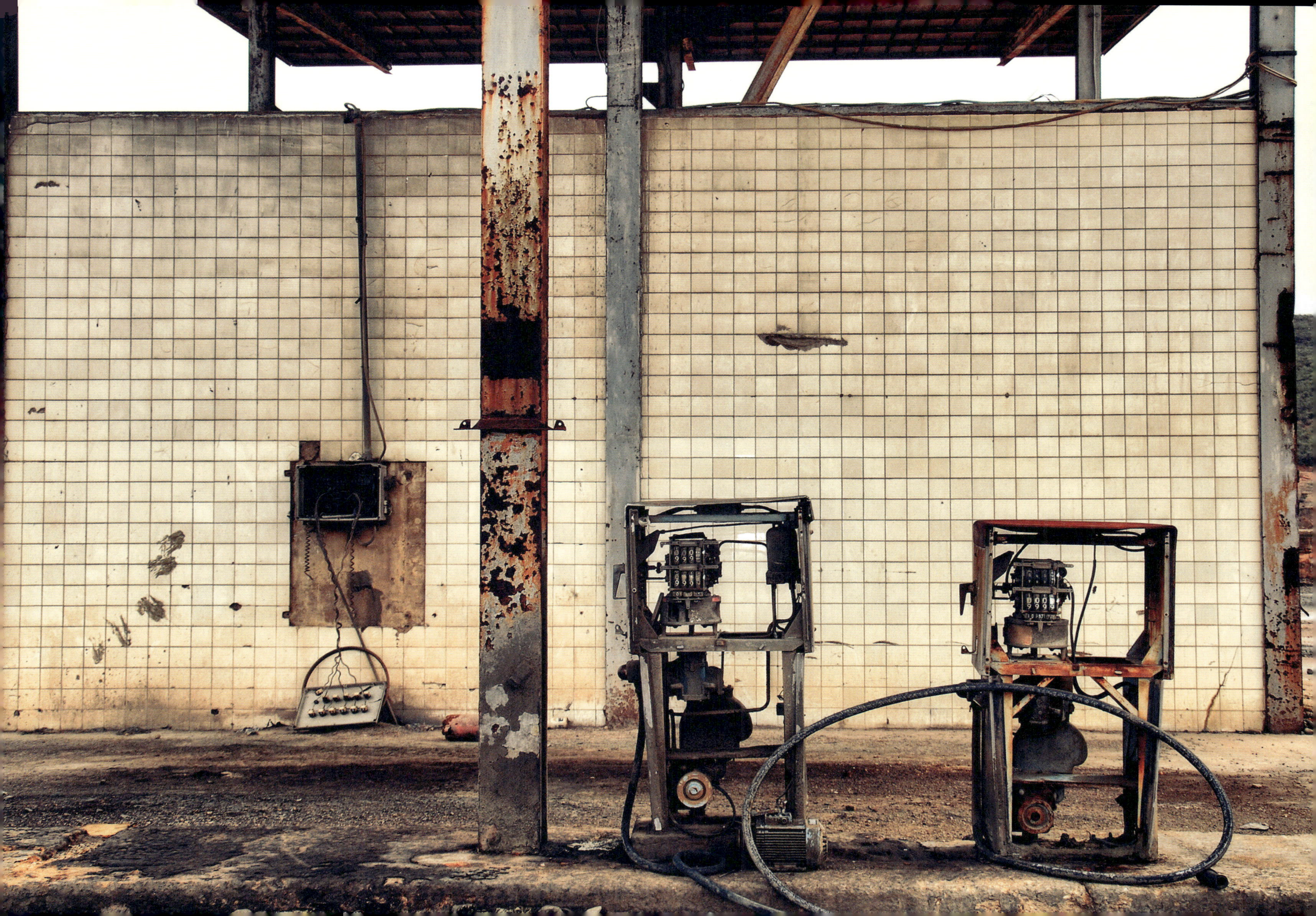

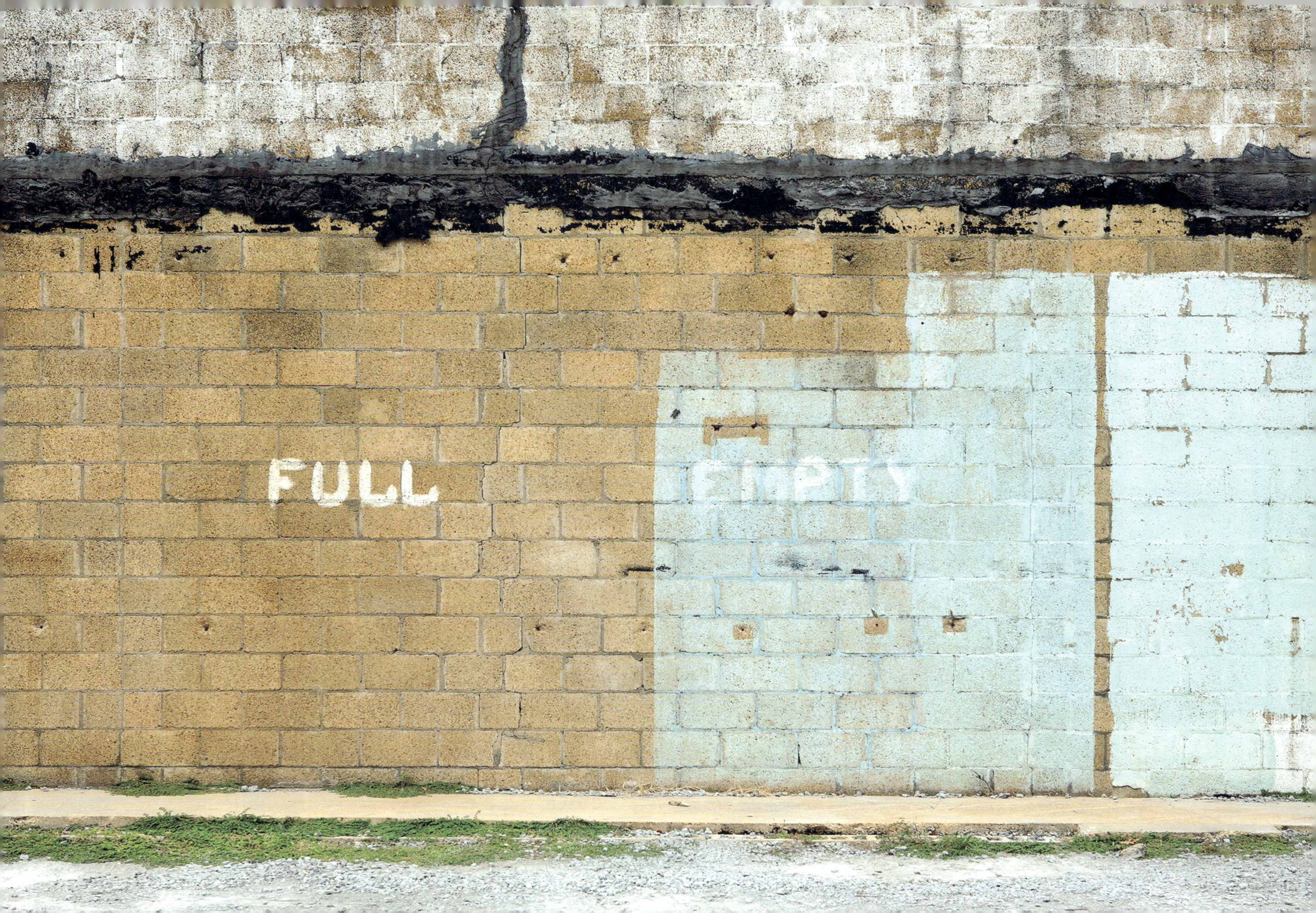

FULL
EMPTY

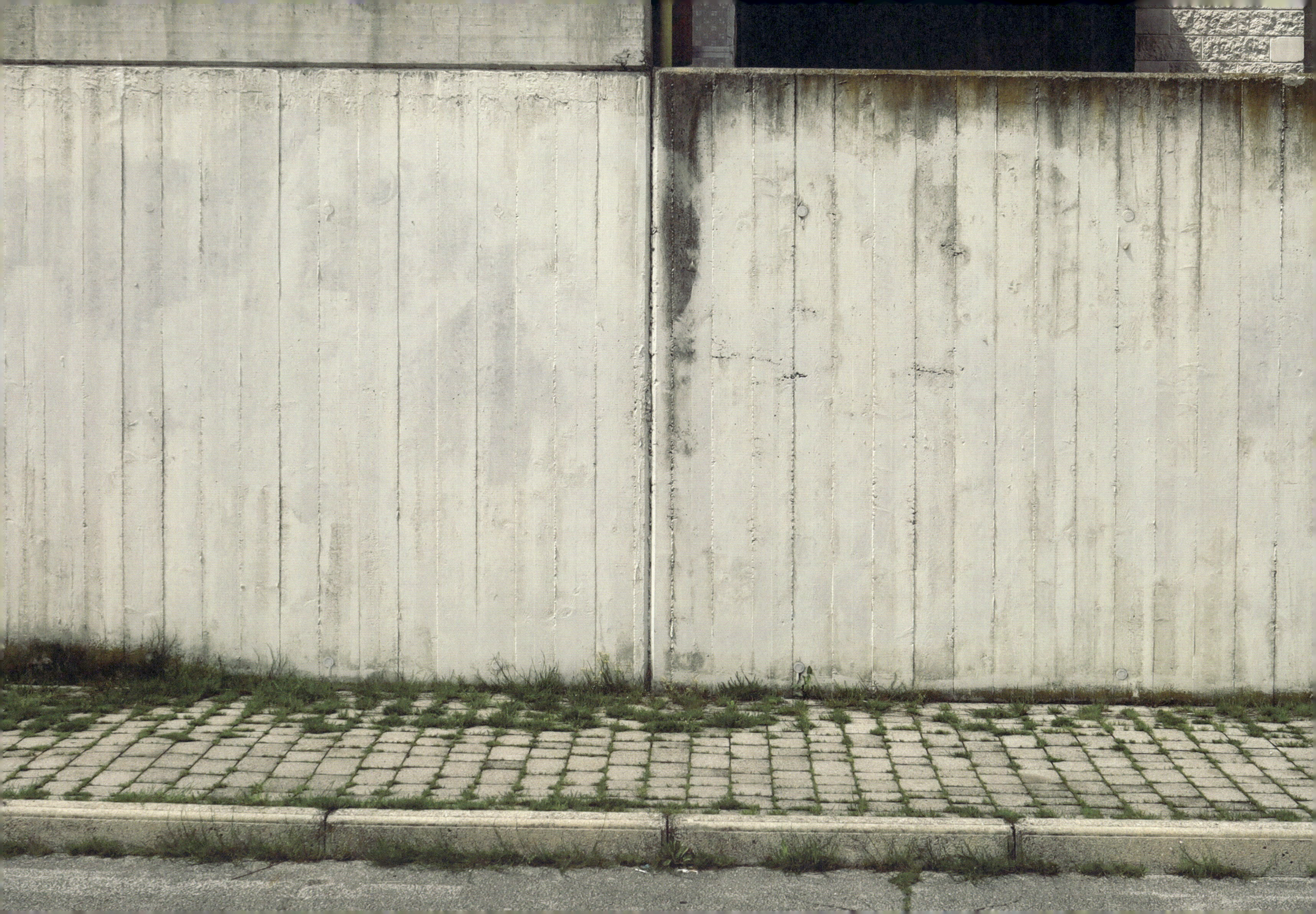

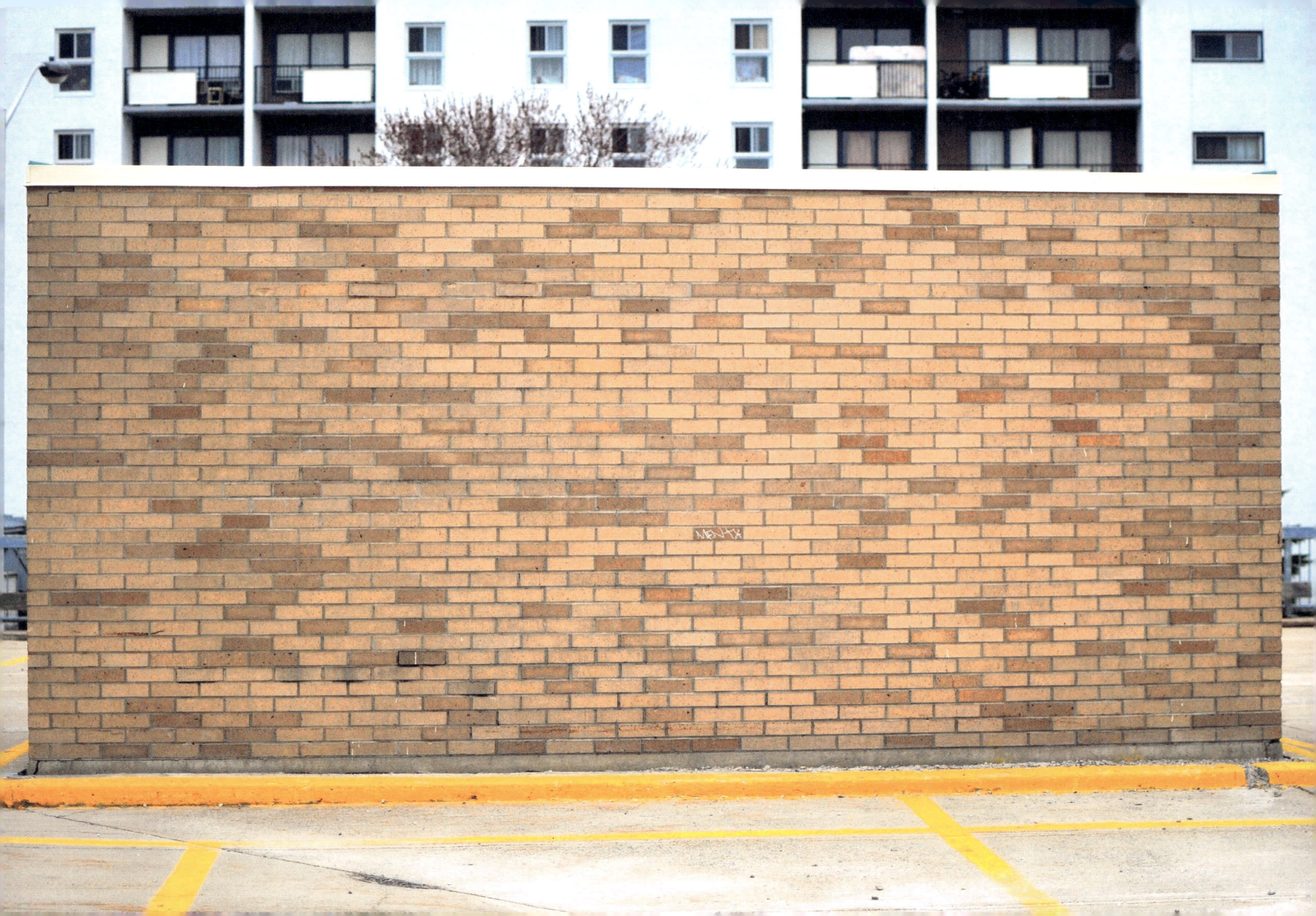

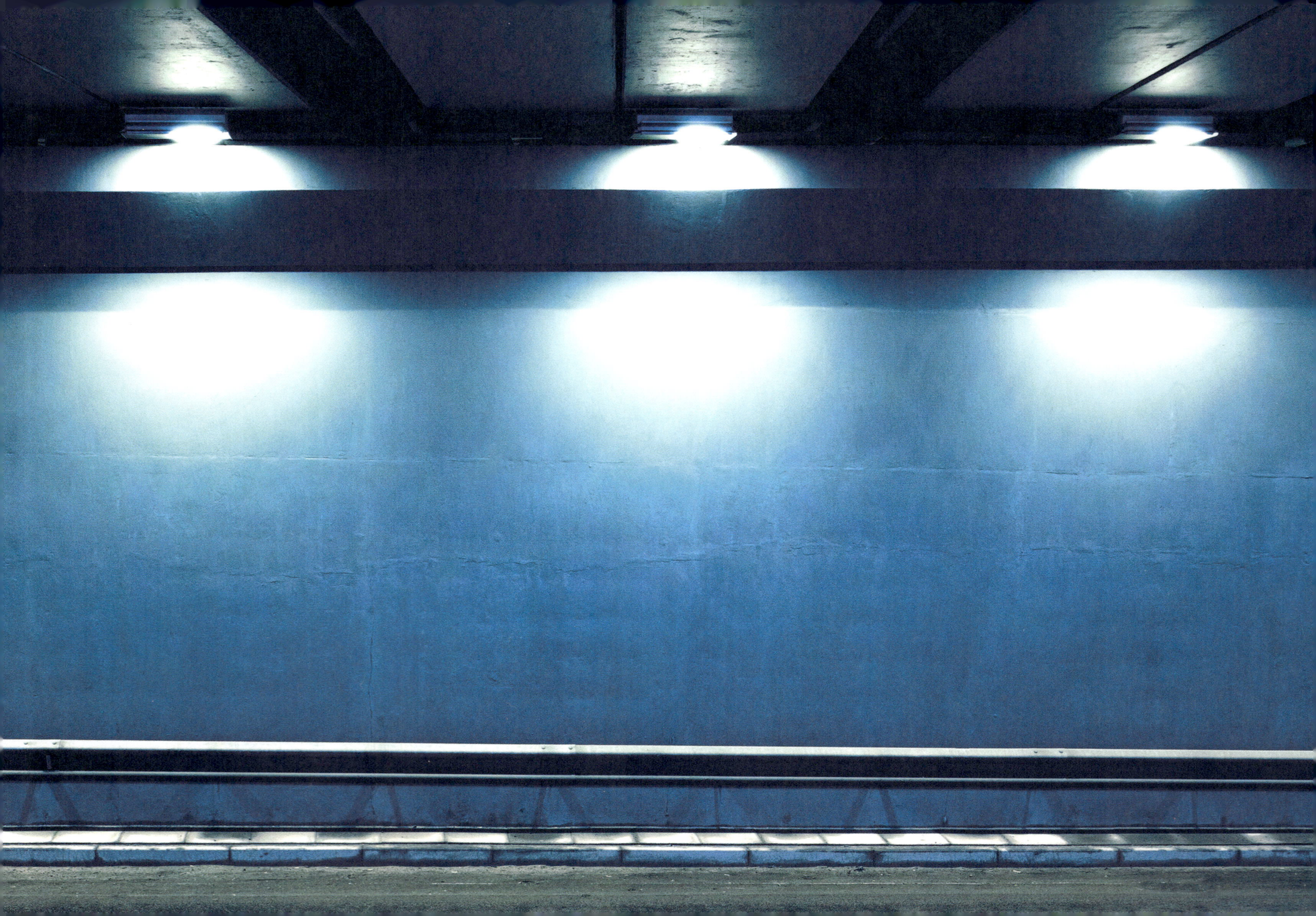

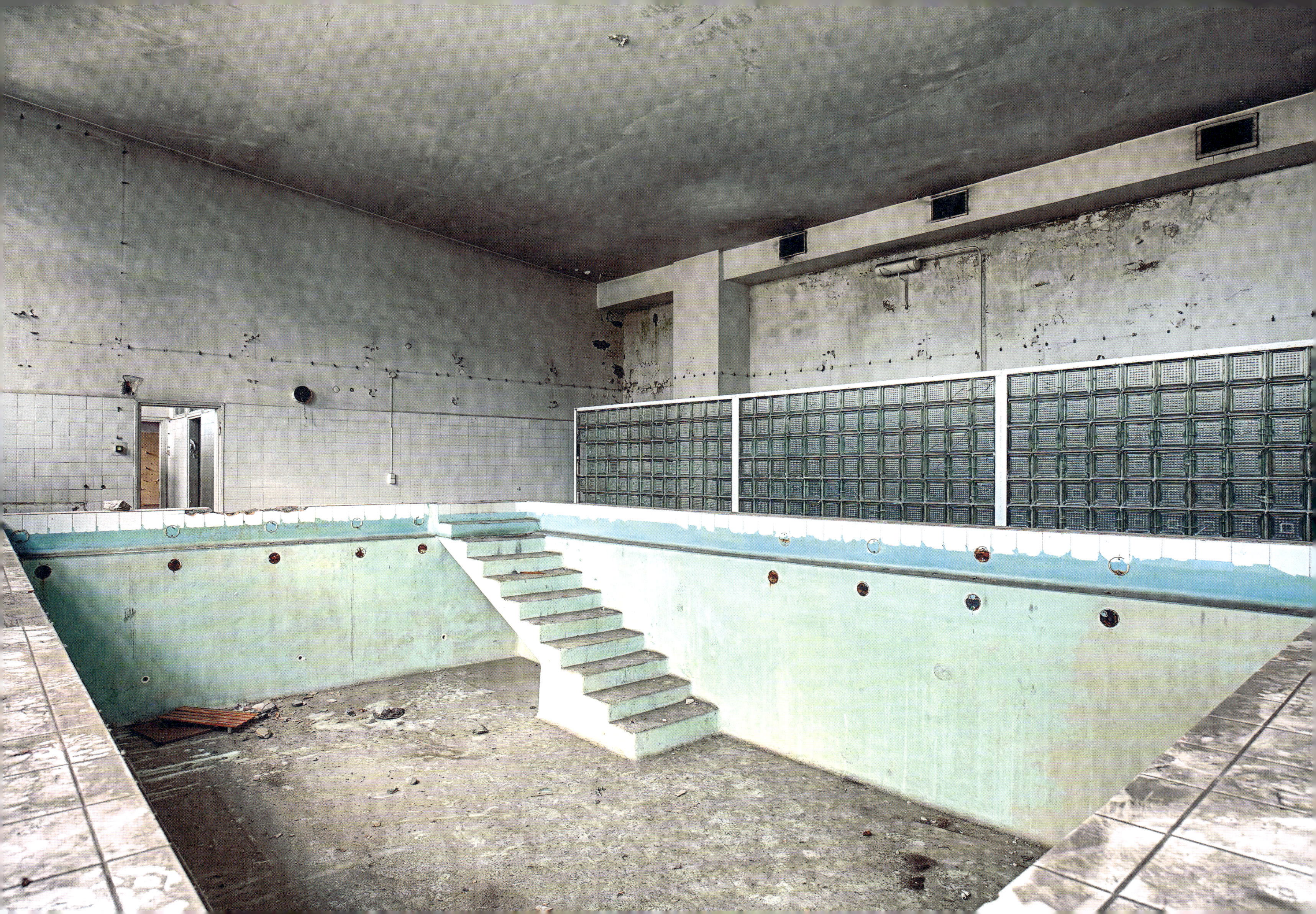

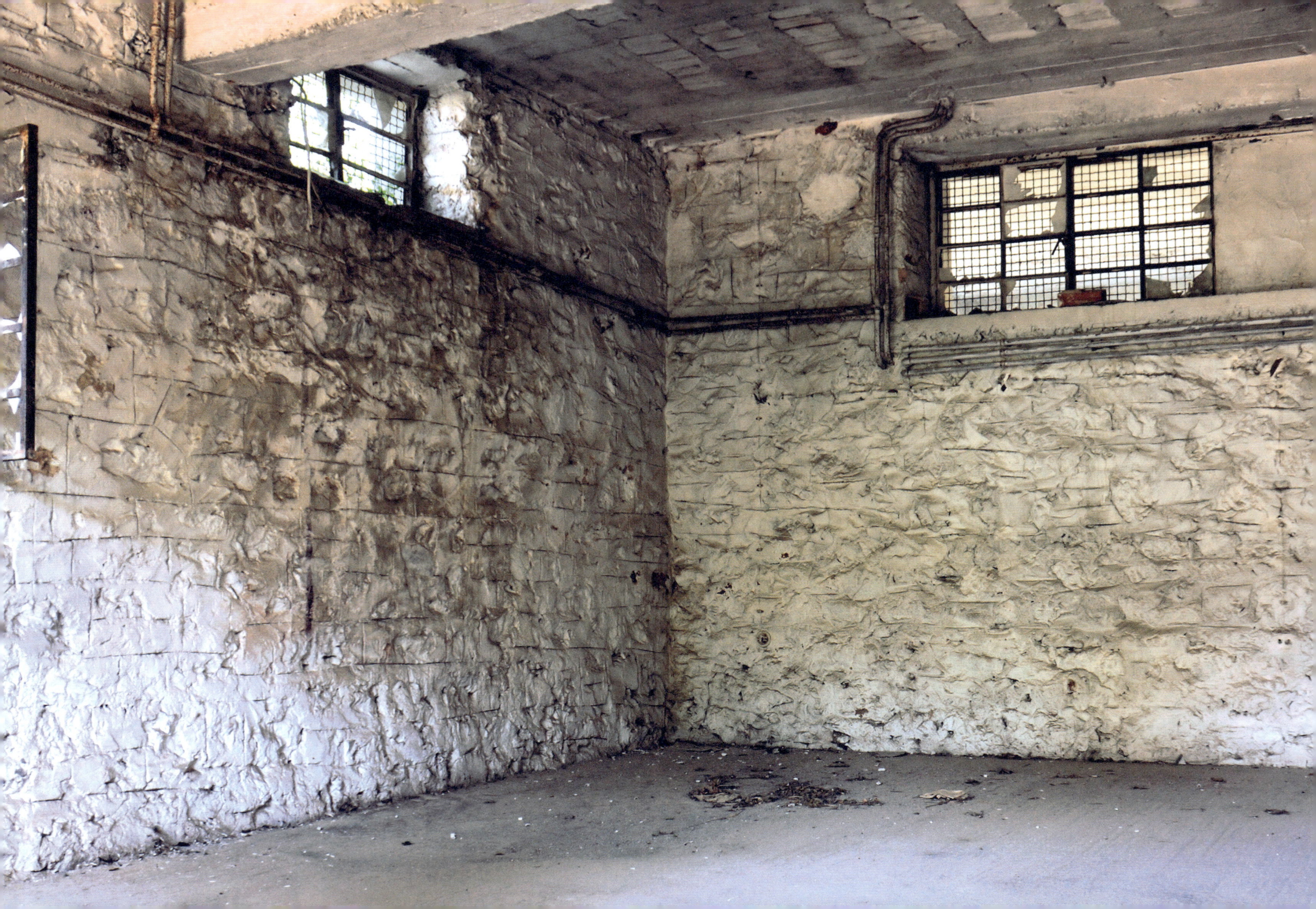

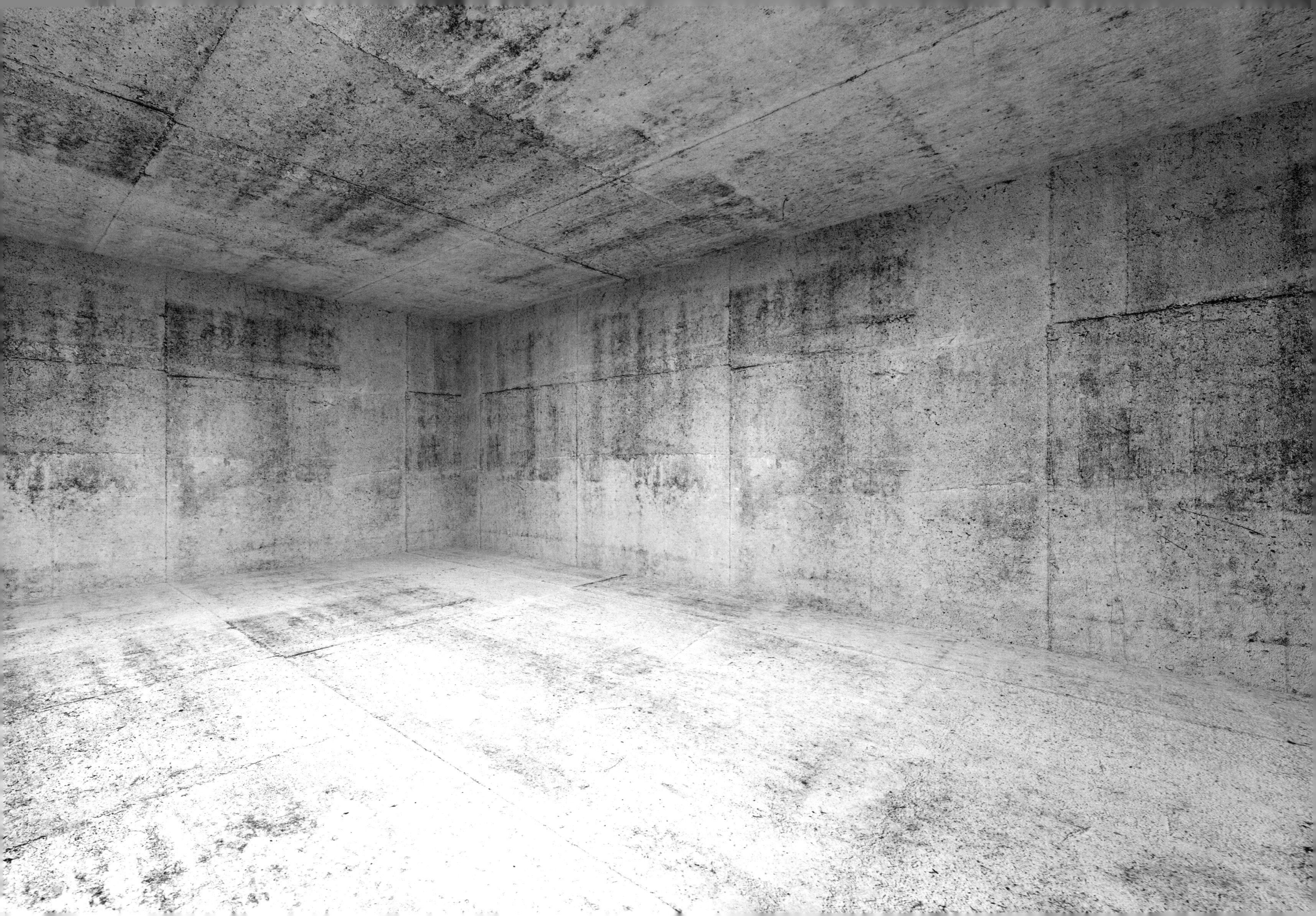

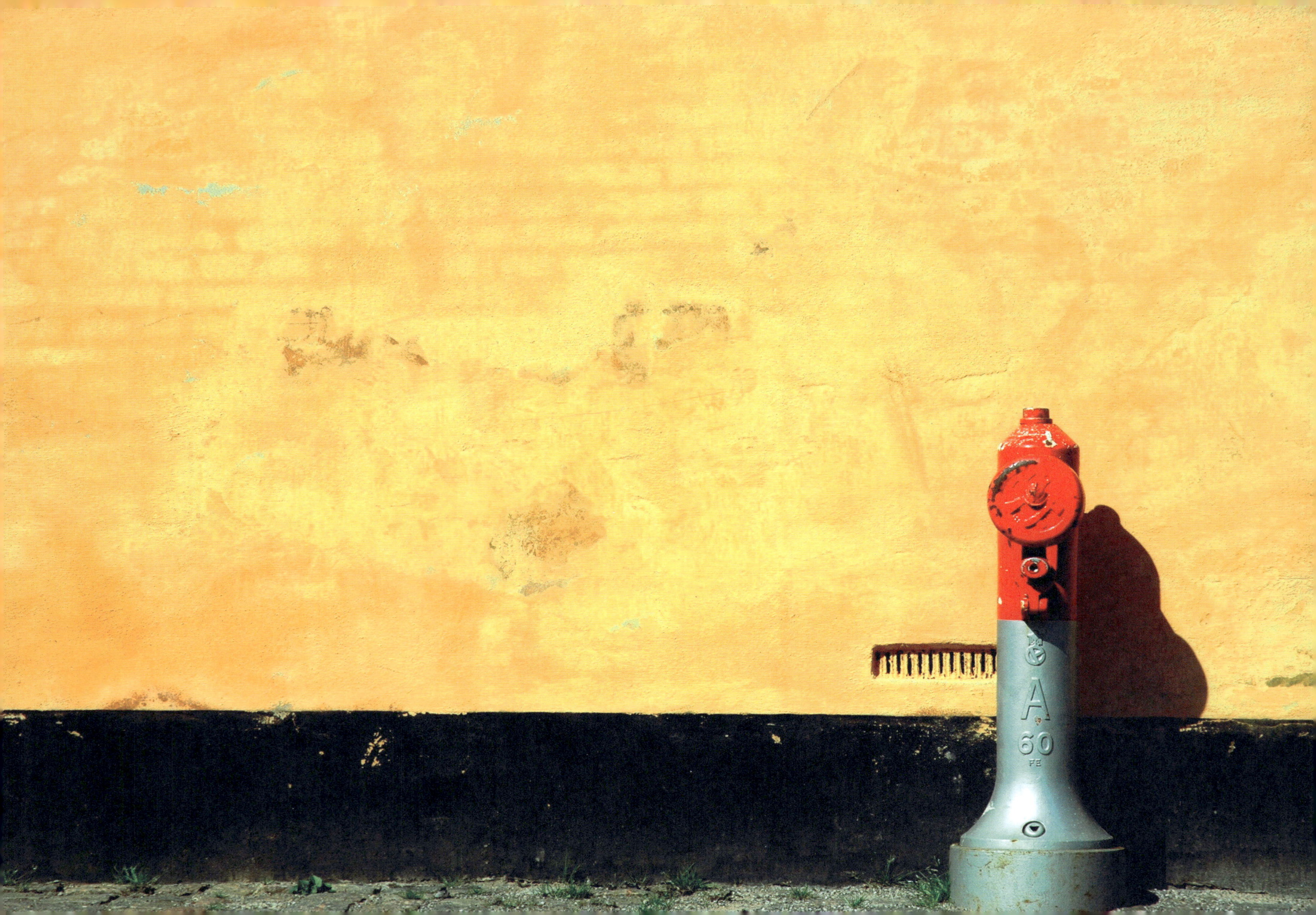

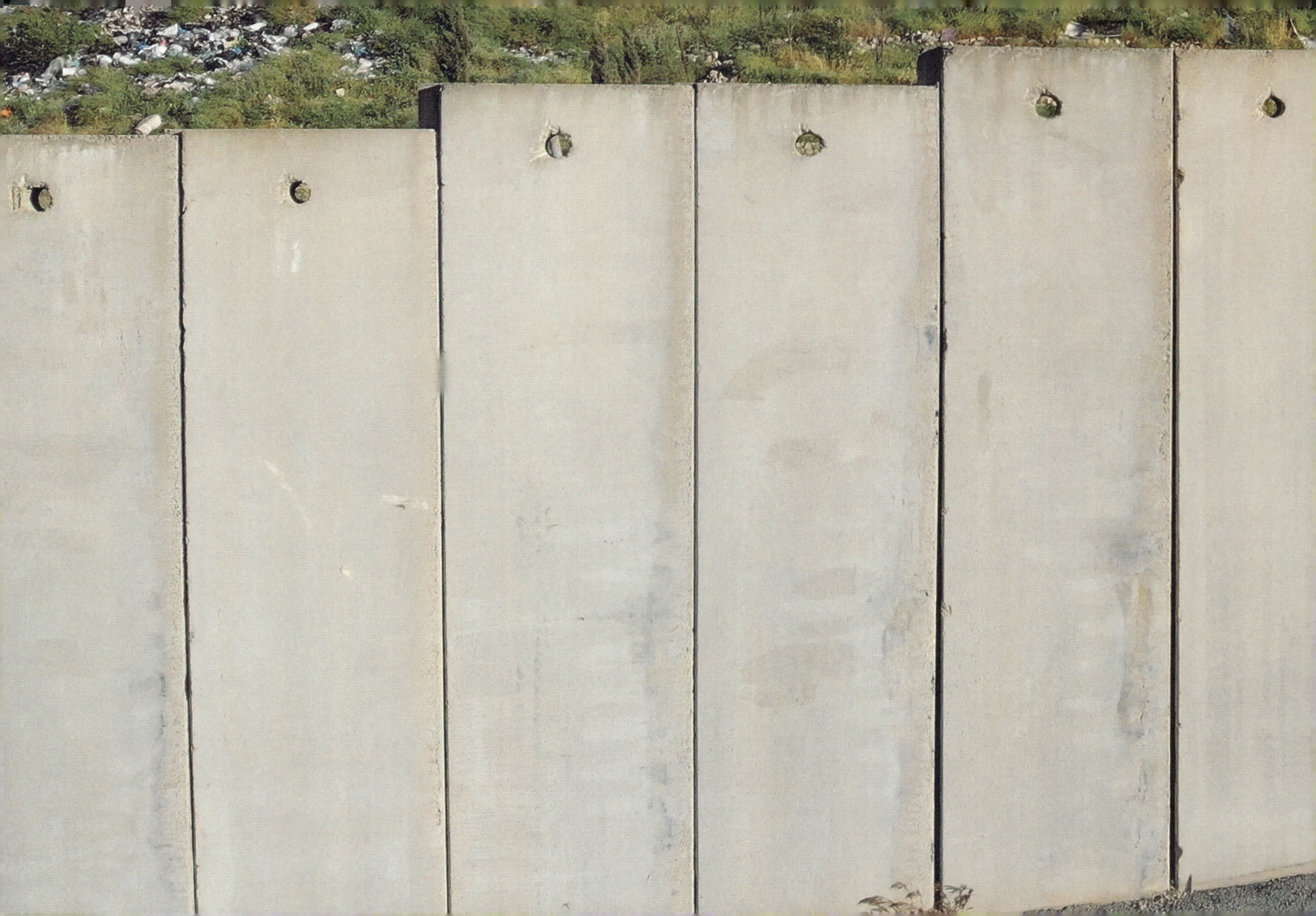

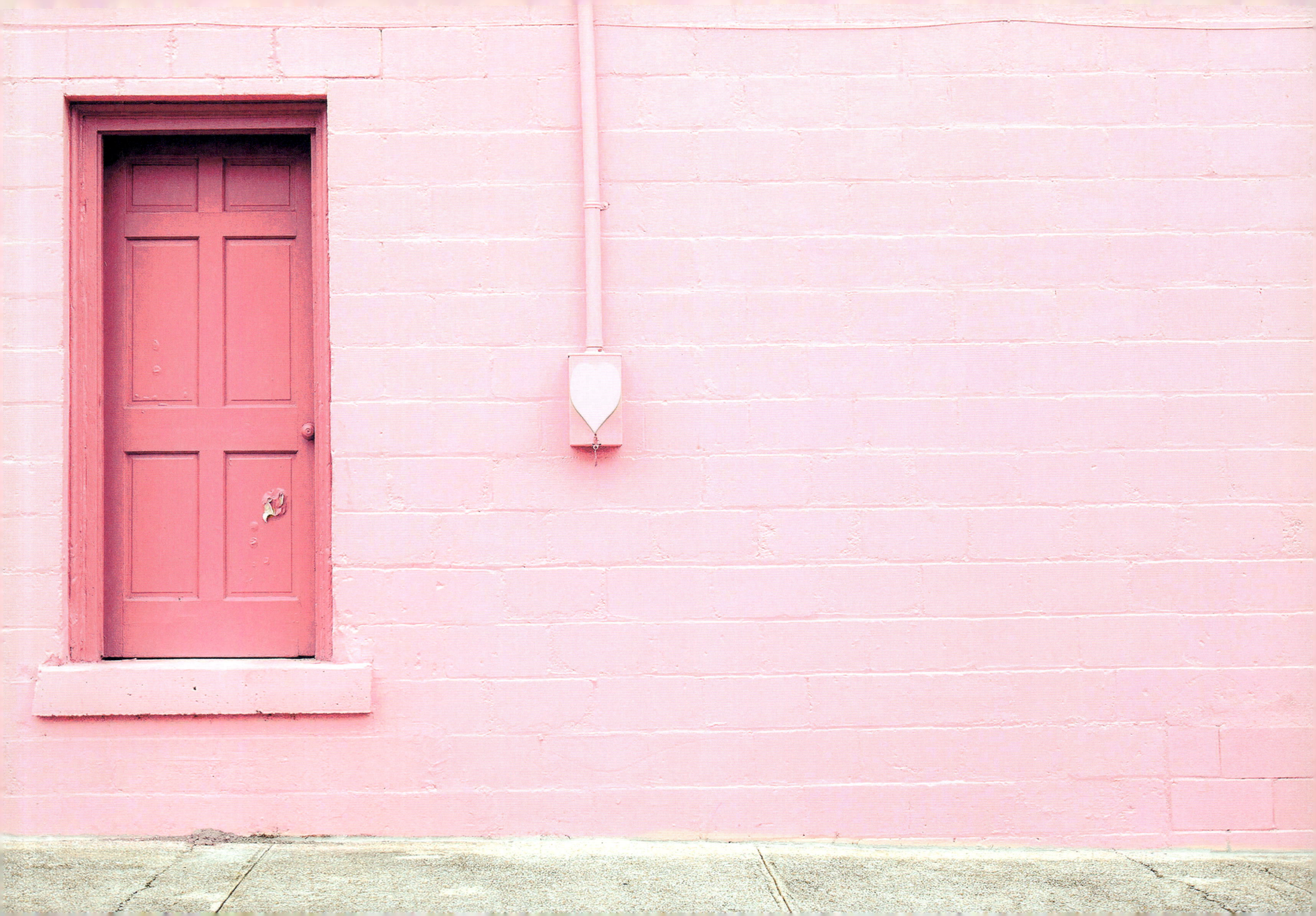

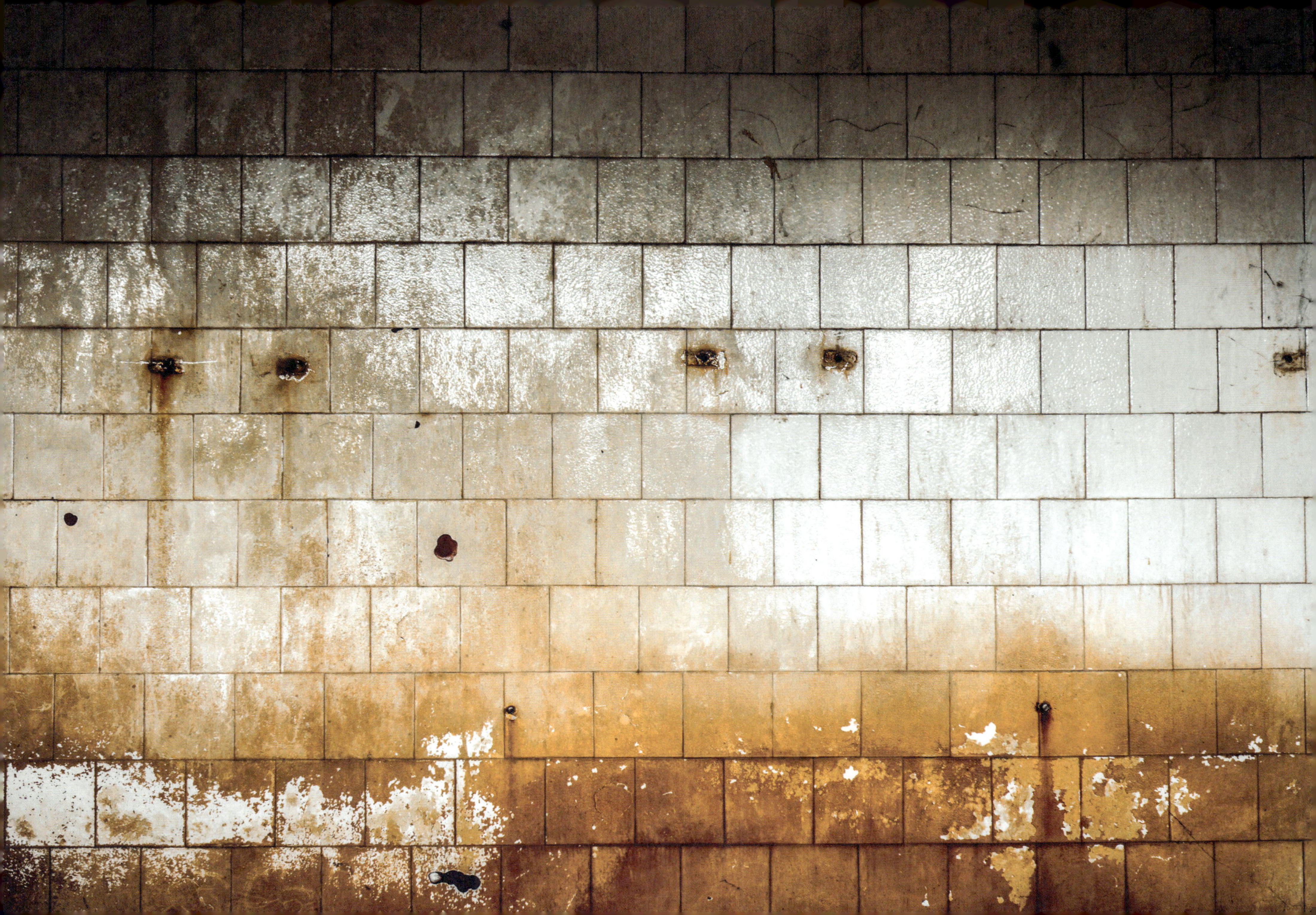

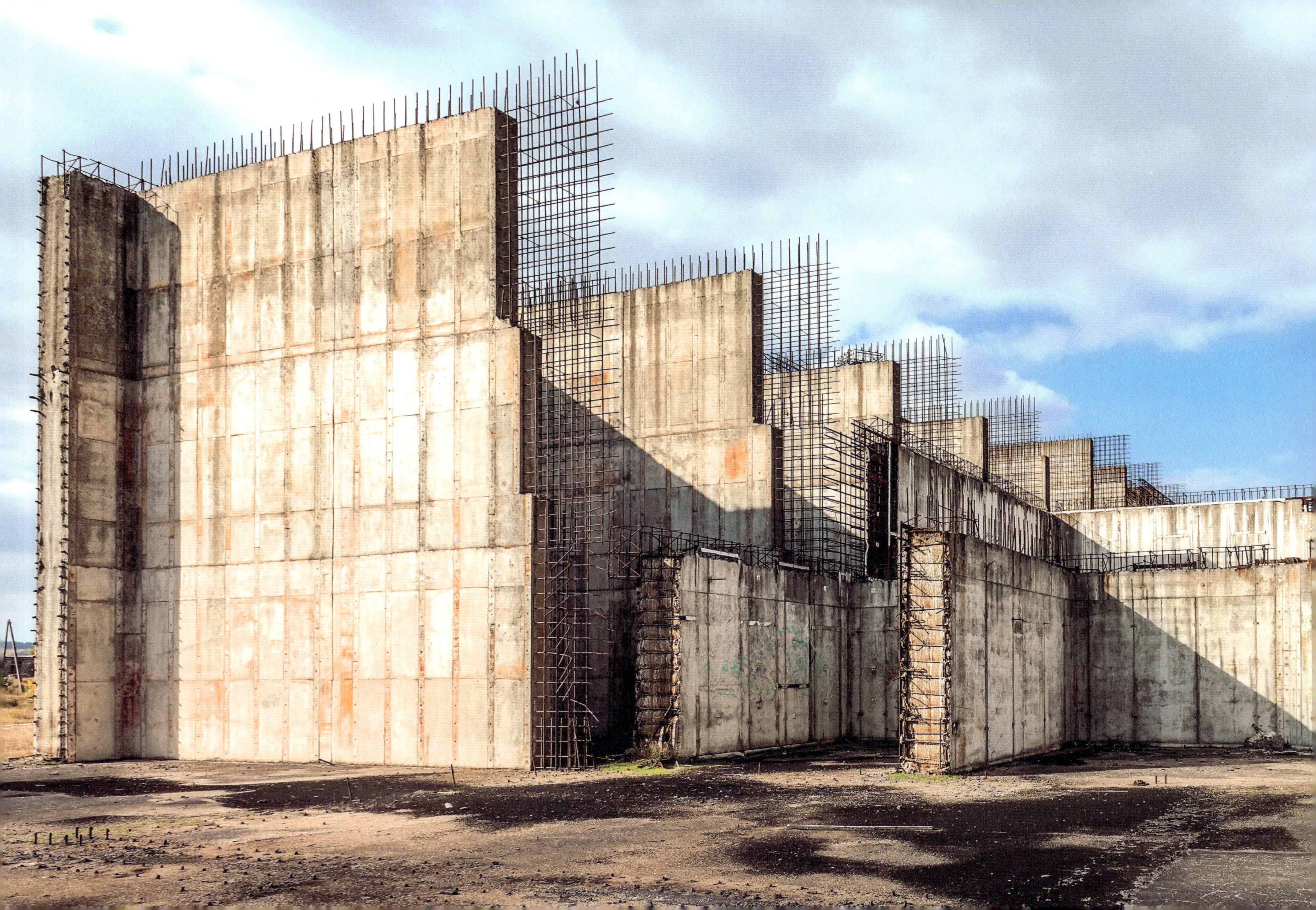

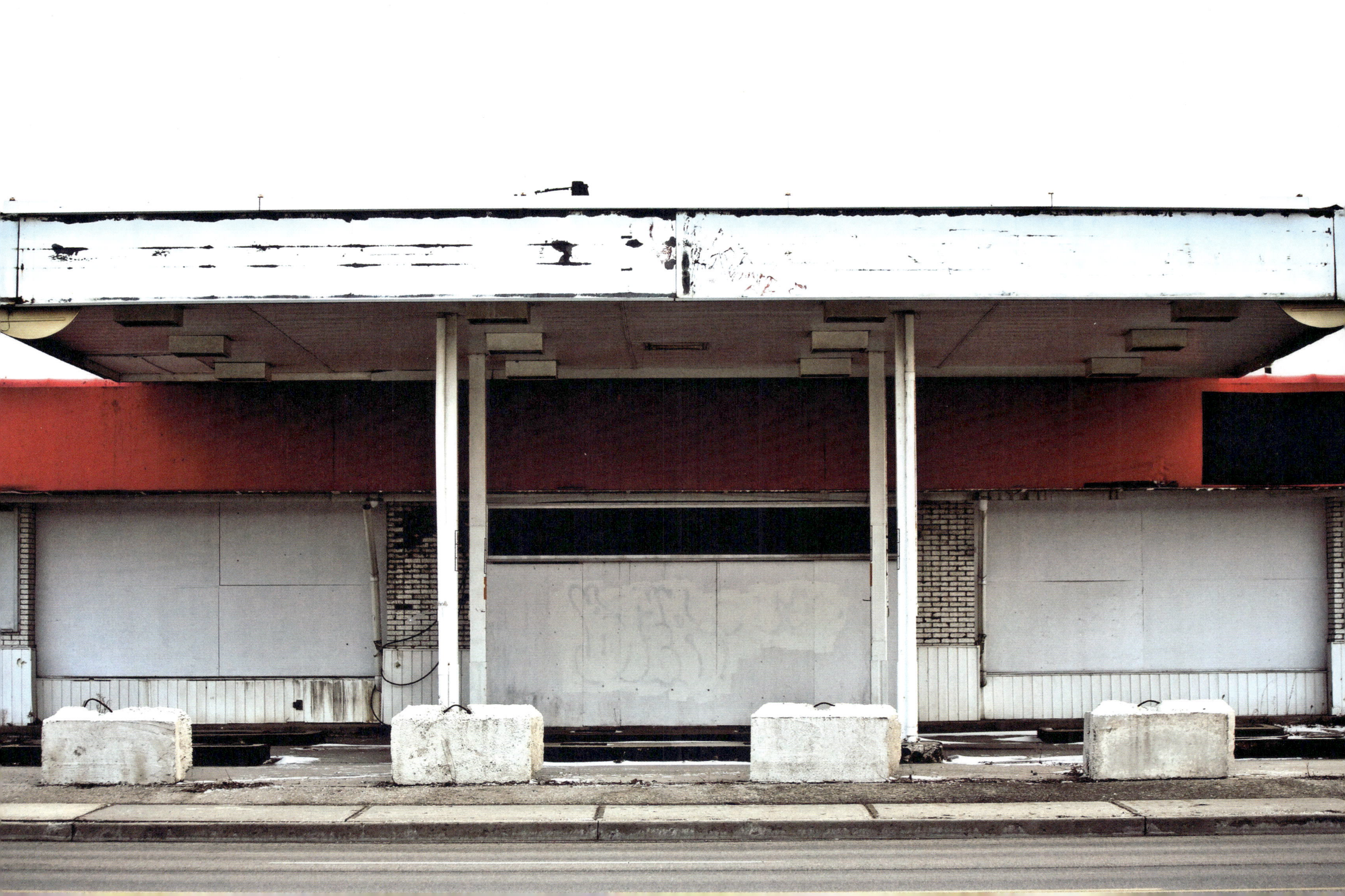

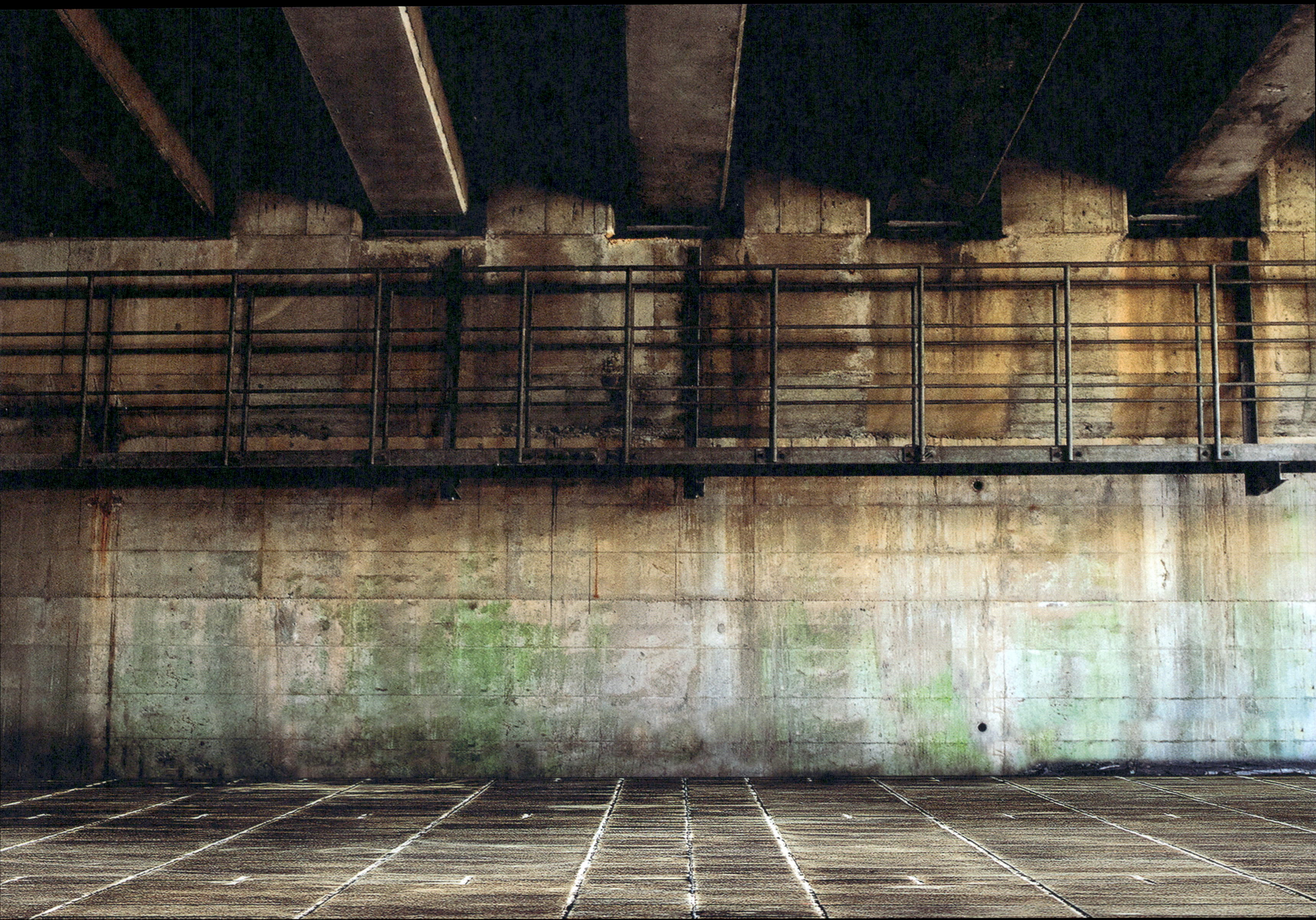

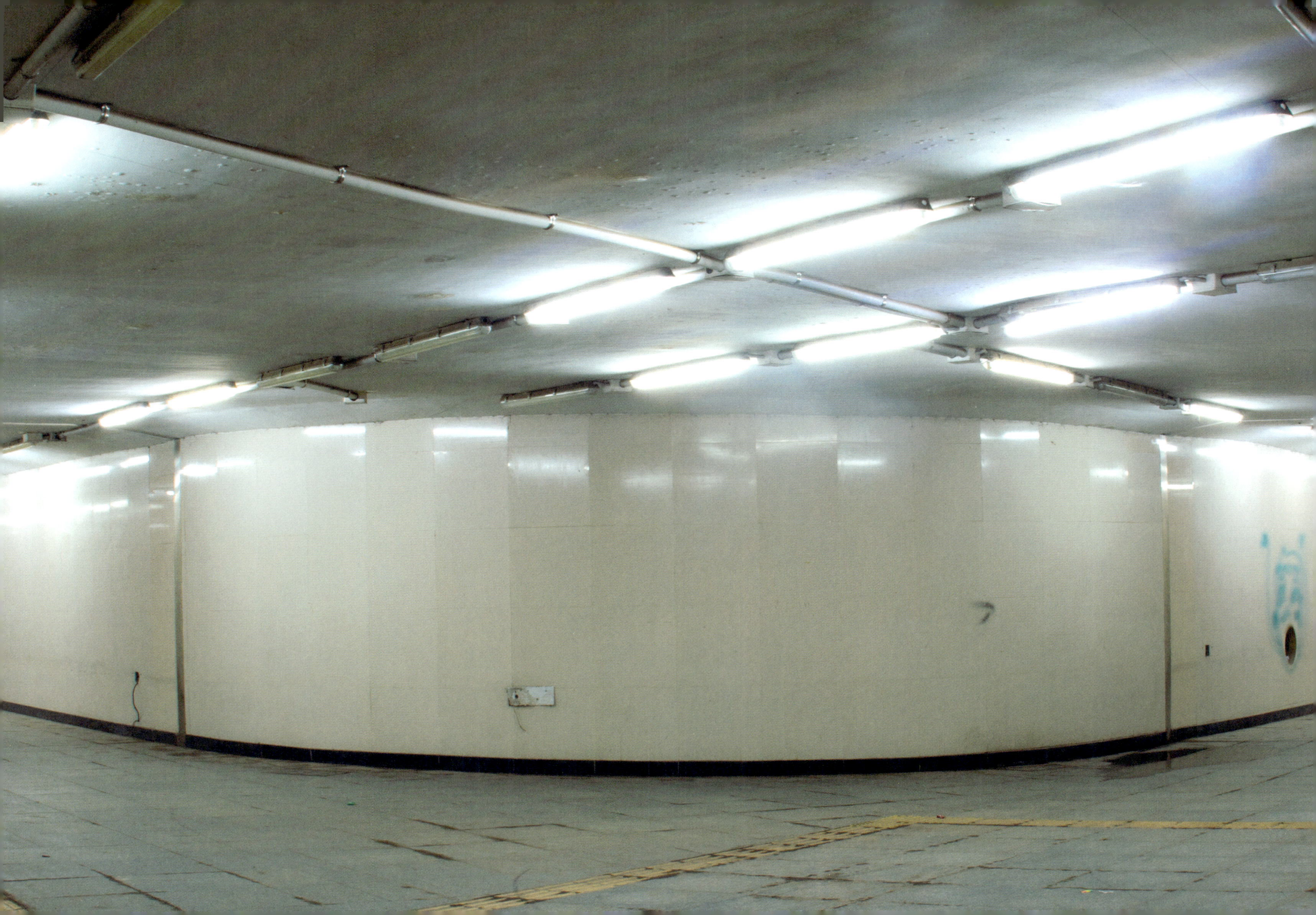

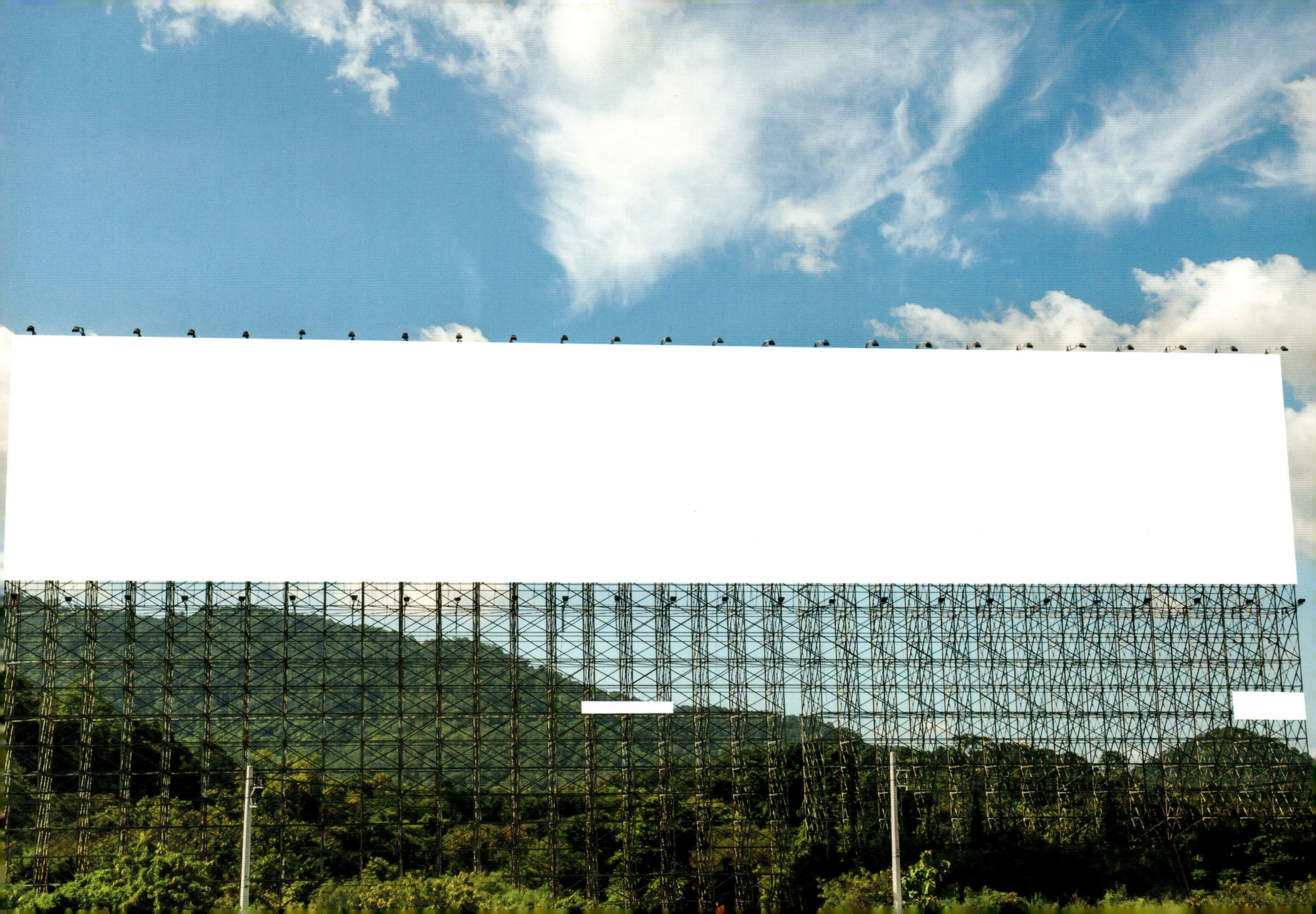

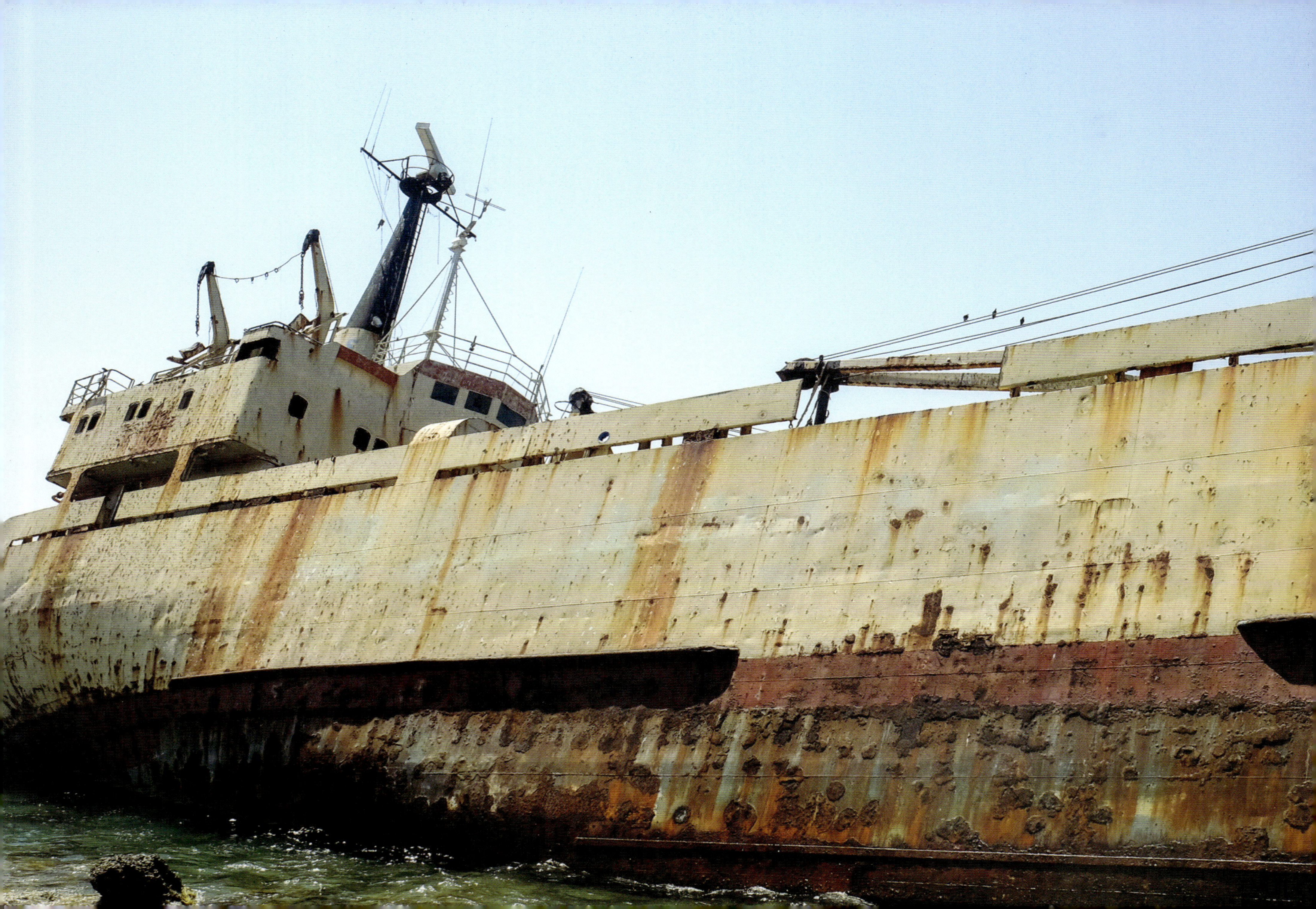

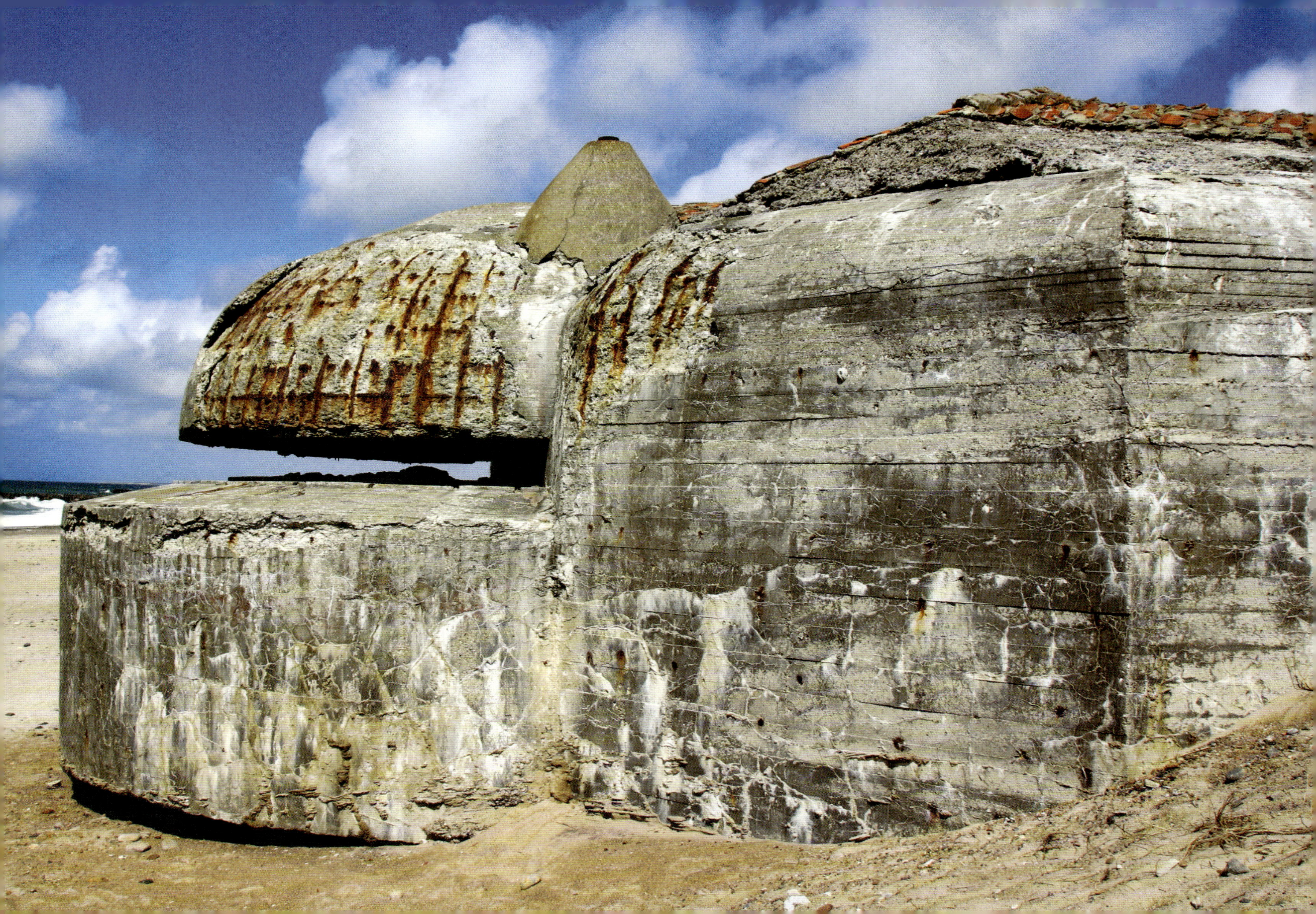

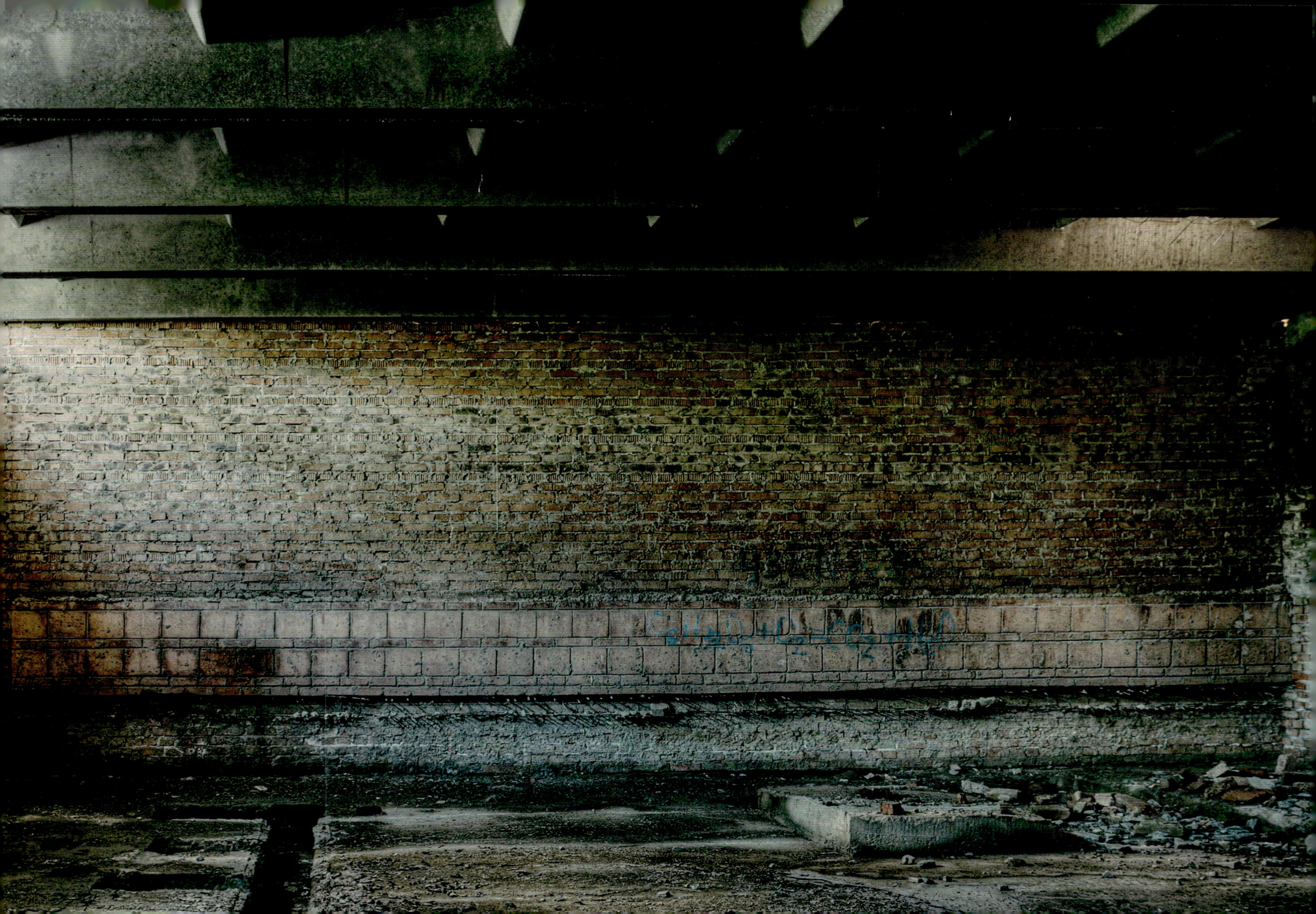

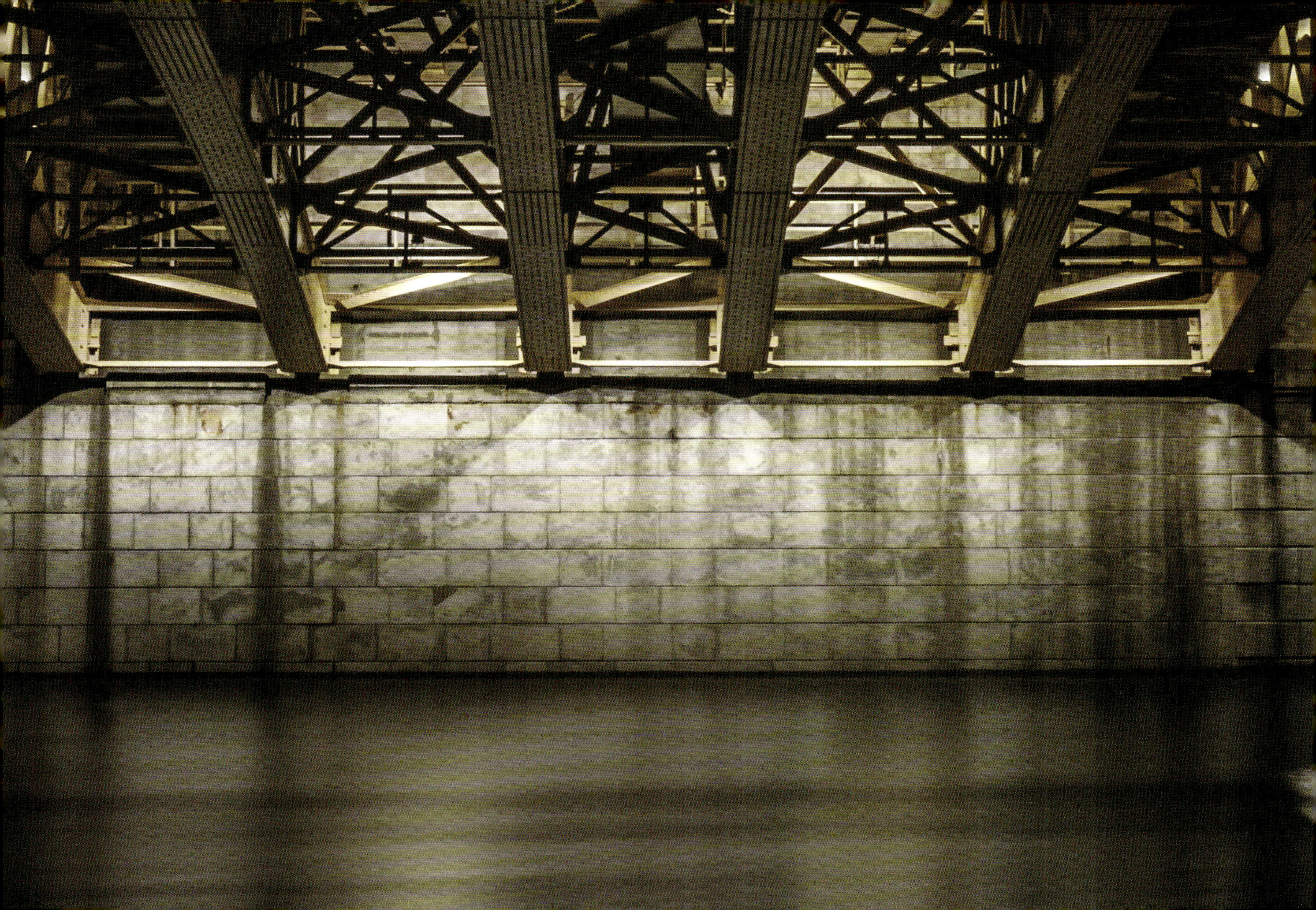

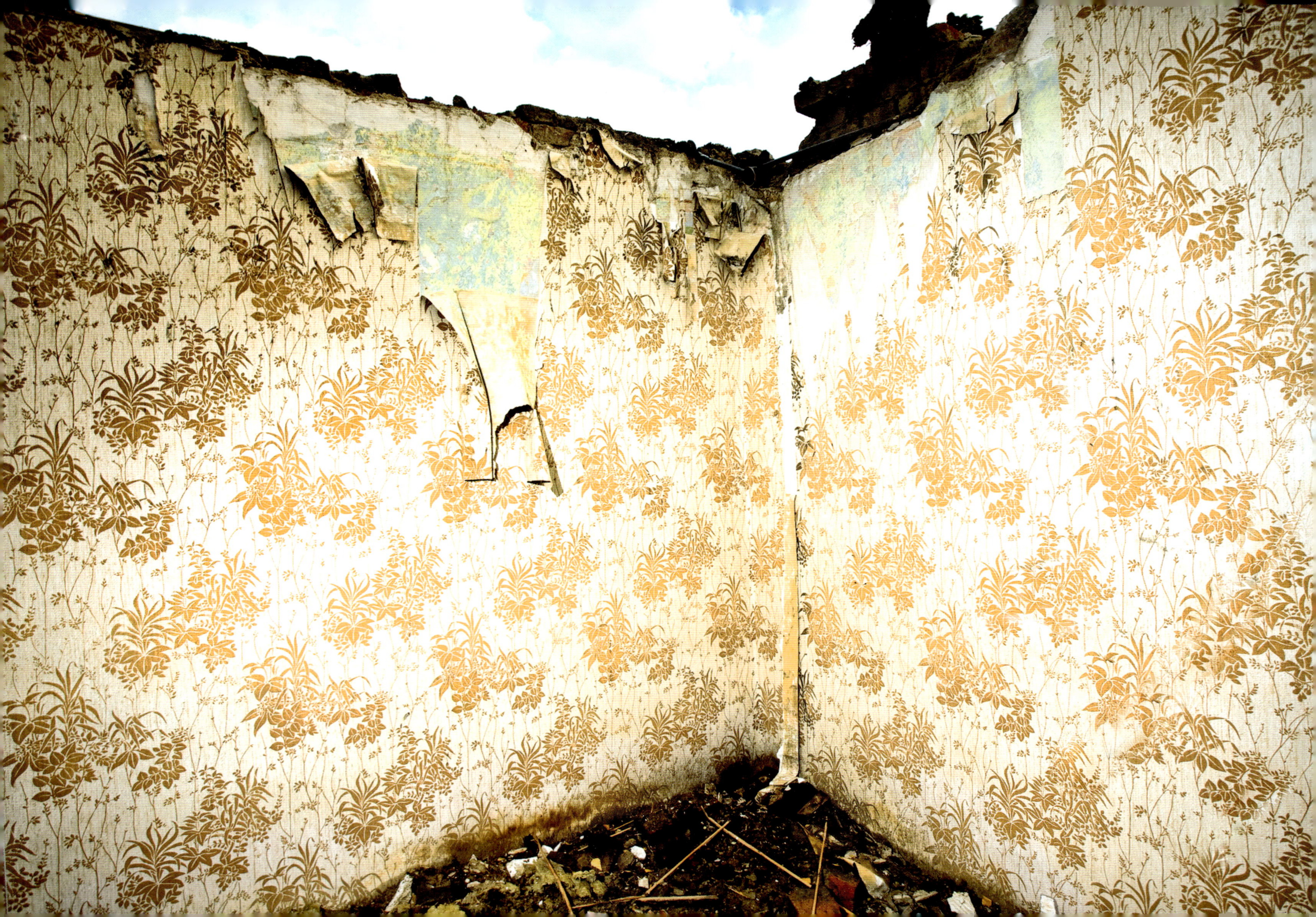

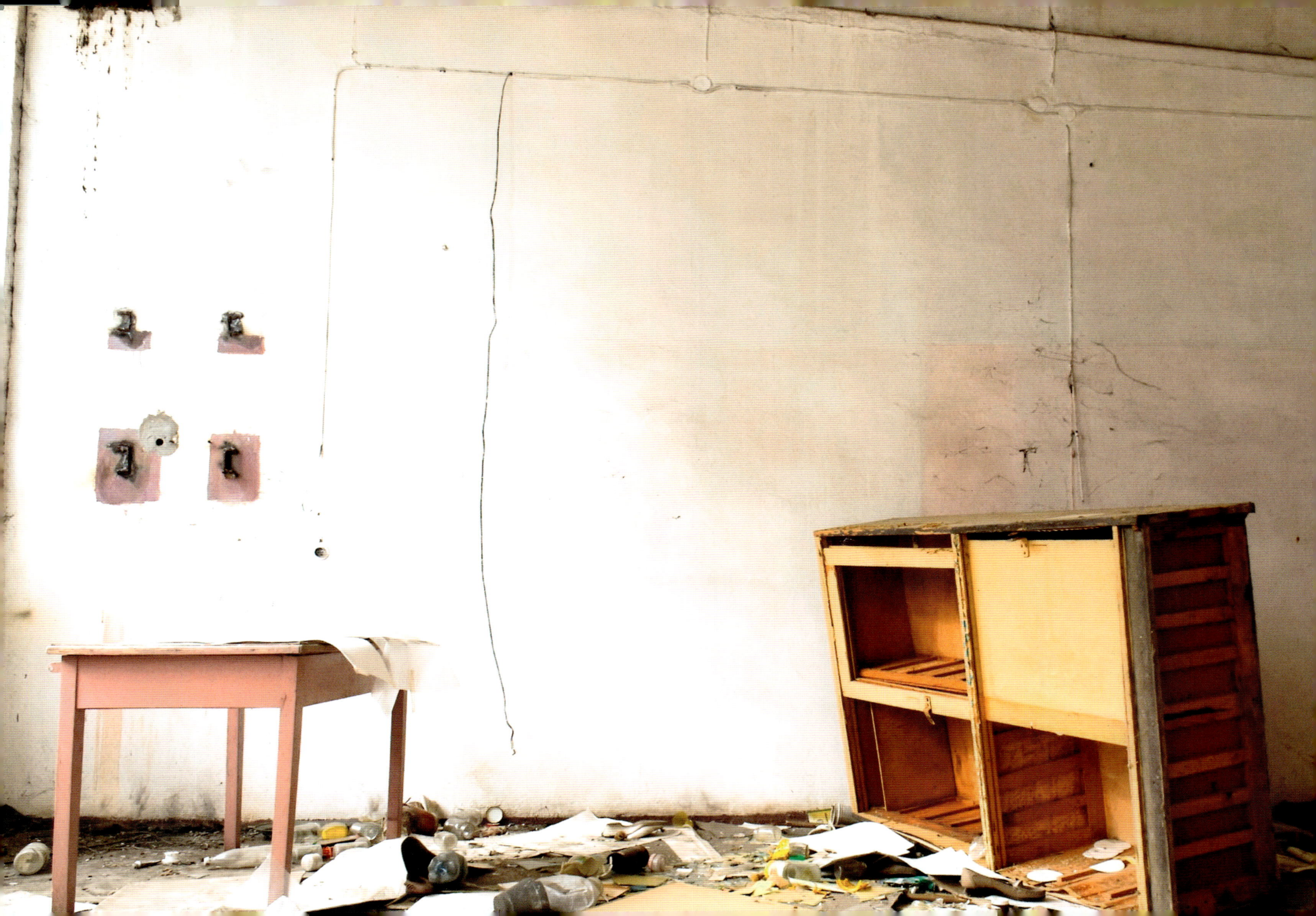

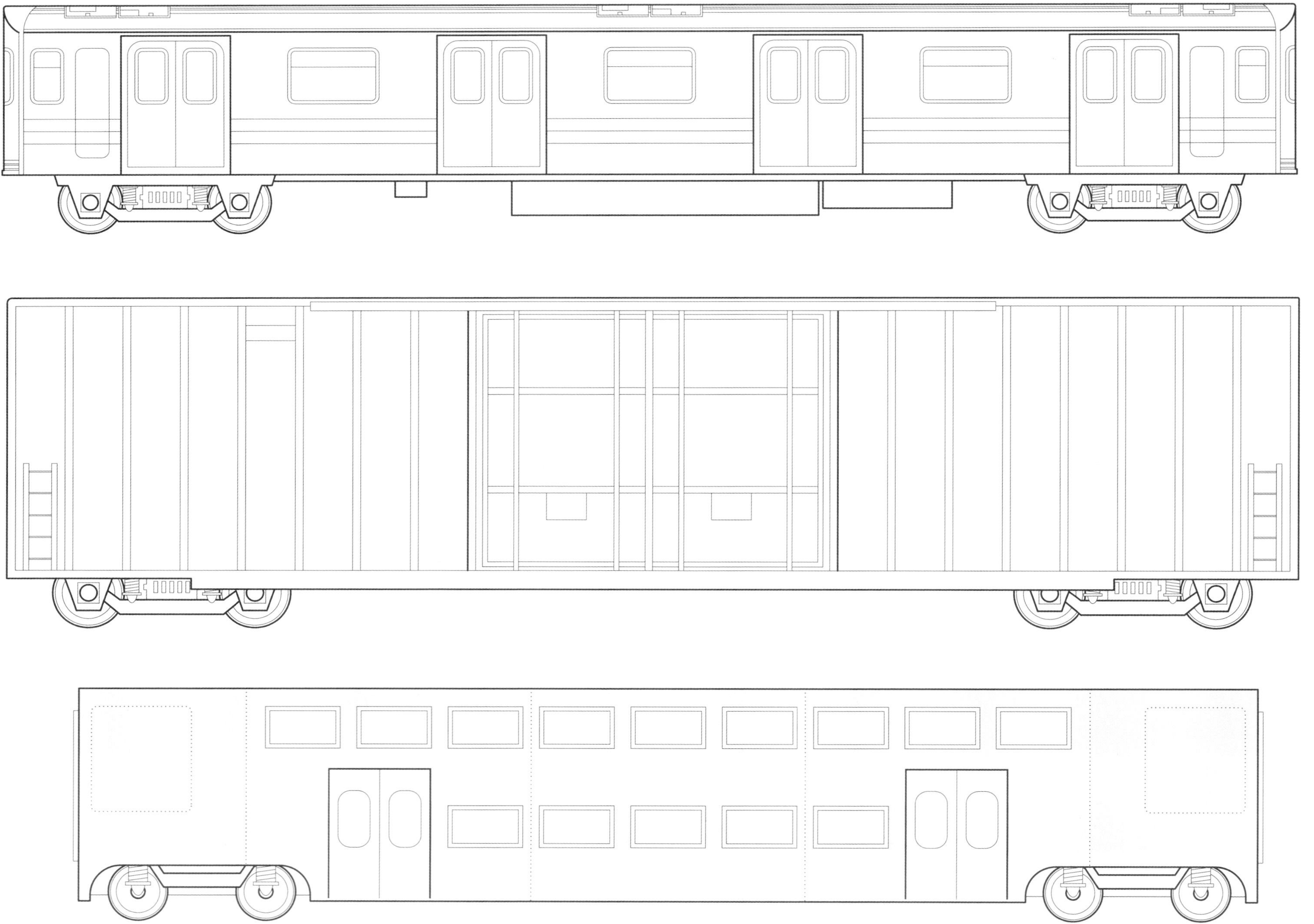

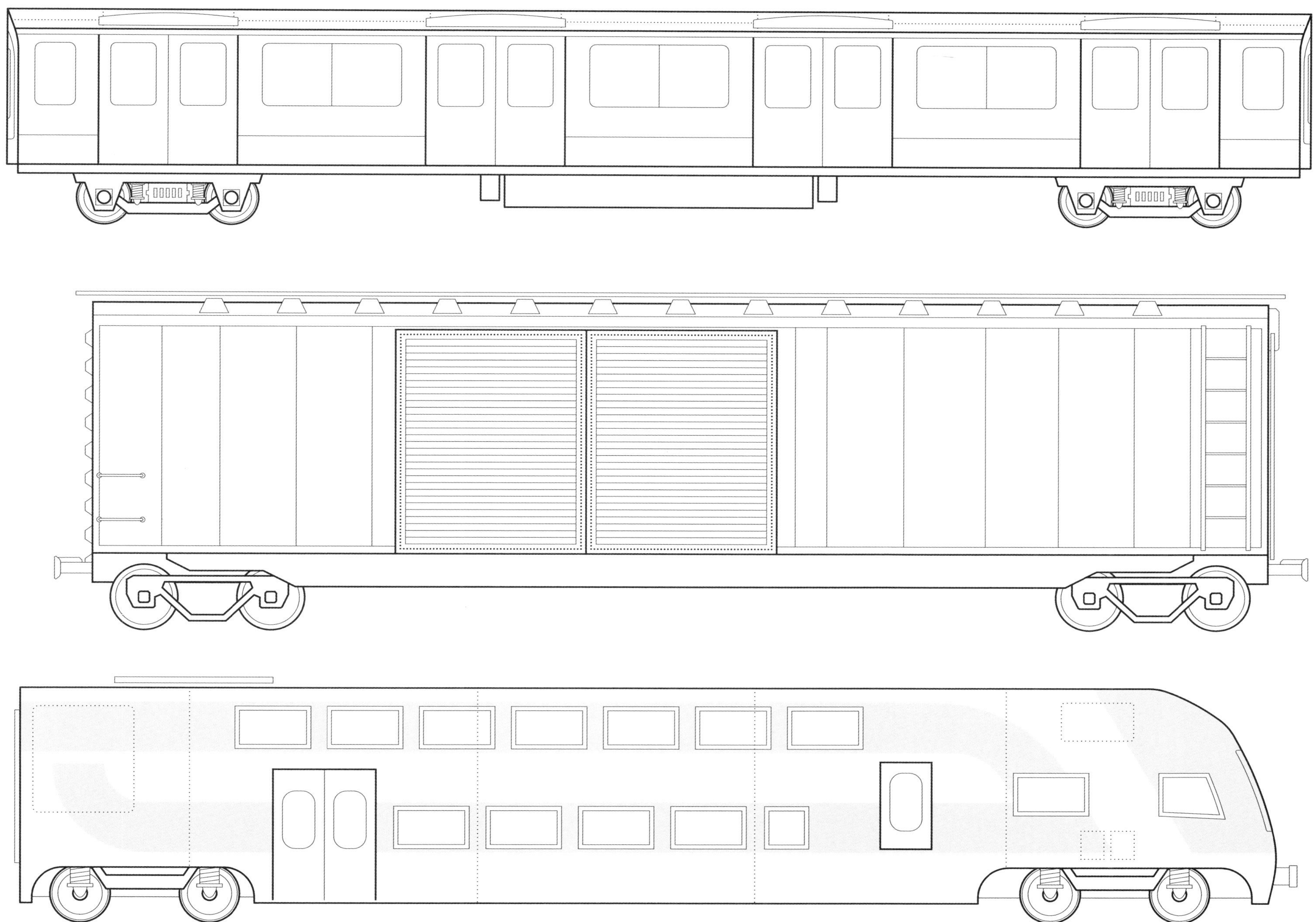

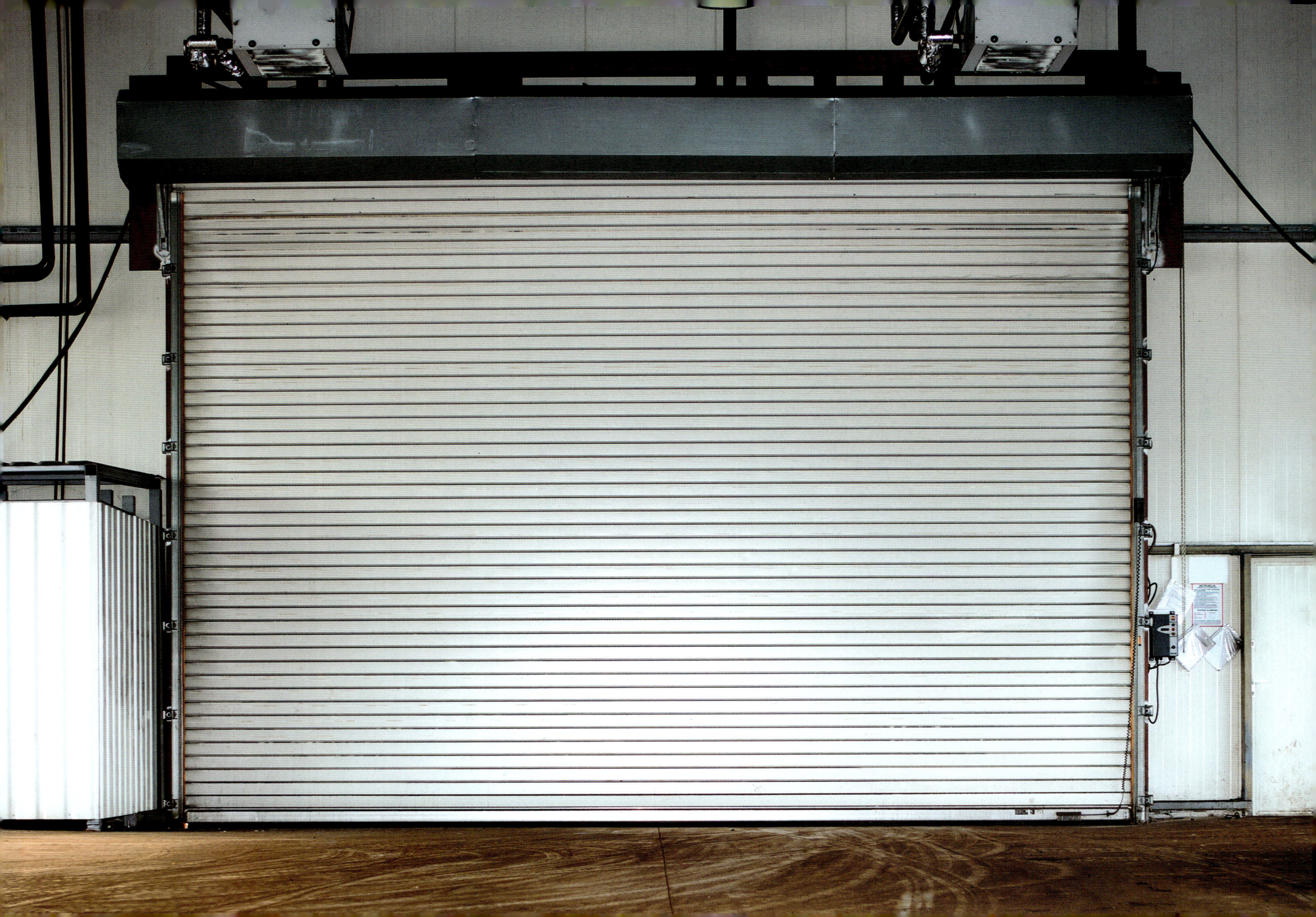

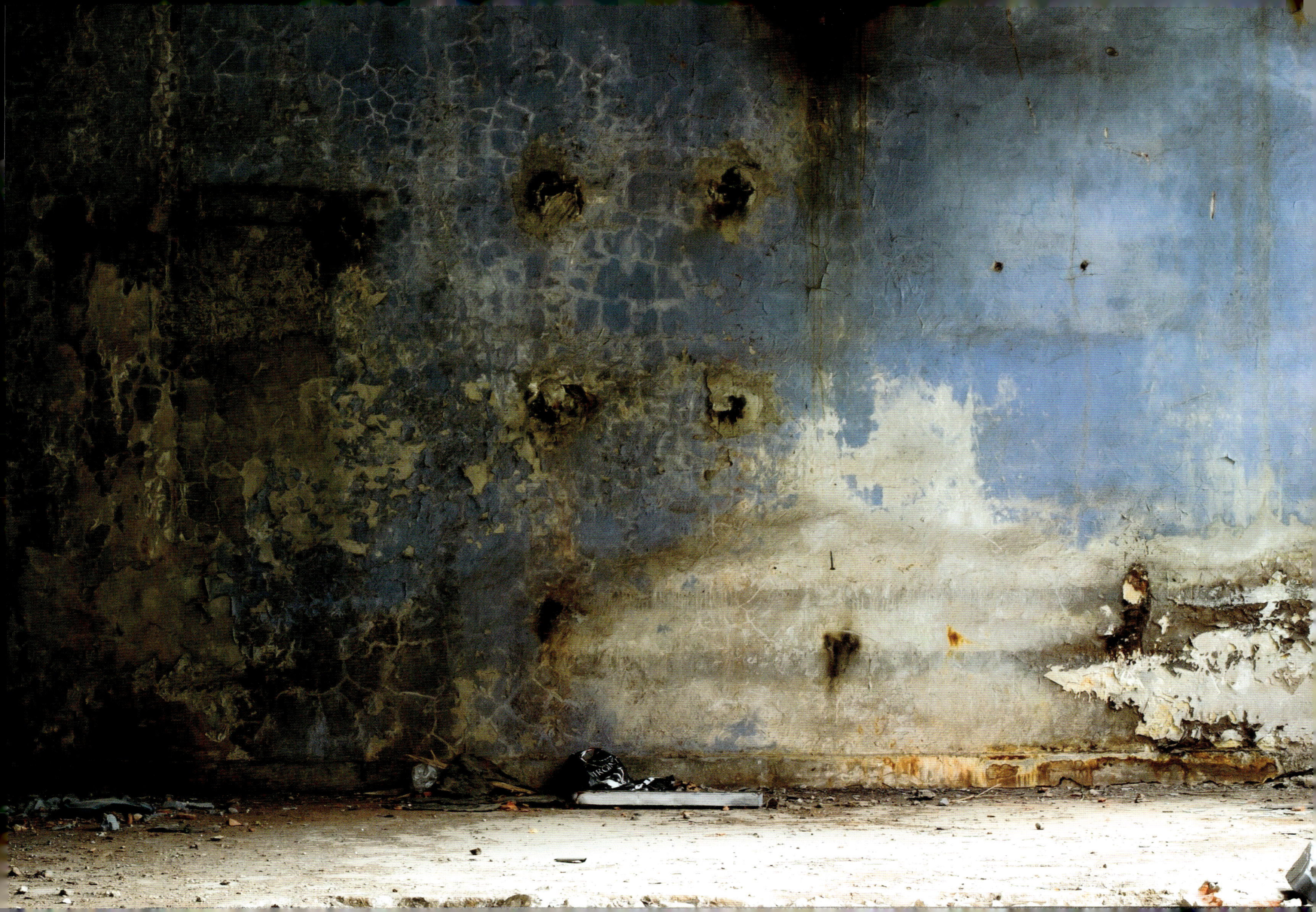

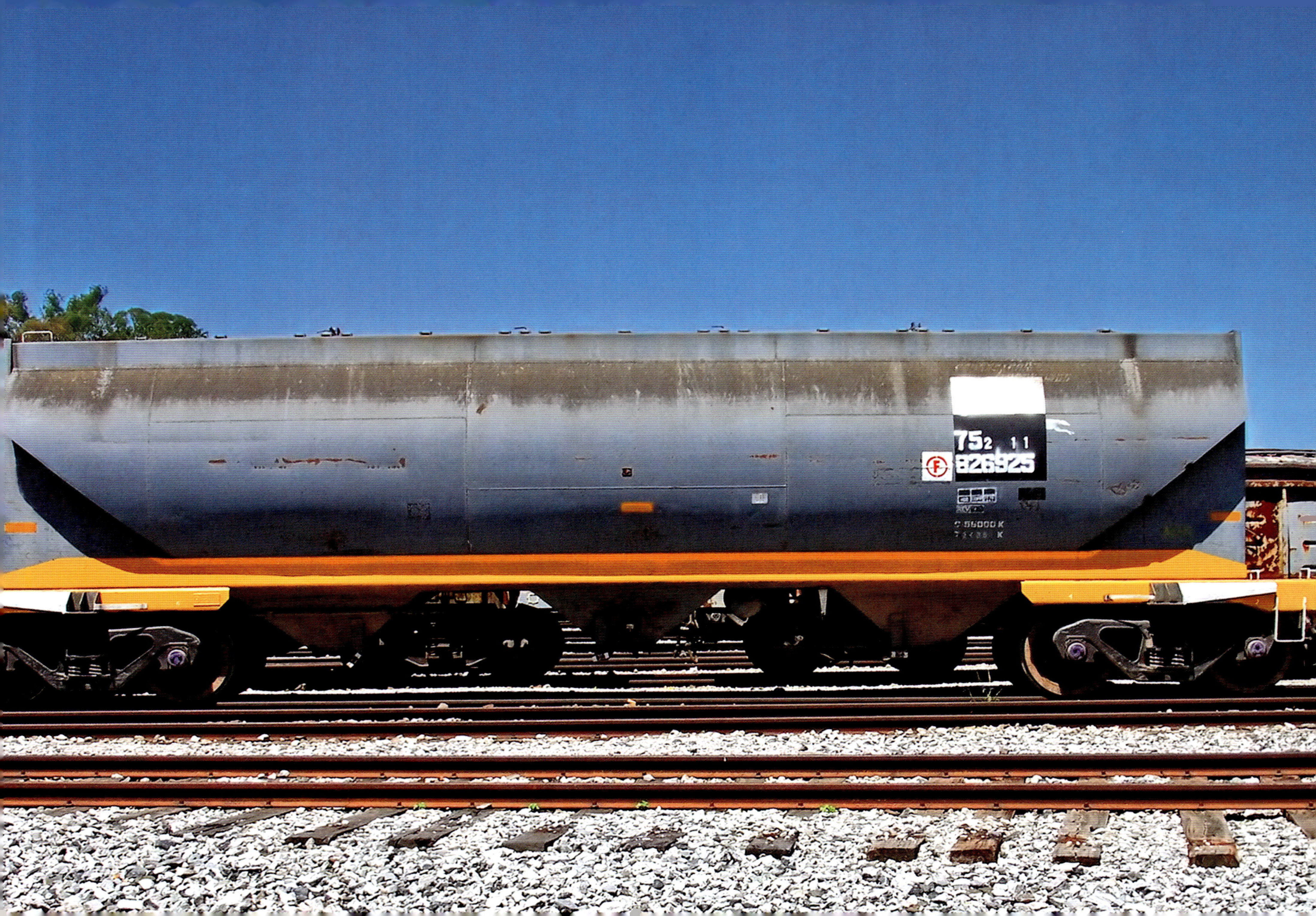

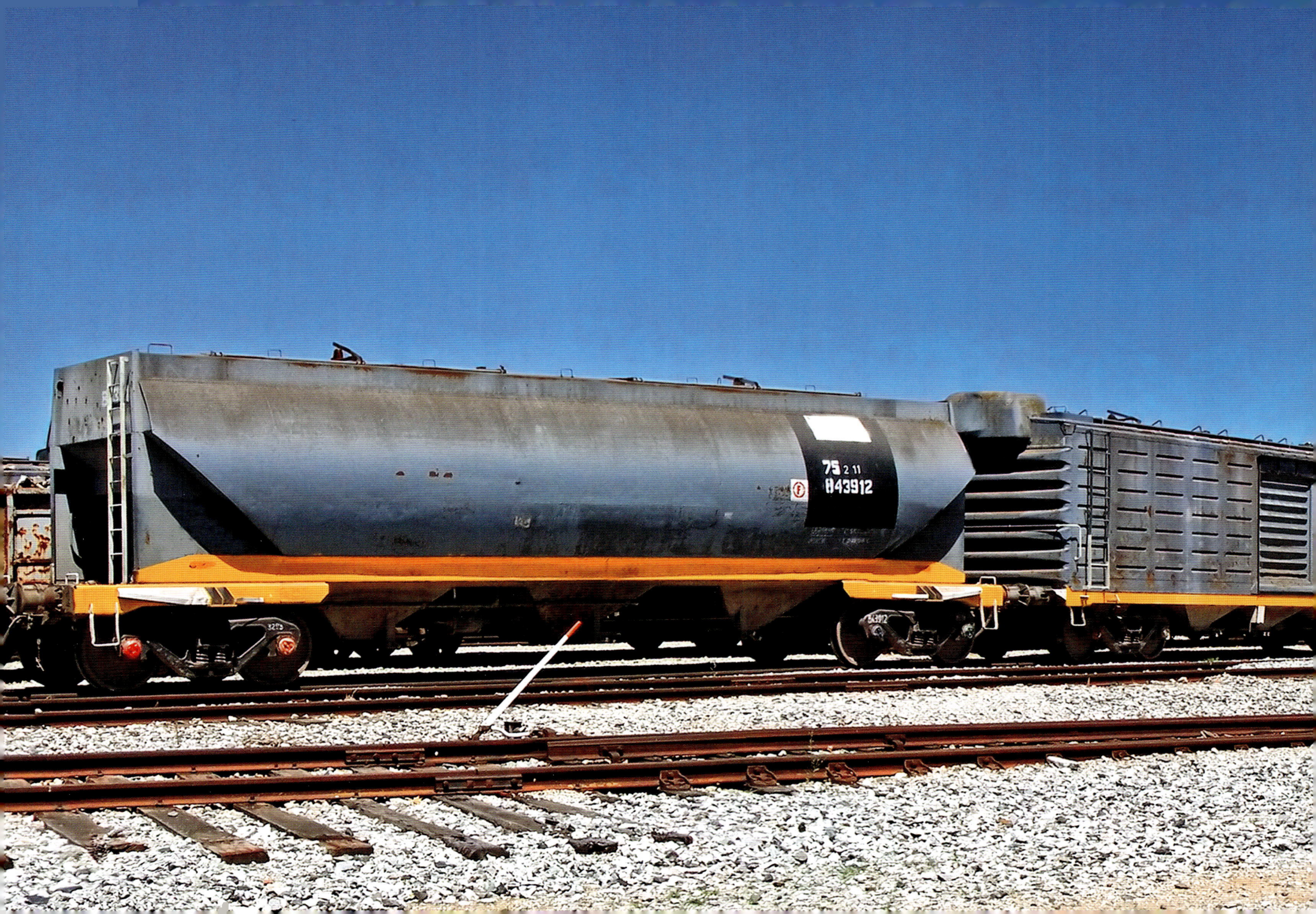
75 2 11
B43912

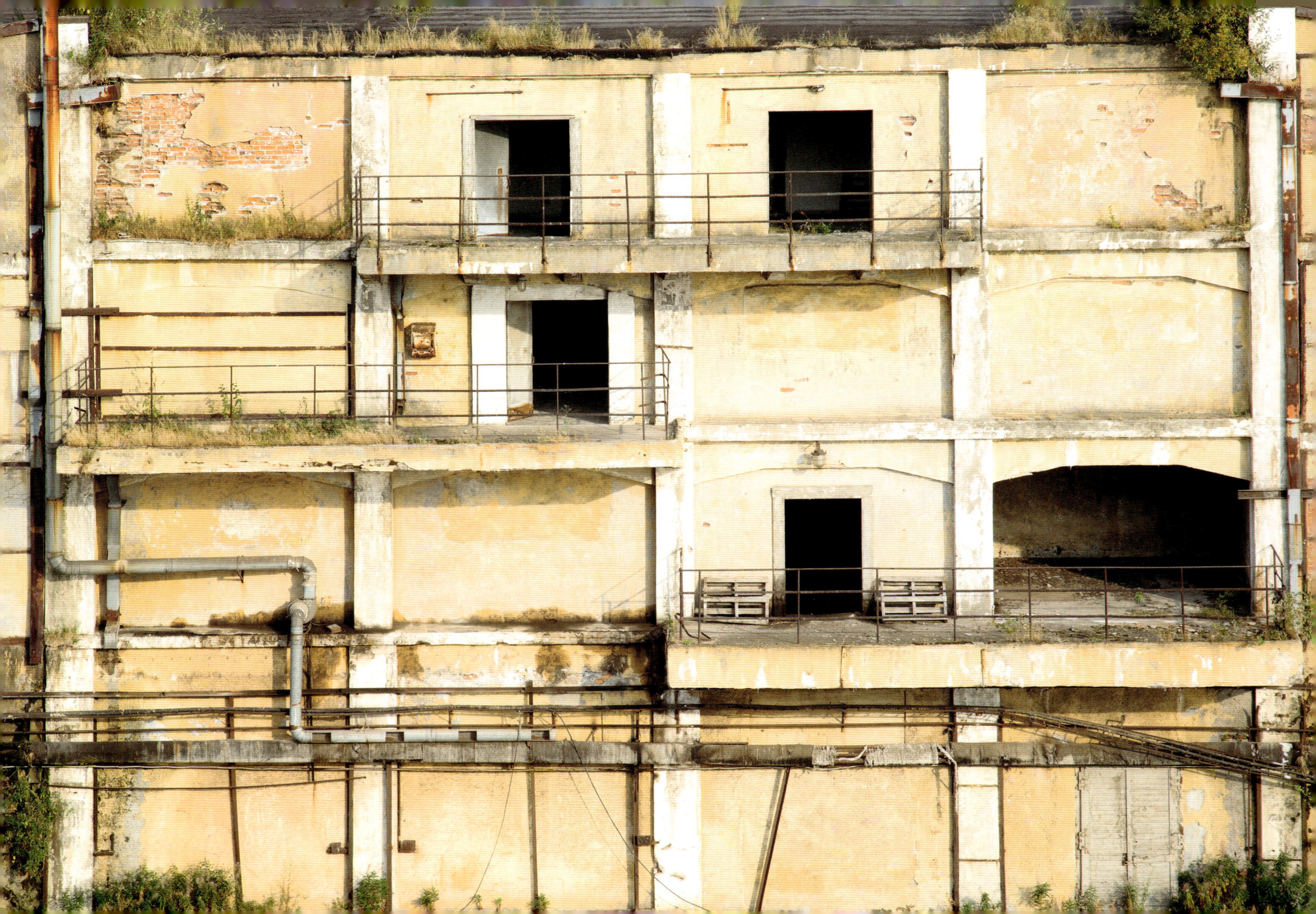

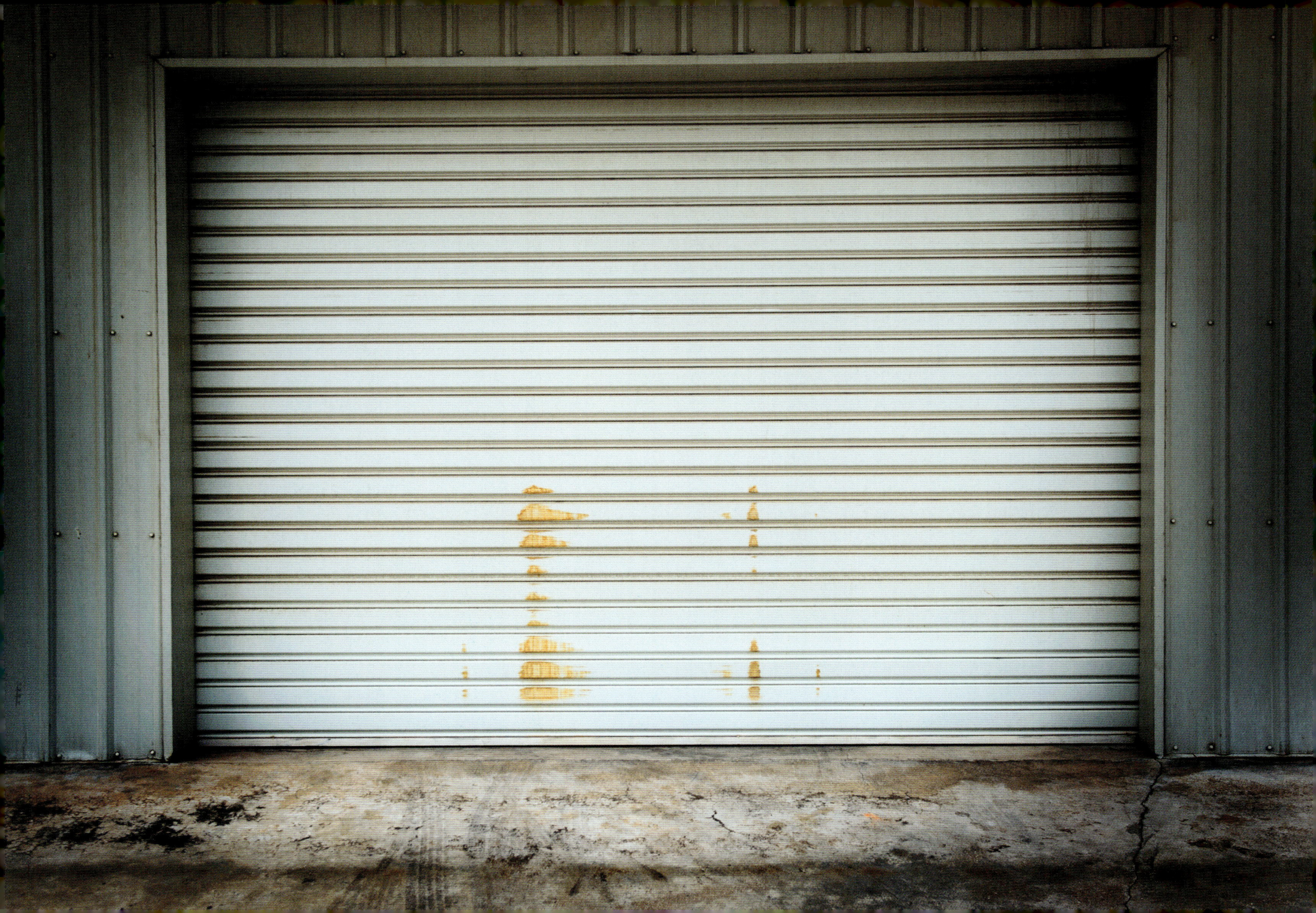

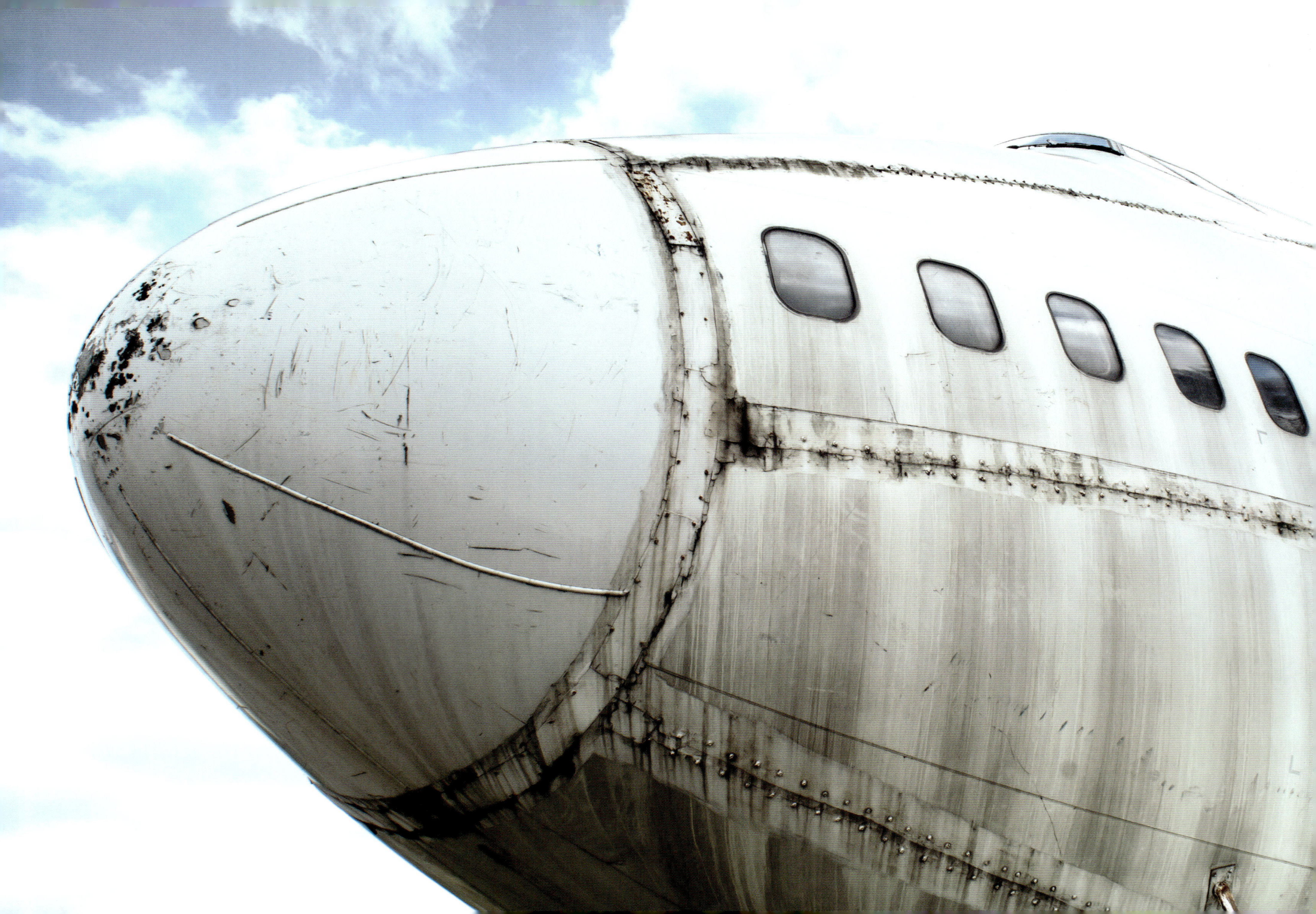

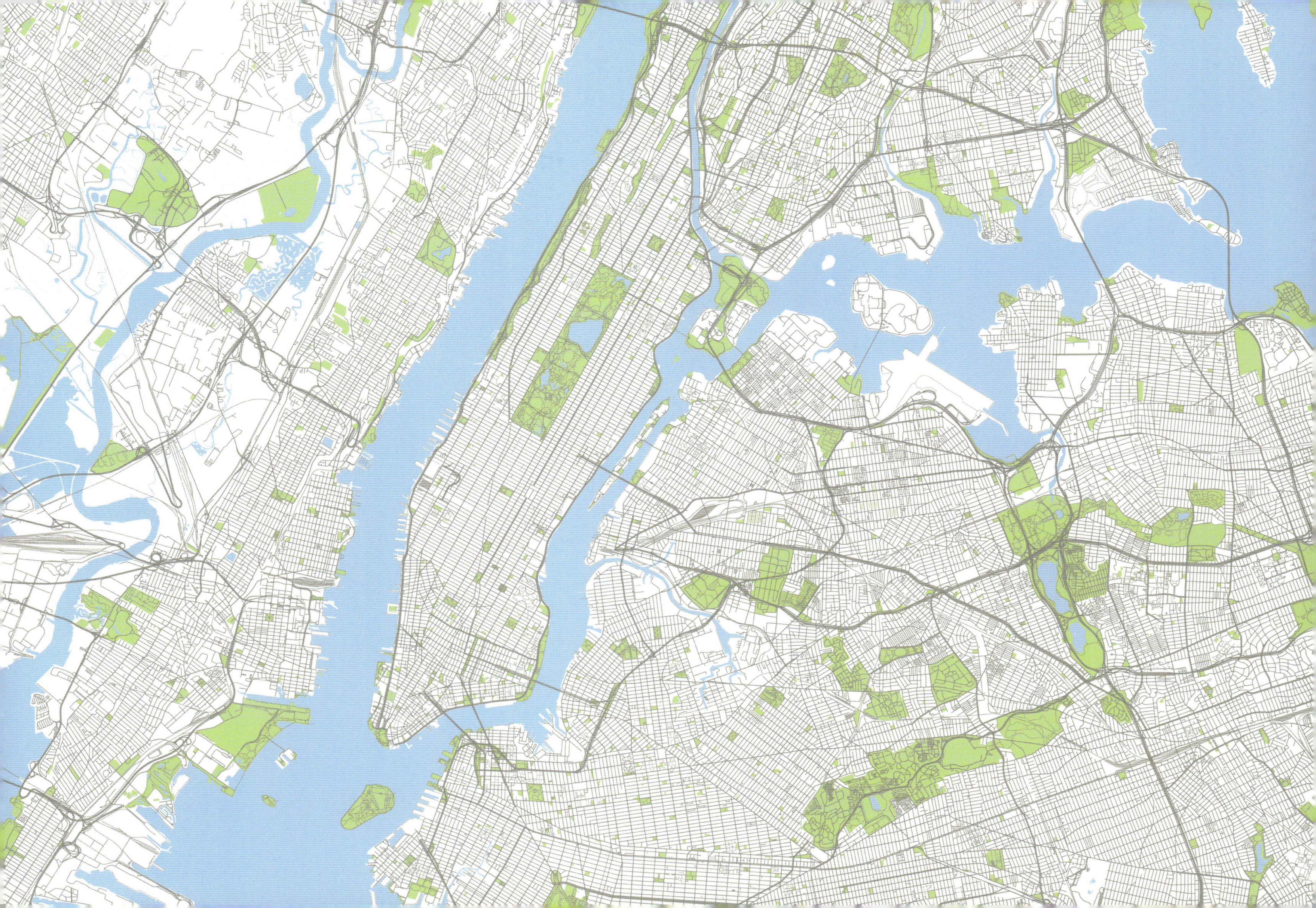

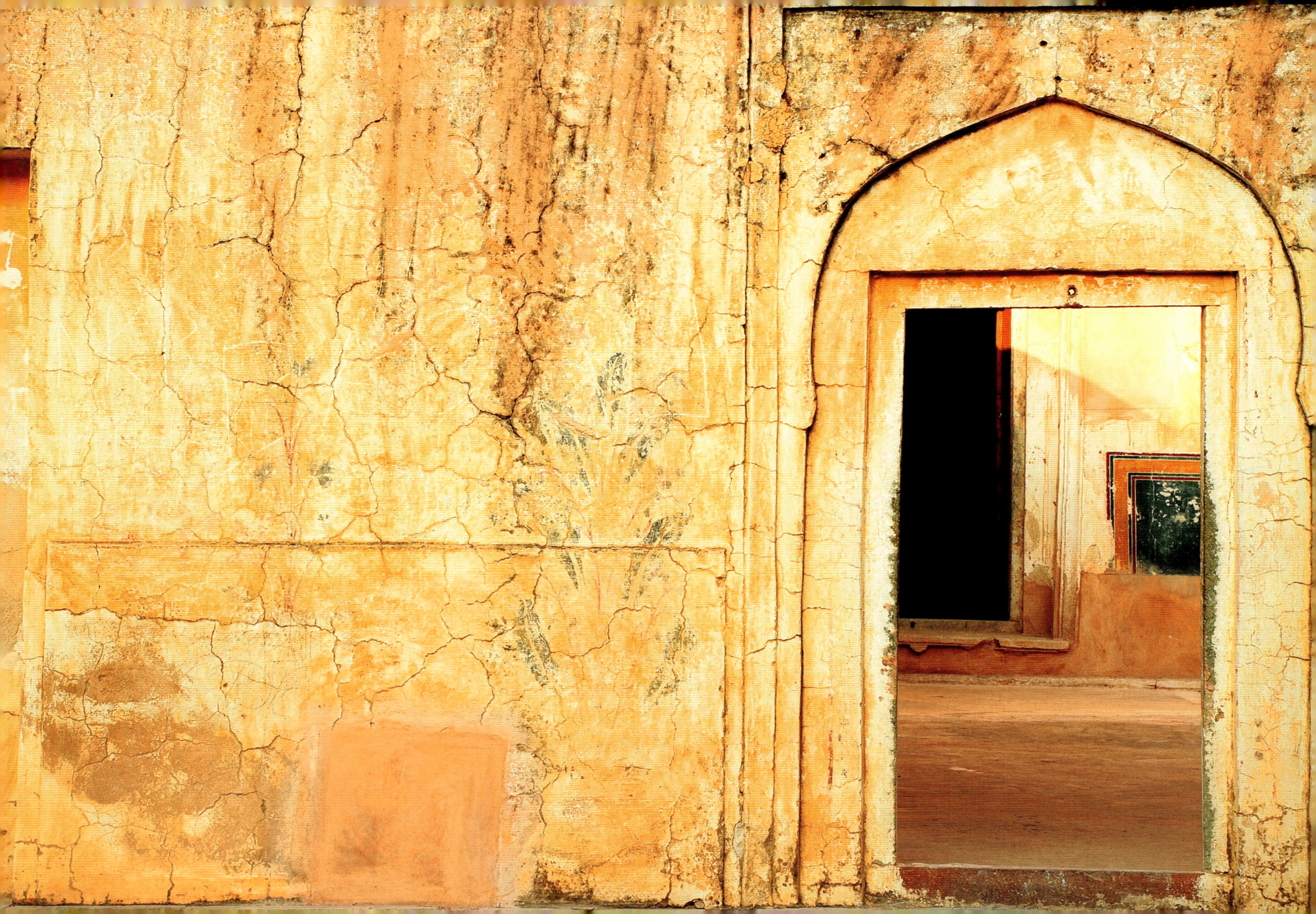

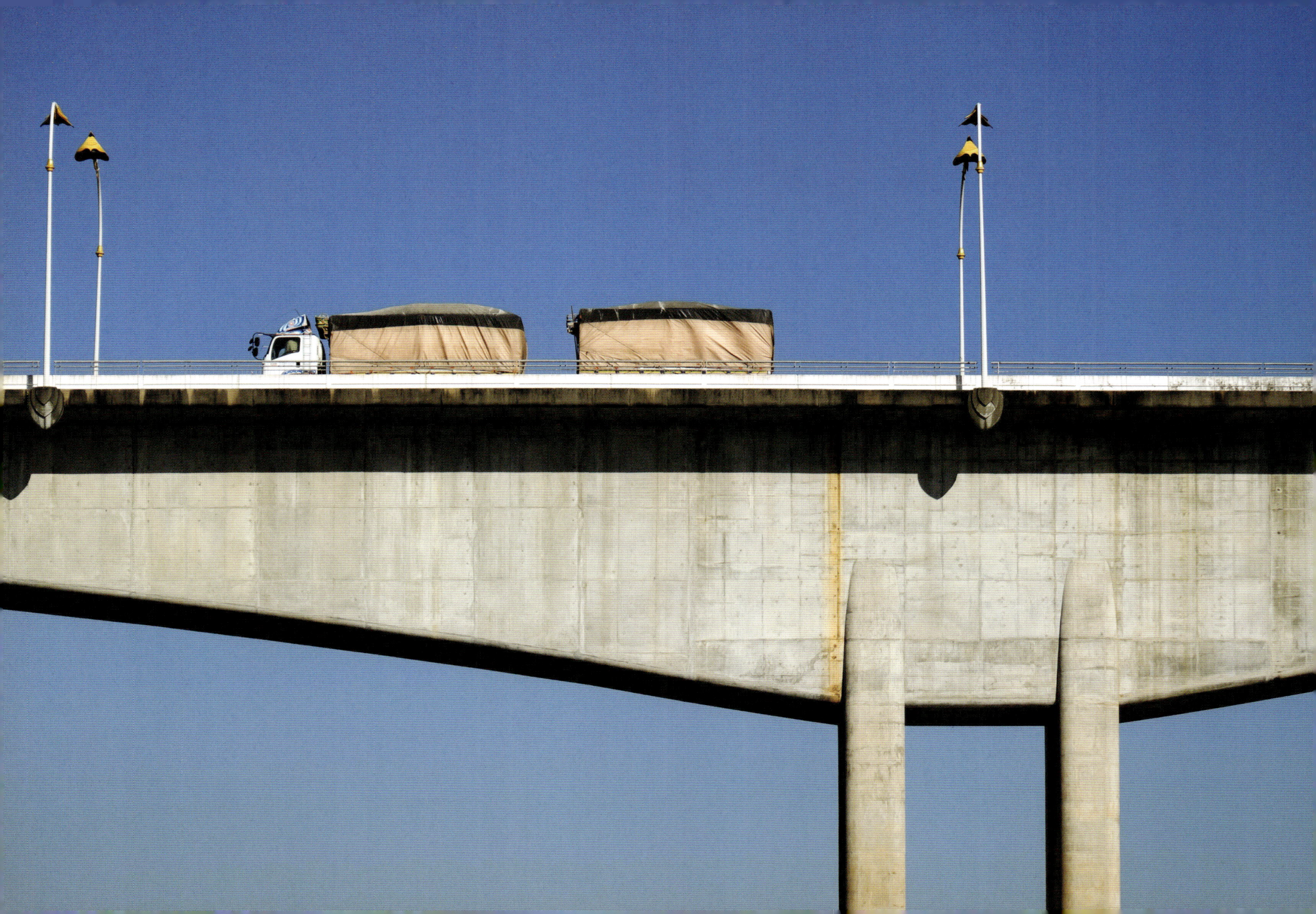

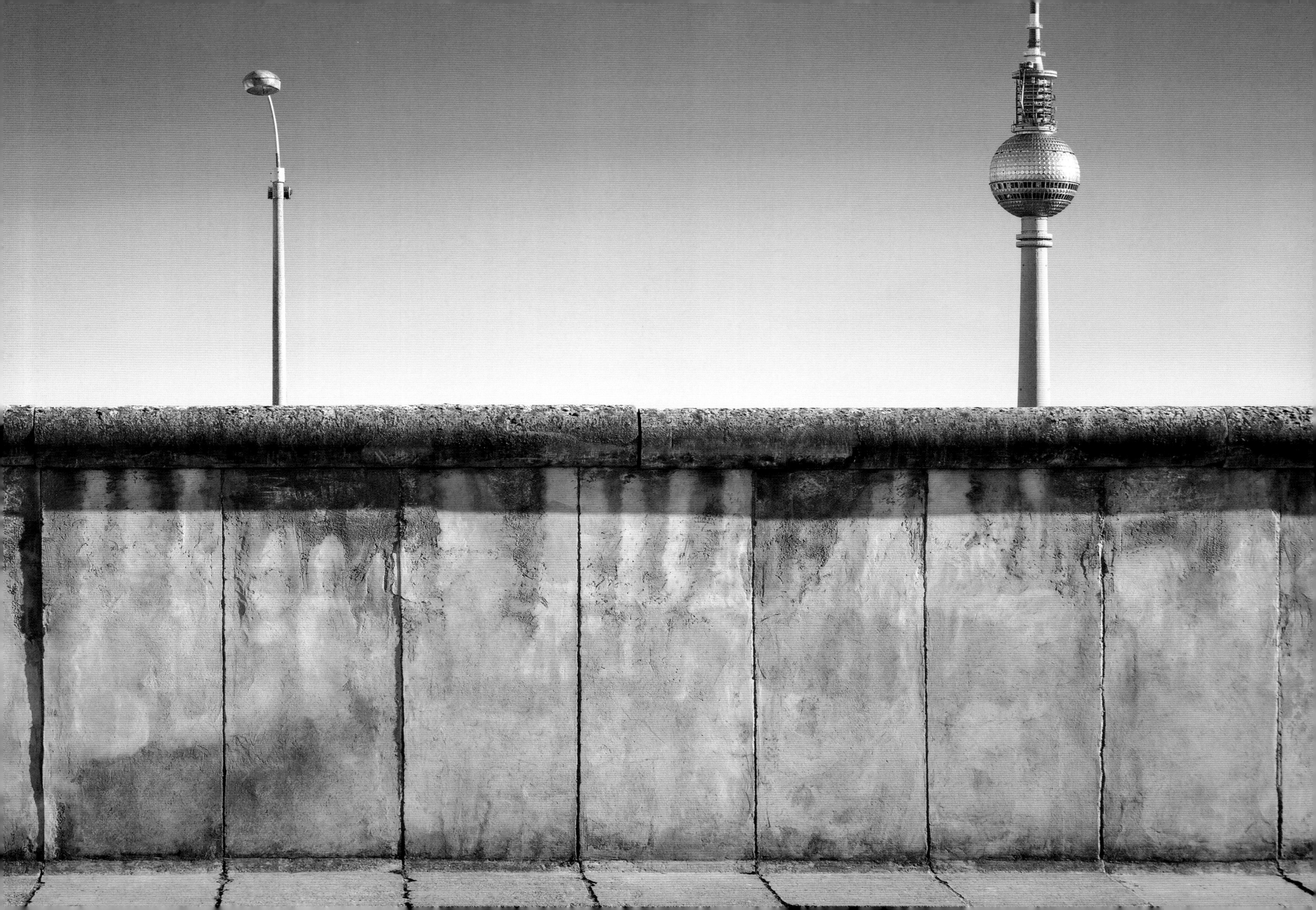

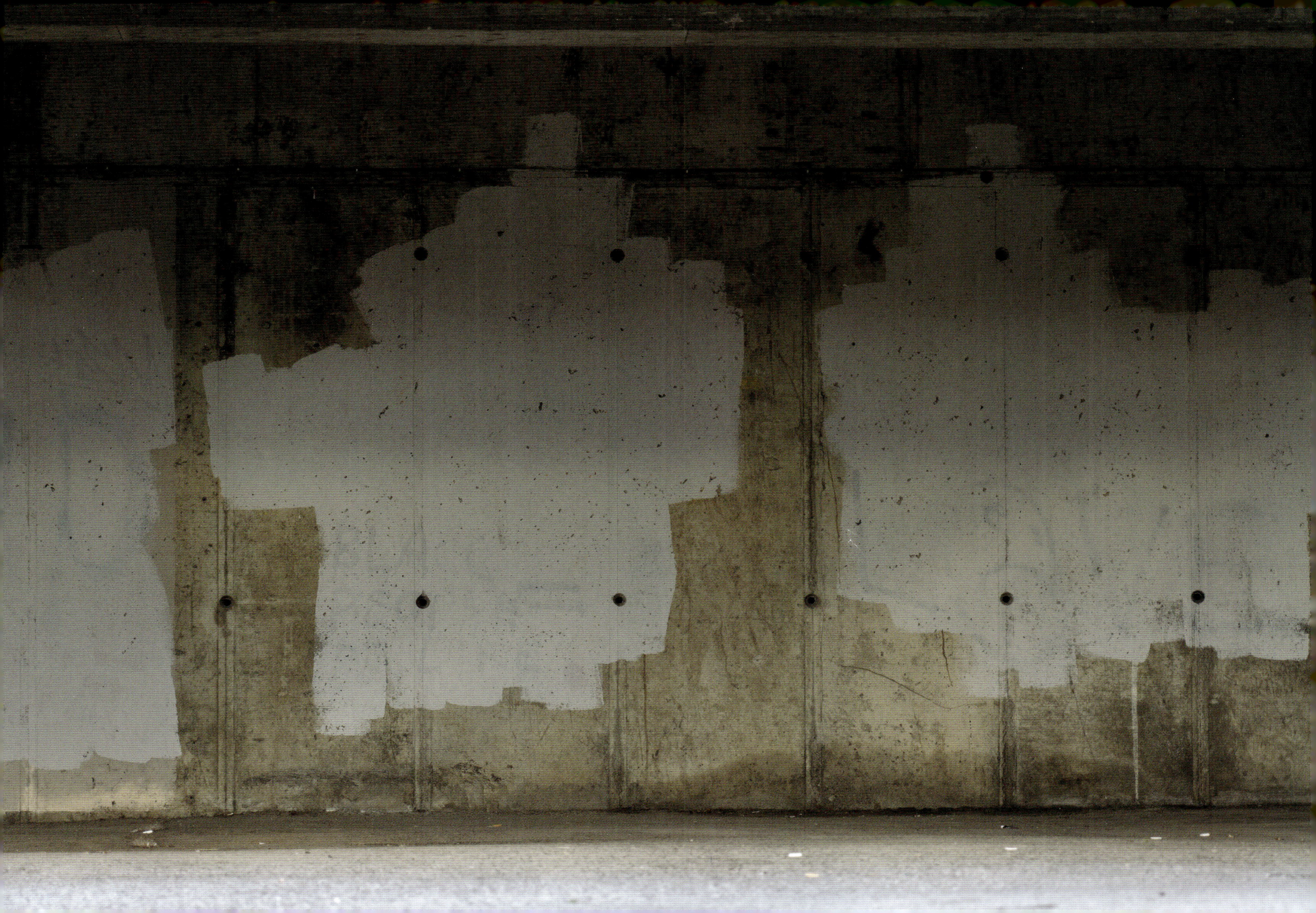

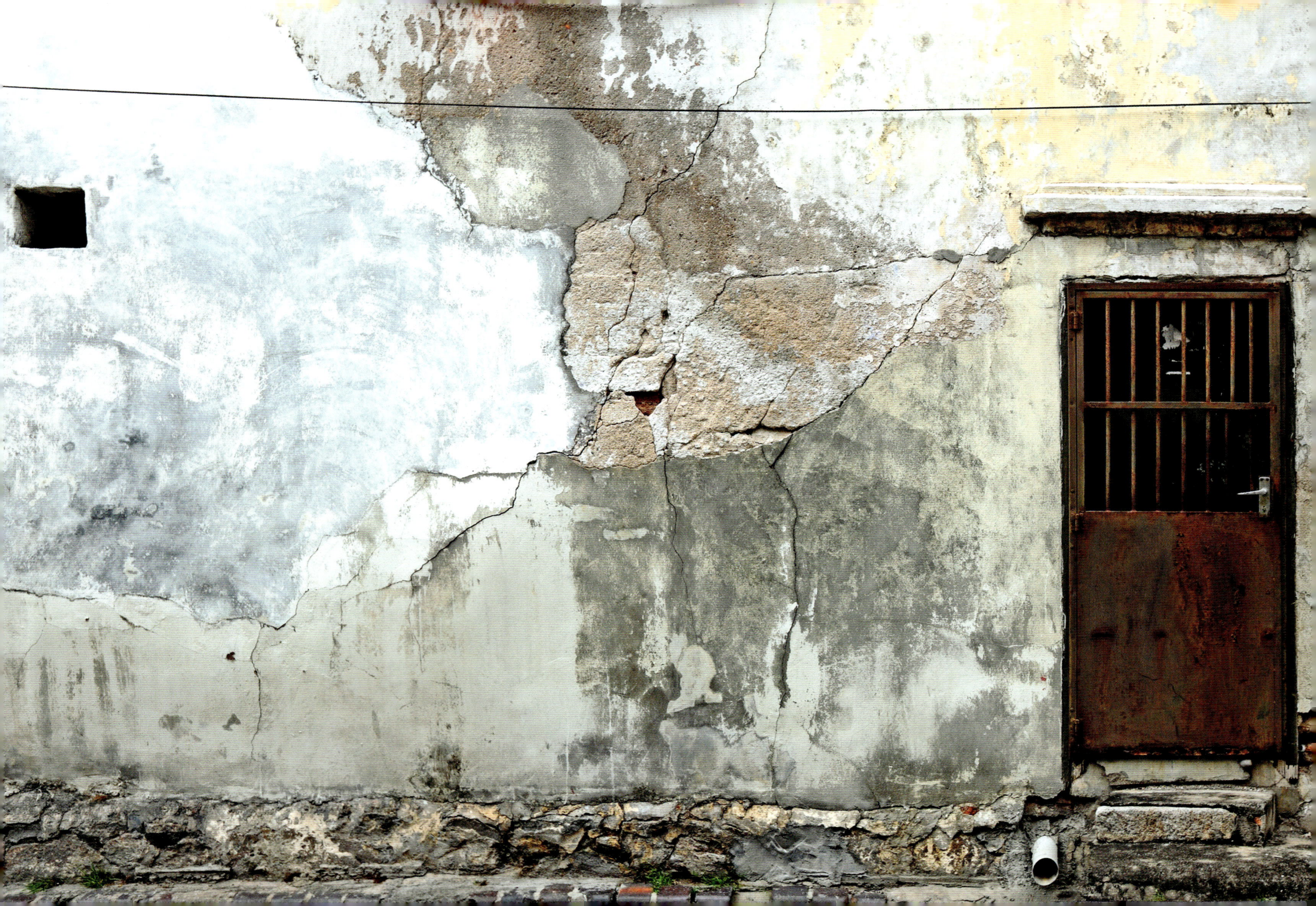

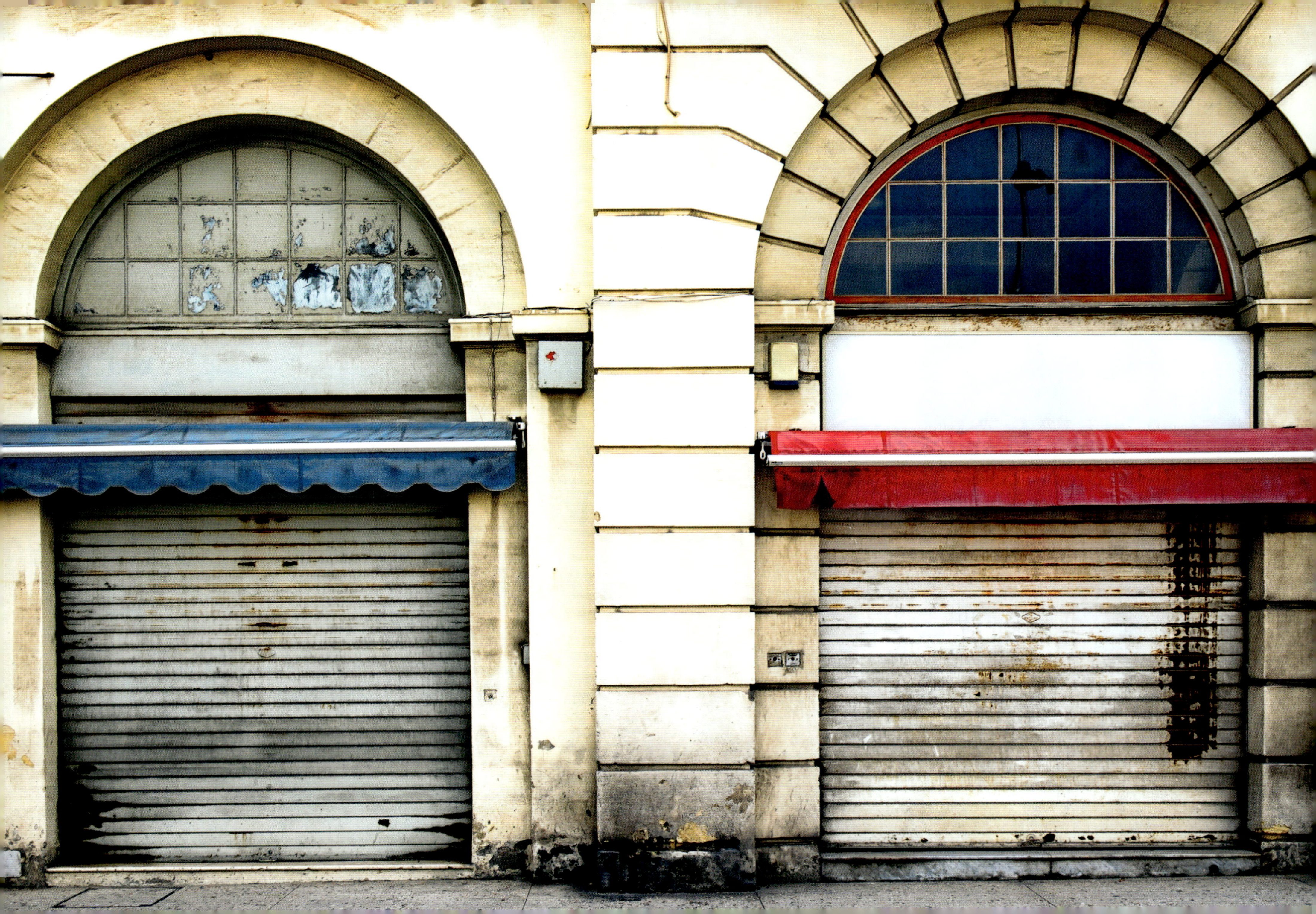

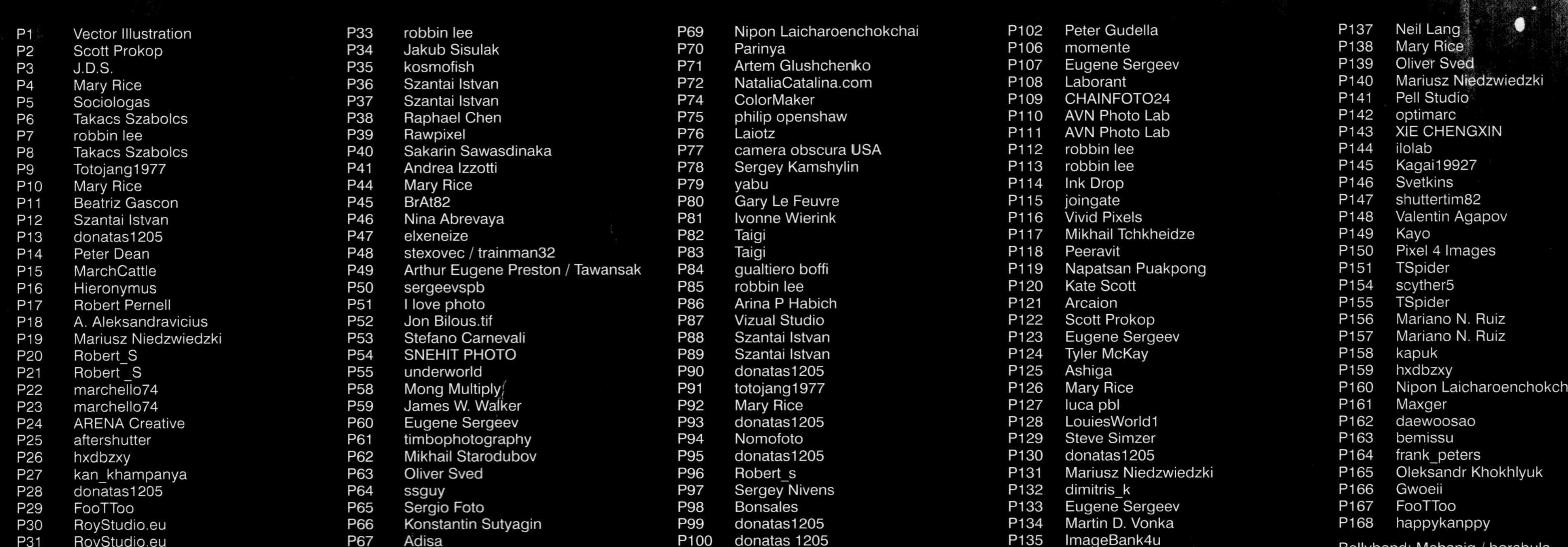

More blank canvas inspiration . . .

GraffBook
ISBN: 9781908211996

GRAFFBOOK

ISBN 978-1-908211-35-4

9 781908 211354 >